Paul Kent has been a journalist for 25 years and covered Olympic Games and World Cups in rugby union, rugby league and soccer. His first book, *Johnny Lewis: The Story of Australia's King of Boxing*, was published in 2010 to wide acclaim. He lives in Sydney.

SONNY BALL

THE LEGEND OF
SONNY BILL WILLIAMS

PAUL KENT

MACMILLAN
Pan Macmillan Australia

For mum and dad, and those Saturday morning sports runs
all those years ago, and the power of encouragement

First published 2015 in Macmillan by Pan Macmillan Australia Pty Ltd
1 Market Street, Sydney, New South Wales, Australia, 2000

Cataloguing-in-Publication entry is available
from the National Library of Australia
http://catalogue.nla.gov.au

Typeset in 12/15.5 Bembo by Midland Typesetters, Australia
Printed by McPherson's Printing Group

The author and the publisher have made every effort to contact copyright holders
for material used in this book. Any person or organisation that may have been
overlooked should contact the publisher.

CONTENTS

PROLOGUE

SONNY Bill Williams is one of the big characters in Australian and New Zealand sport. He deserves a big book. But it is important to note that this is not a biography about Sonny Bill Williams. He is too big a character for that. The real story is around him.

It is a story about rugby league, specifically the National Rugby League, and about rugby union, specifically the New Zealand Rugby Union, and how both organisations moved away from their basic principles to accommodate the large personality of Sonny Bill Williams.

He looms as a mighty figure in both codes. And neither will be the same again now Sonny has walked through them. For the first time, a player dictated entirely to not just one sporting code, but two. For the first time, they bowed.

A precedent was set.

You could list forty reasons why. Rival sporting codes are increasingly struggling to make money and survive. Government regulations now outlaw the easy way to make income, through tobacco and alcohol advertising. Poker machine taxes and new smoking laws both impacted the club industry and the grants they were able to impart.

It forced organisations to find other ways to generate money and it has only got tougher since.

Over time, it became clear just how tough that has got. As we modernise, the world is shrinking, meaning markets are shrinking. First it was teams, and now, in many cases, it is codes competing for the same corporate dollar, the same television audience and their enormous broadcast rights, the same fans. They need money from all of them.

They have been forced to look for different ways to sell their sport.

And in among them are the agents, working their angle, and the media, in daily competition against each other and no longer loyal to just their masthead anymore, but to something else altogether. Rival agents, rival media, in this new world they were perfectly placed to be played off against each other . . . as were the codes themselves.

All that was needed was a little adjustment in thinking, and the one who realised it first was Sonny Bill Williams. He forced them to a place where, when all is said and done, star power eclipses everything.

Welcome to Sonny Ball.

PART I

1

THE CIRCUS COMES TO TOWN

THERE is a fight coming up and nobody knows it.

Most believe the fight is set for 27 February 2008, which is three weeks away. So on this day, with a light rain expected, a press conference is called and due on stage is Anthony Mundine. Mundine is the World Boxing Association super middleweight champion but you can forget anything he has to say this afternoon, the real news is beside him. Ben Cousins was once the Australian Football League's (AFL) best player but is now a drug addict under league suspension and a whole country is watching him slide into abuse.

Cousins is a multiple drug offender who blew it all. His form guide includes stints in rehab and run-ins with the police before finally getting sacked by his club three months earlier and here, this morning, he has promised to talk. Nobody has heard a thing from him since he read a prepared statement months before and, in the days and months since, everybody hears many things about the state of Cousins' recovery.

Still, getting Cousins to a press conference is a big deal in many newsrooms, and that Mundine convinced Cousins to speak as part of his 'KO to Drugs' campaign is one of the small miracles Mundine is capable of performing.

PAUL KENT

Besides large parts of the Australian media, the Australian
Sports Anti-Doping Agency (ASADA), an organisation that
makes a lot of noise without ever truly making a kill, has also
thrown an interested eye over this and promised to obtain a
word–by–word transcript of everything Cousins says. Wish
them luck.

The other big names at the press conference are merely deco-
ration. Nova Peris, the proud Aboriginal woman who won
hockey gold in Atlanta in 1996 and four years later returned to
the Olympic Stadium in Sydney to run the 400 metres, is there,
while our interest here is the other one, Sonny Bill Williams.
Williams is the National Rugby League star with enough good
looks to spark several small wars in the homewares department.
His appearance next to Mundine and Cousins is an odd one,
and more than one person has thrown a concerned eye over it
and asked, what is Williams doing with Mundine?

Sonny Bill Williams is everything Mundine is not. He is at
once the most fascinating player in the game and yet insuffer-
ably boring. He is on his way to commanding a profile that
will dwarf everybody in the game, much of it deserved . . . yet
who really knows him? He almost always knows what to say
and what not to say, and almost always at the right time. And
when he smiles, well, who cares what he says then? He is so
wholesomely correct he drowns any excitement you try to find
in him. The only time he quickens your pulse is when he walks
onto the football field where, finally let loose, something inside
you flutters. Oh, you bet they love this guy.

So while Cousins is most definitely the drawcard this
morning Williams' presence is intriguing. Nobody knew he and
Mundine, Australia's most polarising athlete, were so close.

And it has to be said that right now Williams is in good shape
for the coming NRL season. Without fuss he went into hospital
over the summer and got steel pins removed from his arm. The
pins, he claimed, interfered with his ability to flick pass.

SONNY BALL

To look at him you can forget about any operation. You wouldn't think Williams had missed a day's training in his life. He is twenty-two and punching out three reps on the bench press at one hundred and forty kilograms. It puts him in the top ten per cent of the club's strength men. He stands six-four in the old scale and weighs a hundred and eight kilograms. In other words, Williams is as big as most middle forwards, who we called props in the old days, and brings with him all the aggression and physicality required to play that position. Normally the trade-off for such size is speed, yet he retains the speed and athleticism of what the modern game calls the edge player, which is almost interchangeable between the old-style backrower or centre. He is the fastest at his club, the Canterbury Bulldogs, over forty metres. And he is in such shape his skin folds are almost half the club average. He is such a sight that Wendell Sailor, who never walked past a mirror that didn't admire him back, takes one look at him months before his own return to the NRL and says, 'I'm standing there thinking there's not an ounce of fat. He's strong, he's got skills, he can play any position . . .'

You bet Williams is everything rugby league needs.

He is good looking and humble. He can offload the ball in traffic, hits like ten men in defence, kids love him and women dream he stands under their window. And he has a name you remember forever. Sonny Bill Williams.

Over the summer he has emerged as the strike forward in a Canterbury pack that lost Willie Mason and Mark O'Meley when both signed big contracts with cross-town rival Sydney Roosters. Mason as late as the summer, O'Meley some months before. They joined two other Bulldogs now at the Roosters, Braith Anasta and Nate Myles, and all will go on to play for Australia, if they have not already, revealing how much talent the Bulldogs have lost from their roster.

Yet regardless of all that Williams is finally in the place everybody expected he would be. Perfectly placed to elevate the sport. In other words, Sonny Bill Williams is about to beat rugby league to a pulp.

He is getting a sense of it, too.

His appearance next to Mundine at the press conference is unusual, and when it was announced several days earlier that he would appear at a forum on drugs, with Cousins as the main attraction, a small buzz went through newsrooms across the country. Of course I have no intention of going. Not in a thousand years.

While I have no problem with Sonny I have not spoken to Mundine for years and, for all the publicity around Cousins, who I also have no interest in, him being an AFL player and all, the truth is the whole show is cloaked around Mundine selling his upcoming fight against Nader Hamdan. Already I hear word out of the gyms that the forum won't be nearly so open as it is being assumed and that only certain reporters will be allowed to fire questions. In the competition between my paper, the *Daily Telegraph*, and the *Sydney Morning Herald* over the road, an early version of Sonny Ball is about to be played. The two papers are locked in small combat every day, fighting for bigger stories, better stories and, more recently, bigger names and better names. It is the changing media, the internet age. Mundine has held top spot in this category for some years but like everything that is about to change, although few know it yet. Not that anybody can see it coming in our business, or would share if they could. Whatever healthy rivalry there was between papers disappeared several years earlier during the Super League war, more of which will come later, and so to attend a forum under such conditions is to attend no forum at all. I am at work the afternoon the press conference is on, the *Telegraph* choosing to send editor-at-large Garry Linnell. His focus is Cousins.

For us rugby league reporters, the obvious question was what is Williams doing there alongside Mundine, Australia's most polarising athlete.

Mundine is genuinely hated in some areas of the population and wildly misunderstood in others and treated almost as an absurd sideshow in others, and the pity is all his. Then there is a fanatical group that will follow him through the fires of hell, which explains the pats on the back.

Mundine was once an NRL star like Williams, until he turned his boxing career into vaudeville and, on the strength of his celebrity as a rugby league player, is the only fighter in history to have every one of his fights broadcast on pay-per-view television. Ali, Tyson, both the Sugar Rays – none of them can claim that.

To top it off, Mundine is managed by perhaps the country's most controversial manager, Khoder Nasser. It was Nasser who convinced Cousins – raised in Perth and a star in a game whose heartland is Melbourne – that Mundine's press conference in Sydney was the right platform to break his silence. Who can even pretend to know why? It was an example of Nasser's persuasive powers.

Between all the names present, it is a walking current-affairs program. Williams seems out of place. At least Peris is Aboriginal, like Mundine.

Anybody who says they know what Williams is doing there is guessing, although it is not a complete surprise. Mundine had previously told *Sun-Herald* reporter Danny Weidler, 'Sonny is the rising star in the world of rugby league. In a field of big names, he is right up there and I wanted him to help spread the message about the perils of drug-taking.'

Williams has been spotted ringside at Mundine's fights, but with any number of other local celebrities. His friendship with Mundine was never understood to be so solid.

Originally the press conference, cloaked as this forum discussion on drugs, was to be held at The Block in inner-city Sydney, an empty piece of land in the middle of Redfern known for hard times. All down Eveleigh Street, just one street that borders

The Block, are busted terraces with boards where windows used to be and a lot of graffiti that does not really say anything much at all, and a wonderful big old wall painted with the Aboriginal flag. It is among the city's most powerful backdrops.

Next door Mundine's father, Tony Mundine, runs his gym. Old fight posters curl up the walls and the stain of sweat and hard work is in the canvas.

There are lots of kids, as there always is when Mundine is active. And nearby is a woman whose age they guess is somewhere between thirty and fifty. She stands with a walking stick and a running shoe on her right foot and nothing on the left. Nobody is sure whether she has lost a shoe or found one.

With the threat of rain, everybody is moved inside Tony Mundine's gym.

A cab pulls up and some Melbourne journalists climb out warily. They are there for Cousins but suspect they are at yet another Mundine publicity stunt to promote a fight. Some even doubt Cousins will show. And if he does, they seem convinced, he definitely won't talk. Their suspicion is understandable. Cousins' appearance is a very big deal for the Melbourne press; the AFL is a much bigger game in their city and Cousins was the star of their game. For them, Cousins is bigger than any fight where Mundine will put his belt up against Hamdan and all the bravery he might show.

With interest fading in Mundine after four forgettable fights since he beat Danny Green, over twelve, two years earlier – the biggest pay-per-view fight in Australian history – Cousins, Williams and Peris, most realise, are there as his props. Already it is working. Mundine's press conference is attracting media attention from people who couldn't tell a straight jab from a stiff drink but stand waiting to get in.

That morning Cousins' manager, Ricky Nixon, was on Melbourne radio pouring cold water, saying Cousins won't talk. Forget about any campaign against drugs – Nixon was listening to the gods of finance. Television networks were already putting aside as much as $250,000 for the exclusive Cousins interview and any words uttered about his drug habit and recovery today would significantly dilute that.

But Nixon is no match for Nasser. With numbers buzzing around in his head Nasser has already suggested Cousins could put together his own documentary and then put him in touch with a production company, 50/50 Films. The way Nasser figures it, whatever rights the documentary brings will dwarf any interview fee.

Mundine arrives in a white shirt, a white tie and grey checked pants. White shoes. Cousins turns up in a white shirt and designer jeans, with crocodile boots. Williams turns up in a white T-shirt and arms that take the focus away from whatever else he is wearing that day.

Mundine sees the crowd gathering, the press in front of them, and throws his arm around Cousins – 'You a rock star, man!' – and they bounce up the stairs to Tony's gym for the press conference. In all, they seem to be having a terrific time.

It turns out Cousins' open interview is not nearly so open, as the gym whispers say, but what did Nasser and Mundine care? The media are there and have to report on *something*.

'I think it's very admirable that Ben has come here today to talk about his problem,' Sonny says. 'It would have been a pretty tough thing for him to do and I hope people give him the support he deserves.'

Most wait patiently. Then, just when they believe Cousins is about to speak, everybody is told there is a three-question limit for Cousins. Then it emerges that only selected journalists, apparently clued up beforehand, are allowed to ask questions, so a few soft lobs are tossed in. More serious questions are ignored.

There is little doubt the 'KO to Drugs' campaign was later viewed as a tremendous success if media coverage is anything to go by. And usually it is.

Later, when it is mercifully over, Cousins climbs into a black Mercedes and leaves while Mundine remains outside, holding court, keeping them there for as long as they are willing to stay. Williams, nearby, signs autographs for the kids.

This warmth does not surprise anybody who knows Sonny. Few can see the change growing in him, though.

Not many notice at the time, but subtly Williams' language has begun to change. The first indication comes after a meeting at Mundine's Boxa Café in Hurstville with Channel Nine's head of event television, Gary Burns, several weeks after the 'KO to Drugs' forum. From their meeting, Williams signed a deal to appear on Nine's *The Footy Show*. Not every Thursday night but, when they need a ratings spike, Sonny is the guy.

'Sonny has that special something,' Burns says. 'Given time, I think he can be a spokesman for the players and for Polynesians in the NRL. They need a voice and Sonny can be it.'

Nobody ever saw Sonny as a voice for anything before this date. But change starts with a whisper. Until now, nobody has heard of Williams' ambition to become a leader. Just a month earlier, when asked about various matters such as Willie Mason's defection and captain Andrew Ryan's future at the Bulldogs, Williams tried hard to distance himself from any responsibility above his status as a footballer, 'I'm not a politician, I'm a footy player,' he tells Josh Massoud.

Yet now he emerges from the meeting with Burns fresh with ambition.

'Television is something that really interests me and the chance at Nine is a huge one for me,' he says. 'I hope to develop the role as it goes and in recent times I've been thinking a lot about what I'll do down the track when football ends and this has real appeal. I'd like to take on a greater role in the game and this will help me do that.'

2

ALL CHANGE

EIGHT days after Mundine took the decision over Hamdan, on 6 March, the NRL competition kicked off at a gala opening at Birchgrove Oval. It is rugby league's centenary season and so the game is returning to where it was first played. There were six hundred guests.

'All the players are excited about being involved this year. I mean, rugby league has been such a big part of my life. So to be involved in the centenary season, it's something I'll cherish forever,' Sonny says.

He confirmed as much in Canterbury's opening game against Parramatta, touching the ball three times in the first set of six tackles, for three offloads. Oh, he is going to be hard to handle. The Bulldogs led 20–0 at halftime before Williams was replaced with injury. They lost 28–20. For a brief moment the thought of injury ruling Sonny out for any extended length of time gives coach Steve Folkes a great migraine, until scans later clear him of any serious knee injury. The specialist saying the pain came from strained muscles in his upper calf and behind his knee.

Of more concern right now, though, was what was happening off-field, the slow boil that changed it all.

It started the following Thursday when the public got a taste of the Sonny Bill Williams that Channel Nine's Gary Burns spoke about. Williams made his *Footy Show* debut and the subject is Willie Mason, who we know left the Bulldogs in acrimonious circumstances, released with several years still left on his contract to join the Roosters.

'I was offered double what I'm on at Canterbury to go somewhere else and I stayed because I wanted to stay loyal to the club and keep the boys around,' Williams said, 'but to see him leave like that . . . It's tough because he was a player that I really did look up to and for him to leave like that . . . I had so much respect for him . . . from telling me to stay loyal and what-not . . . and for him to just pack up and leave like that was very hard to take. So, yeah, my respect for him has diminished.'

The next time comments like that worry Mason will be the first time. The following morning he shrugged them off, saying, 'Sonny's entitled to his opinion. We all get offers at different times and there are always different circumstances. I stayed at the Dogs many times for less money as well.'

Williams' protest was reasonable. Mason left for the Roosters in November after falling out with coach Folkes and the club's then-chief executive, Malcolm Noad. Part of his reason was the Bulldogs would not allow him to pursue a boxing career outside his NRL career. He mentioned fighting AFL superstar Wayne Carey in a cross-code money-spinner, a little pocket change over the summer.

'I got a call from Willie's manager last week to ask me whether I was interested,' Carey told the *Sunday Telegraph*, weeks after Mason signed with the Roosters. 'I wasn't at first. But if everything worked out right, I'd certainly be interested.'

They spoke of splitting a potential million-dollar pay-per-view audience. After joining the Roosters, who had no problem with him fighting, Mason tried to squeeze in the fight that January but couldn't organise it in time. It gave him just a few months' preparation for a fight he planned to have at the Sydney Football Stadium, so he switched his plans to the end of the year, once the football season was over.

His departure immediately launched a conspiracy theory. Had he used boxing to get out of his Canterbury contract all along? Were the Roosters, a club that felt no dilemma sharing his services, using the fight purse as a way of slipping around the salary cap, supplementing his income with a bloated fight purse? Certainly some ears pricked at NRL headquarters.

'It was principle – they [the Bulldogs] said I couldn't box. Now it's my decision not to box,' Mason said. 'The [Bulldogs] fans will not be happy but you can't please everyone.'

Roosters boss Brian Canavan denied it was a salary-cap manoeuvre. Canavan said the club simply had no issue allowing Mason to fight. What you can be sure of is the Roosters have never suffered any conflict when it comes to doing what is necessary to get the best talent playing for them.

As for Canterbury, there were many good reasons why they made the right decision. Most of all they wanted Mason, who could be easily distracted, to concentrate more on rugby league. It was still his primary income, and they were paying him considerably. His health was vital to the club's success, some-thing they risked if he slipped right when he should have slipped left in the boxing ring. That his unhappiness was apparent was also a problem. Mason wielded large influence over his team-mates and, left unchecked, it could have a devastating impact on the playing group. Indeed, it already was. It was then the club realised it would be better served letting him go.

The Bulldogs' reasons were regarded as legitimate within the National Rugby League and its clubs, where a clear order was established. The game, the club, the player. The game was not in the business of promoting other sports and, in this unusual way, Mason threatened that. There is no question that if Mason boxed he would be cashing in on his NRL profile to sell the fight.

The NRL felt no need to see one of its highest profile players promote another sport.

Still, his unhappiness at being denied threatened the delicate balance at the Bulldogs, so when his manager approached them for a release it was granted.

All this remained on the periphery as Williams and Mason, the two big dogs, circled each other ahead of when they would meet in round four. Despite Mason's smother, Williams' *Footy Show* appearance lit a fuse that would burn in the media for the next three weeks.

Williams missed the second game of the season with that knee injury suffered in the first round, and as he prepared to return the following Sunday, a small story ran on 28 March, a Friday, in the *Daily Telegraph*. Headlined 'The New Man', it revealed Williams had left manager Gavin Orr, with whom he had signed at fifteen, to be managed by Anthony Mundine's manager, Khoder Nasser. It also speculated Williams might convert to Islam, much like Mundine did when he started working with Nasser.

By now nobody was particularly surprised. More and more, Williams was becoming a presence beside Mundine and his controversial manager.

Williams refused to comment on the management change, not even to confirm it.

Orr was oblivious. 'I haven't been told anything. I will wait until I hear from Sonny until I comment. I think he is big enough to tell me.'

Across town Nasser was indignant when reporter James Phelps called for confirmation. 'I know nothing. I am in a meeting, have some respect,' he said.

Phelps, clearly no mind-reader, hung up.

Bulldogs chief executive Todd Greenberg confirmed the split. 'We are dealing with Khoder Nasser. I haven't spoken directly with Khoder, but I will be very keen to speak to him next week.'

The Bulldogs already knew. Weeks earlier, Williams called club chairman Dr George Peponis, telling him, 'I have got Khoder Nasser to be my manager. Do not tell anybody yet as it will be made public in a couple of weeks.'

The reasons for each response were as varied as the people themselves. Yet what was indisputable was that under NRL rules, player managers must be accredited – and Nasser was not. He had not even cared to apply. With this in mind NRL boss David Gallop sent a memo to every club chief executive reminding them that contracts can be registered from only accredited agents. He might well have sent it to only one, but what was Greenberg to do?

The new alliance was a great concern for Bulldogs coach Folkes.

Folkes had come through the great era at Canterbury. He was a tough backrower when the club was known for its flamboyance, a member of its 1980 premiership-winning side widely called 'The Entertainers'. Half a decade later, when Warren Ryan had assumed the job as coach and transformed 'The Entertainers' into the 'Dogs of War', playing a style others called in a half-complimentary fashion 'Wazza Ball', Folkes was still the toughest going around. He won three more premierships.

They were some club, the Bulldogs. Nobody adapted and succeeded like them. The club was led by club patriarch Peter Moore, who liked to say the winning was in the woodwork. They knew it too. Years later I am sitting next to Bob McCarthy at a grand final lunch. On the other side of McCarthy is Paul Langmack, the lock through the Dogs of War era.

McCarthy played sixteen years at South Sydney and won four premierships before joining the Bulldogs in 1976. He is talking about South Sydney in the 2014 grand final, and the talent through the side, and how he used to watch all these great players at other clubs as the Rabbitohs struggled through the 1980s and 1990s and 2000s, more than thirty years of forgettable football, and he was saying how the whole time, he was wishing some of these great players were playing for the Rabbitohs, when Langmack says, 'Let me tell you something.'

He is leaning across McCarthy, coming straight at me.

'Hang on,' says McCarthy, trying to finish his story.

'No, it's a rap,' says Langmack.

McCarthy was stunned. 'Doesn't anyone say "Excuse me" anymore?'

But Langmack is unstoppable, saying, 'Let me tell you.'

Pointing at McCarthy, he says, 'Him and Gary Stevens started the culture at Canterbury. I'm telling you, they turned Canterbury into winners. They brought it over from South Sydney. It was them.'

There is no reason to dispute any of it. Since McCarthy arrived the Bulldogs have been the most successful club in the League, joined only by Manly. In that time each has won six premierships and finished runner-up six times.

It was no secret Moore and Manly counterpart Ken Arthurson were the two shrewdest club bosses of their era and any other. If that was case, McCarthy and Stevens brought the woodwork with them. Moore, who died in 2000, was Folkes' father-in-law and had given more than half his life to the club. Folkes knew all of Moore's teachings.

The Bullfrog, as they called Moore, had a simple philosophy for success.

'A plus B equals C,' he once told me, smiling.

He let the equation hang there a little.

'A equals "train hard", B equals "play hard" and C equals "party hard",' he said. 'Do that and you'll keep the players happy and the club winning. But you have to get A and B right first.'

When news broke that Williams had joined Nasser, Folkes grabbed him at training to find out what was happening. He did not know Nasser but found little to like about the way he and Mundine went about their business.

'You're not turning Muslim, are you?' Folkes said.

'Seriously, you're joking,' Williams said.

'It'll be a joke if you do,' Folkes said, before offering Williams advice on Mundine. 'You're kidding yourself if you're taking advice off him.'

As simple as that, relationships break down forever.

Folkes had no idea the impact that conversation would have. It stayed with Williams long after he walked off the training field and remained his validation for many days to come. Rather than making Williams cautious of Mundine and Nasser, Folkes played him into their hands.

'I start to think, "Who is he to question my friends?"' Williams said later, although he chose to say nothing to Folkes at the time.

Williams was experiencing great change in his life at this moment. Until now, he had never really had to think. He trained, he played. He went along with the crowd. It was perfect at the Bulldogs, with their train hard, play hard and party hard philosophy. Sonny never had a drink of alcohol until he started playing first grade at Canterbury and teammates encouraged him. When he started, he took to it with some enthusiasm.

Now though, his close contact with Nasser saw him begin to think differently. Williams started to question things. And it would take a long time before we found out who he was truly unhappy with.

Nasser and Mundine's influence was emerging. Sonny might have always wanted to be a leader in the Polynesian community, and there was nobody better suited, but he lacked the confidence to express it. A few months earlier he was just a footy player, remember, not a politician. Now he wanted to take his place in his community, and spoke of a television career as a platform towards that.

And while Nasser couldn't tell you the pointy end of a football, when it came to making an athlete feel loved there was nobody better.

The Bulldogs were about to find out just how much.

3

MARSHALLING TROOPS

EVERYBODY was looking towards Canterbury's showdown with the Roosters as Sonny Bill's big moment. After Sonny's comments that his respect for Willie Mason was 'diminished' the rugby league world stood back and waited for the inevitable collision. His teammates got on the front foot, too.

'To be honest,' said Willie Tonga, 'there's that feeling within a lot of the players.'

Mason, not exactly the retiring type, welcomed this. His personality is too large, and Roosters coach Brad Fittler acknowledged as much when he confirmed Mason had the green light to 'get personal'.

Mason was the most destructive player in the game and Williams the next good one coming through. He might already be there, and some were hoping this game would go some way towards answering that. Nothing is as exhilarating as two big guys going at it. Mason plays in the middle while Williams usually occupies an edge, which is just semantics for the commentators. At some point they would find each other and when they do, you can be sure, a little extra will be put into it.

The game was two days away and Sonny Bill was relaxed.

He pulled up at an intersection on Anzac Parade in his sponsored Jeep. A windscreen washer was working the cars.

'I used to do that when I was a kid growing up in Auckland,' he said to his passenger, pulling a couple of gold coins from his centre console and reaching out the window with his big arm.

The windscreen washer was delighted when he recognised him, saying, 'I should be the one paying you for letting me do your windscreen.'

Williams was on his way to the city between photo shoots for a new sponsor, Bolle sunglasses. He came from Maroubra beach, where he stunned the production crew when their equipment trolley got stuck in the sand and Williams, shy but wholly decent, simply picked up the equipment and walked ahead with it.

Bolle's signing was strategic. He replaced Australian cricketer Brett Lee as Bolle believed Williams would help them sell their sunglasses in New Zealand as well.

'I've actually been amazed by the reaction, it's probably the biggest response I've had to a signing and that includes the cricketers we've had,' said Fiona Marty, Bolle's publicity and sponsorship manager. 'When I first met Sonny I was struck by how gracious and humble he was. He's very sweet. But he's just such a massive brand. He's almost like Australia's answer to David Beckham.'

Williams was interviewed by the *Sydney Morning Herald* during the shoot. The story is to preview Friday's game, his first against Mason. The *Herald* got access to Williams because of Mundine and Nasser. Williams knew he was news, and had not spoken since word broke of his signing with Nasser. A different Sonny was emerging. A spokesman.

'I just think it's beneficial for us because if we don't speak up, we're going to be . . . not walked over, but treated like we are treated,' he told the *Herald*.

Roughly one-third of the game, at NRL level, were Polynesian players. By 2017 it will be half.

'That's why, this year, I'm talking a bit more in the media and trying not to just give the same old clichéd answers but opening up a bit more. Now that I'm a bit more mature, I feel like I can.

'I started from a young age, when I was eighteen, and I've seen a lot of things. I'm twenty-two now and it's been a big learning curve. I'm not saying that I've been treated differently, but people think the islanders, or the darkies, they . . . not necessarily do what they are told, but they will just accept what they are given. So I think it's beneficial to speak up.

'It's just the nature of the boys. They're quiet and humble and not used to speaking up and people take that the wrong way. But there's a lot more of us playing now, and some of the players are the most dominant players in the game, so I think we need to have our opinions heard, and that's probably the reason I've decided to talk a lot more.'

He refused to address speculation he was considering converting to Islam.

Williams and Mason made this game a dream for the ponytail brigade that run marketing departments. Nothing sells like bad blood and, to add to the menace surrounding the game, ANZ Stadium officials realised they had a little problem. When Mason was interchanged he would sit with his back to five thousand Bulldogs members. So naturally they told everyone about it. This was wonderful publicity for the game. Bulldogs fans immediately tried to be part of that five thousand, and ticket sales surged.

At the ground, Stadium boss Ken Edwards hired three private security guards to specifically watch Mason's back, a small price for a game that was selling itself. The NSW Police were about the only ones now unhappy. Roosters and Bulldogs fans had brawled four years earlier, clearing an entire bay and injuring two policemen.

As the game drew closer Mason found himself in his environment. A day before the game he turned up at a press conference organised by the League.

Sonny's dislike for him was no big deal, he said. 'I have played plenty of big games. I have played in Tests and Origins and bigger [club] games. I have had countries hate me and states want to kill me. It's just another club game. I was expecting this from the time I signed with the Roosters. I've known what the build-up was going to be like and I've prepared myself for months now. This is it.'

He didn't care what Sonny thought.

'I understand fully why's he's upset. People make decisions in their life. One day he's going to probably have to make a tough decision as well.'

Like everybody else, Mason had no idea how near that decision was.

The *Footy Show* sought to capitalise on the feud. It organised Williams and Mason to appear together the night before the game, right up until Williams told Gary Burns he wanted to be separated from Mason.

'Sonny Bill has specifically asked to be kept away from Willie,' Burns said. 'He doesn't feel a television studio is the right place for them to sit down and talk about what has happened.'

Mason left the studio before Williams was introduced. Sitting on-set during an ad break, co-host Matt Johns was surprised how nervous Williams was. His hands were shaking.

'If our paths cross, no one will be taking a backward step,' Williams said on the show.

The following day the *Australian* broke the only real news of the week, revealing Mason had lost the support of his Bulldogs teammates while at Canterbury and Williams was part of the senior playing group that had fronted Bulldogs officials saying they were increasingly frustrated by his behaviour. It was part of the reason the Bulldogs were so willing to release Mason to join the Roosters. And Sonny, now so outraged, was part of it.

Like all the great games, there was a crackle in the crowd. There always is when it's personal. The Bulldogs fans turned up with their intentions clear, hand-painted signs proclaiming 'Money talks, traitors walk' or 'I feel like chicken tonight'. Failing that, they went for the blunt approach: 'Bash Mason'. The Roosters received the ball from the kick-off and Mark O'Meley, the former Bulldog, hit the ball up first. Second tackle was former Bulldog Nate Myles. Third tackle came Mason, another Bulldog, and if the message wasn't clear by then it was after the next when, against any sound reasoning because he played in the backs and this was not part of the job description, along came another former Bulldog, Braith Anasta. This was a statement.

Eyes were getting tired in the grandstand waiting for Mason and Williams to finally come together. Nobody wanted to get distracted and miss it. It finally happened in the eighteenth minute. It was a moment for the crowd. Mason took the ball right through the middle of the Canterbury forwards and Williams saw his opportunity and nearly knocked Willie bow-legged.

It was a tremendous tackle, and the joy of it lasted less than a minute.

That was when Mason scored. And that's the way it went. By the time Mason scored his second try early in the second half the Roosters were on their way to victory, the final score 40–12. Mason was close to best on ground.

When fulltime sounded the two men found each other.

'Good game, catch you around,' Mason said.

The following day coach Steve Folkes called in captain Andrew Ryan and the club's leadership group, including Williams, and told them he was quitting at season's end. Immediately Todd Greenberg, the Bulldogs chief executive, said the hunt was on for a new coach. Anybody who knew anything said assistant coach Kevin Moore would get the job but Greenberg promised to look as far as needed to find the right man.

It was becoming apparent, even after four rounds, the Bulldogs were a club in serious trouble. Without O'Meley and Mason, particularly, they were stuck playing a style of football they no longer had the horsepower to maintain. Any new coach needed to understand the job ahead and the culture within the club. In a bow to growing player power, Greenberg confirmed the leadership group would be consulted.

Things began moving behind the scenes, and not just on the coaching front.

Weeks later a curious paragraph appears in Danny Weidler's column. Former Wallabies coach Eddie Jones, now a coaching consultant at Saracens in England, nominated Sonny Bill as the man the All Blacks should sign 'if the Kiwis are even half serious about trying to win the World Cup'.

Where did this come from? The All Blacks were a year past their 2007 World Cup failure in France but were already favourites for the next in 2011 in New Zealand.

'He was never an option for me at the Wallabies,' Jones said, before he was asked how much Williams was worth in rugby. 'That's hard to say. Because he is so marketable, he'd be a player who could earn close to one million dollars. Somewhere around that would be very worthwhile.'

This is the way it starts. A throwaway line in a column.

Williams wouldn't be the first to switch to rugby. Andrew Walker left the NRL to sign with the ACT Brumbies in 2000, five years after rugby became professional, and was not missed for five minutes. Back then Australia was planning to host the 2003 World Cup but administrators realised they needed to sell to a broader audience to make it a financial success. Cross-promotion was needed. So a year before the World Cup the NRL's Wendell Sailor and Mat Rogers signed with the ARU, declaring their desire to play in the World Cup. Sailor knew what it was all about. As he said while walking through the turnstiles at an empty Ballymore Oval, about to start his rugby career, 'Watch these babies swing.'

Four days later Jones' ponderings to Weidler began to take form. Williams confirmed to the *Sydney Morning Herald* that he would not rule out switching to rugby. This was a great shock to the Bulldogs. If nothing else, Todd Greenberg had a document in his filing cabinet that told him Williams was in the first year of a five-year, $400,000 deal. Why was he thinking about something that was five years away?

By now the Bulldogs had confirmed Kevin Moore as coach the following year, Greenberg's exhaustive search needing to go no further than the office down the hall.

Weidler took it a step further the following week, contacting the New Zealand Rugby Union to ask about its interest in Williams. NZRU boss Steve Tew listened 'intently', Weidler reported.

While the Bulldogs stayed quiet as a club, not everybody did. Or could.

Steve Mortimer is considered the greatest player in Bulldogs history and six years earlier was running the club as chief executive, taking over when it was in crisis after being caught cheating the salary cap. Nobody could question his love for the club or his integrity.

'When I first came to the club as CEO I took a particular interest in Sonny Bill Williams,' Mortimer said. 'He was at Belmore and he brought his father over from New Zealand. He came across as a kid who was very principled, very decent. That's why it sickened me to hear him talk about playing for the All Blacks.

'The fact is, Sonny has signed for the Bulldogs for another five years. I know he's got a new manager, so maybe there's something to that. I am curious about the motivation for Sonny to suddenly be saying he wants to play for the All Blacks. What's the motivation? It certainly didn't enhance the spirit of Bulldogs supporters. It sickens me full-stop to constantly hear about coaches and players coming and going before their contracts finish. I've had quite a few Bulldogs supporters ask me what I think Sonny Bill is doing. He is still quite a young man and quite impressionable.'

Adding insult, Williams' comments came days before he was to play for New Zealand in the Centenary Test against Australia. He flew his mum Lee in from New Zealand for the Test.

'I wanted to bring my mother over for Mother's Day,' he said. 'She was pretty excited to come and I was excited to have her. I'm close to my mum and it's always special when you can do those things. I don't get to see her that often, maybe just a couple of times a year, so it's good to be able to spend time with her.'

It was a big week for rugby league. A black-tie dinner was held as part of the centenary celebrations and the Team of the Century was announced. The most modern career among the seventeen named was Andrew Johns, who retired two years earlier. The names went all the way back to the game's original superstar, Dally Messenger, who signed to play the game from rugby union in 1908. The coach was Jack Gibson.

The dinner was timed as rugby league's official one-hundredth birthday, the Test a part of the celebrations. It was to be played at the Sydney Cricket Ground, where a hundred years earlier New Zealand beat Australia 11–10. If anything else was needed, Williams was due to come up against Willie Mason again.

Days before the Test the *Sydney Morning Herald* called Parramatta legend Ray Price for a preview. Price is one of the all-time greats and, it's a funny thing, but he views the game now with much the same single-mindedness he did as a player. Price won four premierships, played twenty-two Tests for Australia, and had a capacity for work that earned him the nickname Mr Perpetual Motion. And still he refused to go quietly, on anything.

'The thing about Ray,' Jack Gibson once said, when he was coaching Price to three premierships at Parramatta (1981–83), 'is Monday to Thursday nobody cares about Ray. By Friday, it's "Anybody seen Ray?" Then it's the weekend and it's "How's Ray feeling? Ray okay?" Everybody wanted to know Ray on the weekend.'

Price retired in 1986 when rugby league was semi-professional. Good players were playing for $30,000 or $40,000 on top of their wages. He would not have made in a career what Williams was being paid for that season, a little piece of accounting that had not escaped him.

'Sonny Bill is a good player,' Price said, 'but he doesn't spend enough time on the paddock. Willie Mason could be a good player. [But] if we can get those bastards playing eighty minutes then we'll see how good they are.'

Price could not understand why Mason did not play longer. The game had completely changed since his playing days. 'He plays twenty minutes a half and gets a motza of money to do it,' Price said. 'He'll get better and better if he stays out on the field longer.'

Not necessarily, and that is being kind. Rugby league was an endurance game in Price's day, when a player ran onto the field with a high knee action and socks up, and stayed onfield until he got injured or dropped so many balls teammates pleaded to the coach to get him off. Not all did.

Rugby league today is a power game. Instead of permanent replacements, players are allowed to go off and have a short rest and return. It has made the game more dynamic, and attracted a larger television audience, but not necessarily better.

Yet Australia won the Test 28–12 and Price's words proved prophetic. The Kiwis started slowly and the Test was as good as over after twenty minutes, when Australia led 22–0. Somewhat hollow, but with a World Cup at year's end, afterward the Kiwis tried hard to focus on the final sixty minutes when they outscored Australia 12–6.

'In our last sixty minutes we showed what we were capable of,' Williams said. 'We just have to build on that for the World Cup. We tried our best. That first twenty they got on top of us. It just shows how lethal they are.'

SONNY BALL

The night was a sombre one, though. Less than an hour before kick-off it was announced at the game that Jack Gibson, just weeks earlier named the greatest coach in a hundred years, had passed away in his nursing home.

IT started a week later. The *Australian* broke the news Williams had 'sounded out' former Wallabies coach Eddie Jones about a potential rugby union career in Europe. While no quotes supported the story, not even attributed to an unnamed source, you could be sure it was a thousand per cent correct.

And it worried the hell out of those at NRL headquarters. A year earlier they would have giggled at such news. It would have seemed absurd. But in the past year Craig Gower had left the NRL to start a career in French rugby union and Luke Rooney, one of Gower's teammates, was set to join him. Gower fled the NRL for the reduced scrutiny of French rugby. That, and when he did his numbers, French rugby looked very attractive indeed.

As League officials tried to digest what Williams was trying to achieve they knew that over at St George Illawarra Mark Gasnier was also unhappy that several third-party deals built in to top up his contract had failed to come through, leaving him $300,000 short. Gasnier's plight was beginning to be mentioned in support of Williams' stance.

Under NRL rules clubs are not allowed to guarantee third-party sponsorships, for the very simple reason that forty deals could be written into contracts and, for mysterious reasons that would not be mysterious at all, fail to materialise. At which the club would feel deeply sympathetic and decide, out of goodness of heart, to compensate the player. It would make the salary cap redundant and push power to the wealthier clubs. With no guarantee, clubs could only promise to make 'best endeavours' when it came to third-party deals.

Gasnier's problem came when his contract included a deal with Channel Nine, the game's free-to-air broadcaster. The way it worked, his manager would kick a few doors and bring advertising revenue to Nine under the happy understanding that the money would pass fluidly through Nine's books and into Gasnier's pocket after he made a couple of appearances. It was some good deal, only nobody wanted to pay it. Nine had nothing to pass on because nothing was coming in.

So at the time Williams revealed he would consider playing French rugby Gasnier was taking advantage of a one-month window written into his contract that allowed him to research options, French rugby being one of them, if no endorsement deals came through. Still, nobody believed he would go.

The NRL salary cap is a complicated animal. Few understand it properly. Almost nobody in the media did because it was not their business. They learned what they needed to know at the time of reporting and tried to report as much as they could before making the reader fall-face first into their newspaper through boredom.

But it would soon prove vital in Sonny Ball.

Only a brief understanding would explain why Gallop and salary-cap auditor Ian Schubert were angry at St George Illawarra for the Gasnier situation and why they never truly believed Williams would leave because the money was there if he was truly as marketable as he claimed to be.

This assumption would soon prove costly to the game. So much of this kind of work goes on behind the scenes every day. Few know it, but in NRL headquarters they knew it well enough to presume that by now there was every likelihood Williams had had several discussions with Jones about playing at Saracens, not just one.

The great concern for the League was Williams' new manager. Khoder Nasser never played by the rules and, if there was one manager capable of carrying this through, Nasser would be the one. Nasser still remained an unaccredited NRL player manager and showed no sign he would formalise his position. Williams was his only NRL client.

And, as far as anybody could tell, Williams was unhappy for the biggest reason of all. Money.

It had already been mentioned several times in 2008 that when Williams was nineteen he knocked back a million-dollar deal – a year – to play in England out of loyalty to the Bulldogs. It was a fact well reported, if not as well supported. There were suspicions the deal was leaked by someone close to Williams as he negotiated his new Bulldogs contract. Its validity could not be verified; for one, nobody from the English club, St Helens, was willing to confirm anything on the record.

Such behaviour is not as uncommon as it sounds. There isn't an agent worth his Gucci loafers who hasn't talked up a rival interest in a bid to bump up a contract's value. And say what you like about player managers, they catch on quickly. As one chief executive said of another player manager, he could peel a pear in your pocket and you wouldn't even know.

Regardless, things were about to go crazy, and not much of it would make much sense.

Williams was about to play hard ball with the Bulldogs and the NRL. The rules were about to change.

Williams was about to play Sonny Ball.

4

BURNING BRIDGES

THE first details revealing the depth of Williams' unhappiness broke in the *Sun-Herald* in May. The first line in Adrian Proszenko's story is a sledgehammer for Canterbury and the NRL: 'Bulldogs superstar Sonny Bill Williams is fed up and wants out of the club.'

Williams was quoted, but said only, 'I don't want to comment,' which left no doubt he was aware of the contents of the story – and was comfortable with it going to print.

Once again Eddie Jones was tapped, saying, 'Certainly, if Sonny was interested in playing rugby, we'd be interested in talking to him, He's undoubtedly one of the most talented league players we've ever seen. He'd make a fantastic twelve [inside centre] in union. He's got pace, he's got speed, he's got a step. He has the ability to distribute the ball and he's tough. They are all pretty good qualities that make a good twelve . . . I have had a chat to a number of people about a number of things. We haven't gone down that track to any formal extent.'

By now it was clear Sonny's agenda was being run through the media. The details were designed to make the Bulldogs shudder. Pressure was being applied, indirectly. He did not believe his show of good faith in knocking back that million-dollar contract in England was reciprocated. He was concerned he was not being treated as a senior player, and not given a greater leadership role at the club. Nor was he consulted on Moore's appointment as coach.

His grievances were hard to accept as legitimate concerns. Indeed, some of the concerns are rebutted just a day later, with Bulldogs sources saying Williams was heavily involved in Moore's appointment. They looked increasingly like ambit claims, but they were giving chief executive Todd Greenberg significant pain behind the eyes.

The chief executive did not know of Sonny's concerns for five minutes when office staff told him about the day he signed his current contract, just the previous year, and walked out of then chief executive Malcolm Noad's office so happy he hugged them all. Everyone seemed happy. At the press conference held later Williams smiled throughout, and in the next morning's *Sydney Morning Herald* was buoyant.

'I always wanted a five-year deal because I don't want to go through this ever again. I haven't been sleeping too well the last couple of weeks. I've been getting headaches,' he said.

So after reading Proszenko's story Greenberg went back and checked the contract. It was still there. Still signed. Though it had to be said he could not believe the good job Malcolm Noad did to sign Williams to such a deal. At $400,000, for the 2008 season, Williams was at the market rate for a player with the potential to be the biggest name in the game. In five years, still on $400,000 a year, he would be the bargain of the year.

How did the Bulldogs pull off such a tremendous deal?

Simple. Sonny wanted it.

The contract was negotiated the previous year, in March 2007. The great stumbling point in the entire negotiation was the contract's length. The Bulldogs had concerns about Williams' long run of injuries and wanted a three-year deal, worried mostly about the disintegration of his knee. He was already doing reduced work during the week to spare the knee's wear and tear.

But Williams wanted a five-year deal. 'I don't want to go through this again,' he said.

The Bulldogs were prepared to offer more per season for the three-year deal, but reduced the annual amount if Williams wanted the surety of five years.

The deal carried inherent risk on both sides. Malcolm Noad brought up the reduced terms for the longer contract at the meeting and Williams, according to the *Sydney Morning Herald* at the time, 'seemed content'.

So Noad asked Williams and his managers Gavin and Chris Orr to leave the room. Closing the door behind them, Noad turned and looked at head coach Steve Folkes and Canterbury recruitment manager Keith Onslow.

'Did I hear right?' he asked. He then wrote the deal down and called Williams and the Orrs back in.

'Are you happy with this, Sonny?' he said.

'I am,' Sonny said, then uttered the same line he would repeat to the *Herald* the next day. 'I don't want to go through this again.'

At that they shook hands and Williams walked out and hugged everybody in the office.

'Are you coming to training now?' he said, turning to Folkes.

Clearly Williams was thinking differently now. The Orrs were gone and Khoder Nasser was his new manager and he believed, after Willie Mason's departure, along with Mark O'Meley, Nate Myles and Braith Anasta, and with Steve Price having left some years earlier as well as Johnathan Thurston, he should be upgraded. In the world of modern sport, this is called 'Where's Mine?'.

Yet Williams failed to understand why many of those left in the first place. Canterbury could not match the offers from the Roosters for one very simple reason: their salary cap was full.

Why?

A large reason is they knew Williams was coming off contract and began planning their future by creating space in the cap, diverting money previously intended for those players to Williams and other emerging players. Have no doubt that Sonny Bill Williams was on the top of that list, though.

And now he was asking for more.

The Bulldogs were shocked at the report Williams wanted out. The NRL believed it was absurd. Williams had four more years on his contract. Not only that, the club had already met some of those courtesies he was complaining he did not receive.

'He endorsed Kevin Moore,' a source at the club told the *Daily Telegraph*. 'His only concern was recruitment but he agreed to play a major role in bringing players to the club. [But] after doing so he missed a meeting with a potential player, instead choosing to promote a sponsor.'

The same meeting is revealed in the *Sydney Morning Herald*, which told of how Moore met with Melbourne's Jeff Lima with players Reni Maitua and Ben Roberts. The *Herald* gave no reason why Williams was not there. The *Telegraph*'s claim was an unnamed source, highlighting the growing quandary of Sonny Bill Williams. Who to believe?

It seems unlikely Moore would have invited Maitua and Roberts to a dinner to appeal to a potential player without inviting Williams. Both men are of Polynesian descent like Williams, as was Lima; there are good reasons why Williams would have been the first player invited, the best being he is the biggest attraction of the club.

When we step back here we see more Sonny Ball being played. A big part of Williams' reputation and his ability to promote himself is his ability to remain likeable. Smile a lot, be modest in public.

If Williams was going to extricate himself from his Canterbury contract he needed support to put public pressure on Canterbury to release him. He needed to control the media message, and the tried and proven way was through selective leaks to a media organisation that Nasser and Mundine regard as sympathetic – the Fairfax group, publisher of the *Sydney Morning Herald* and the *Sun-Herald*.

There is nothing new or original about a strategy to control the media message. Nearly a hundred years ago American political commentator Walter Lippmann coined it the 'manufacture of consent' and more than twenty-five years ago Noam Chomsky and Edward Herman documented how government selectively leaked information to steer public opinion in *Manufacturing Consent*.

Controlling the media message was crucial in Sonny Ball. So the same day that a club source revealed to the *Telegraph* Williams wanted to be involved in recruitment but missed the first player meeting he was called to because he preferred to promote a sponsor, we see the same meeting was covered in the *Herald* as an example of *how* Sonny was not being properly respected – while not reporting that his absence could have been his own doing.

Despite their differences, the tone of both reports is that Williams believed his wage proved that he was under-appreciated at the club and was serious about his threat to walk.

NRL boss David Gallop, a former lawyer, immediately pointed to the sanctity of the salary cap. 'We want to see players like that stay in our competition,' Gallop said. 'But making exceptions to the salary cap rules is not the way to go.'

Greenberg raised the threat of legal action if Williams walked out. 'It would certainly be something we look at. But it hasn't come to that and we are expecting Williams to honour his deal. We are one year into a five-year contract. We have made a lot of plans for him and he is seen as a huge part of our club going forward.'

Still, the Bulldogs were concerned. Williams was once Sonny by name and sunny by nature around the club. Day after day, turning into weeks, he became increasingly withdrawn. Greenberg and chairman George Peponis approached him but he was reluctant to talk. Andrew Johns started to notice that Williams no longer wandered to the end of the field after training sessions where he was doing extras with the club's halves. He had stopped without explanation.

Teammates were concerned. 'It would be good to see what he does think,' said Luke Patten. 'I'm sure in the next however long it will all get sorted out. He's one year into a five-year deal so I guess he's still got four years to go here.'

Coach Steve Folkes had no doubt why. He believed it was Mundine and Nasser's influence.

Privately, the club believed there was a clear motivation behind Williams' demands. Contractually, Orr was still Williams' manager. For the next five years of his contract his commission went to the Orr, not Nasser. And Nasser couldn't negotiate any money on top because he was not an accredited player manager.

'Even if they meet with the Bulldogs and the Bulldogs agree to give more money, the NRL is not allowed to register the new contract,' said Paul Osborne, the boss of the NRL's agent accreditation scheme.

'I think he has been made aware that he needs to be accredited,' Osborne said of Nasser, 'but I've received nothing.'

By changing codes Williams could circumvent that.

Greenberg made his reputation as the unflappable chief executive and saw no reason to change. 'We are not going to get drawn on the articles and headlines,' he said, referring to Proszenko's exclusive. 'Sonny is a big part of our club going forward. We expect Sonny to honour his contract. Sonny is one year into a five-year deal and our expectation is that he will fulfil that. There's no meetings. There's no discussions taking place.'

But there were meetings. For the first time there was a belief this could be genuine. Privately, the Bulldogs panicked.

Williams was unwilling to talk to the club the day the story broke, leaving Greenberg and Peponis with no option but to talk to Nasser.

This was difficult. Nasser was in Melbourne overseeing Mundine's preparation for his title fight against Sam Soliman on 28 May, more than a week away.

'I've made contact with Khoder Nasser today and we'll be meeting when he gets back to Sydney,' Peponis said. 'We need to come together and broker something and get on with it.'

Who knows what they will come up with? Gallop, the chief executive, had already said there would be no salary-cap concessions to allow Williams to earn more, no matter how much he thought he was worth.

The first rule of any negotiation is to find a competitor. The second rule is, if you can't find one, invent one. Who knows the difference? After that, all you need is luck, and Williams was about to get plenty of that. It came their way when the conversation started around them. Newspaper columns were filed. It meant others were about to do their heavy lifting for them.

Sure enough, Australian Rugby Union boss John O'Neill stepped forward to claim the ARU had no interest in rugby league players, saying the ARU was more interested in junior players the League had coming through. Rather than rule Williams out with a simple declarative denial, though, O'Neill talked and talked until eventually it seemed more possible than ever.

'What we are seeing at the moment is the force of the UK and European clubs,' he said. 'We have been talking about it for a while in terms of our talent being under attack, but it's clear if you see great rugby league players like Sonny Bill and Mark Gasnier talking about going to play rugby in France, it gives you some idea of the size of the dollars on offer.'

While Craig Gower was still the only player to leave the NRL for European rugby, O'Neill warned the money was legitimate. 'It is a genuine threat. I don't think we are going to see it go away. We are seeing second-division clubs in France like Toulon paying extraordinary money for [former Wallabies captain] George Gregan and others. Dan Carter, the great All Black five-eighth, has been offered €700,000 for half a year to have a sabbatical in France. The entrepreneurs who are running those clubs see the world as one big market place for them. All I'm saying is the world is a smaller place now.'

Throughout this, few picked up on Williams' newly found stance that he was underpaid and under-appreciated, along with his threats to walk out unless the club addressed them . . . and then sat them against his criticism of Mason just two months earlier for essentially doing the same thing.

The *Australian*'s Stuart Honeysett noticed, though. In May he told Williams to buy a dictionary and 'look up the word hypocrite': 'Williams' loyalty has a price – it's just a little higher than Mason's. What message does that send to Polynesian players? Obviously stay loyal until you get a better offer.'

I wrote a similar column in the *Daily Telegraph* the same day. 'Sonny Bill lost respect for Willie,' I wrote, 'and yet he is now threatening the same thing'. Until now, there was nothing in our relationship that might have caused a problem. After this column, there was everything.

The *Herald* covered the story by reporting tensions between Williams and the club were set to escalate and then repeated his grievances listed by Proszenko. Sonny Bill Williams was serious.

In other words, Sonny Ball.

Honeysett's criticism was an indicator of greater change. There came a backlash Sonny Bill had not experienced before. When he was caught drink-driving or fined for urinating in public in June 2007, or when photos emerged of him having sex in a hotel cubicle two months before that, Williams maintained unprecedented public support. It was a testament to his popularity, and to the modern culture of pop celebrity. Bulldogs fans supported him entirely. In place of any disappointment they felt at Sonny Bill's behaviour, essentially the result of poor decision-making, they instead attacked the media for sensationalising each incident. Such is the advantage of celebrity.

Now, fans were turning. Williams was losing his most loyal group.

This all happened over the weekend. The following Thursday Williams appeared on the *Footy Show* to explain. Fans wanted answers. The *Footy Show* was a soft forum to get his side out, but what few expected was how evasive he was in his answers.

Williams was normally polished on television. This time, he looked confused. 'There's a few issues I need to sort out with the club,' he said. 'It's nothing to do with the players. It's not all about money, but money is an issue. It's about money but it's also about opportunity – I see rugby as a challenge.

'I'm a sportsman and I definitely see it as a challenge, the whole rugby union thing. It's also about opportunity and I see rugby as an opportunity. If I did decide to do that, there would be a lot of goals I could try to achieve. I have achieved a lot in rugby league but this is all just talk at the moment, there has been no formal offer or anything but what I have said is that if rugby did come knocking on the door with a serious offer I would definitely consider it.

'I definitely don't think I am bigger than the game, but I think I have a right to do what's best for myself and my family. Say a guy earning $80,000 a year is offered $200,000 a year, what's he going to do? Is he going to weigh up the situation? It's just the same for me. I'm just a normal bloke and if people come and want me, I don't think I'm worth that but if they say "Look, we think you're worth this amount", of course I'm going to think about it. I'm not a dummy.'

Williams deflected the criticism. 'People have come out and jumped to conclusions and said I am a hypocrite. That one word is affecting me a lot. I hate that word. I guess above all, that is one of the things I would hate to be called. I'd like to think I am a pretty honest person. What I said about Mase [Willie Mason] was that if someone you respect tells you to do something and then turns around and does the exact opposite then of course you are going to lose respect for them.'

Kind of like signing a contract and then reneging on it.

Only once did Williams offer a peek behind the curtain, at what might be driving him. Again it revealed his confusion.

'I guess in most other professional sports, the players have had a pay increase over the last couple of years so I guess something has to be done,' he said. 'I'm all for a salary cap because it evens out the competition but . . . if a sponsor wants to pay me something to play league it gets poured back into the salary cap and affects other players so I can't do that. I guess maybe rules like that need to be changed, I don't know, but if we don't see that happening then more players are going to leave.'

This was a tremendously emotive argument. The moment everybody heard that, they argued why shouldn't a man be allowed to go out and earn what he is worth? Everybody realised Sonny was a brand all his own. Who is the game to stop him earning money for being SBW?

Sadly, here Williams is making the basic mistake of being uninformed. The NRL has two levels of sponsorship funding for players.

The first is a marquee player allowance which, under NRL rules, says, '. . . any or all of the Top 25 players at each club can share in payments made by club sponsors seeking to use a player's intellectual property. These may be guaranteed in the playing contract by clubs.'

It is a commonsense rule that lets companies sponsor individual players on top of their club sponsorship. It allows them to pay players to wear their brand of shoe or drive their car and appear in club colours to help make the sale. It is capped at $600,000 per club and the entire amount can go all to Sonny or be split between him and his teammates.

That is the sponsorship money Sonny seems to be referring to that gets 'poured back into the salary cap and affects other players'.

But there is another sponsorship agreement that is completely uncapped under NRL rules, its website stating: 'Players can earn *unlimited amounts from corporate sponsors who are not associated with the club and who do not use the game's intellectual property (no club logos, jerseys or emblems) provided these are pre-approved. These agreements may not be negotiated by the club as an incentive for a player to sign a contract, nor can they be guaranteed by the club. In other words, sponsors can pay a footballer as much as they believe he is worth to advertise their product, the only stipulation being they are not allowed to use the NRL or club's intellectual property.'*

In other words, Bolle could have paid Williams a million dollars a year if they believed he was worth it, ten million a year if they thought that was value for money, and their only obligation was they could not have any NRL or Canterbury Bulldogs branding in the campaign when Sonny appeared smiling in the glossy magazines. That they chose to pay him much less suggests he was being paid market value.

The point here is not so much the claim for more money or even what Williams was saying, but to understand Williams' transformation. Then it all makes sense. The Sonny we all thought we knew was the man there just a few months earlier, still humble, with an inherent sense of fairness so ingrained he understood the reasons for the salary cap. Now, that was beginning to change.

Once Williams' troubles were raised Mundine became the most vocal campaigner about how unfairly Williams was paid. More than once Mundine declared that he returned to St George in 1999 for $600,000 a year and here was Williams, ten seasons later, on two-thirds of that. It sounded woefully short in those terms.

Yet it completely ignored the obvious point. Mundine was paid in the aftermath of the Super League war. *Every* big name was on bigger wages then. Super League nearly broke the game and one of the first priorities when the game got back together was to bring club expenditure – the one Gallop was so stubbornly sticking to through his support for the salary cap – back under control. It saved the game.

If nothing else, though, Williams' comments on the *Footy Show* put the salary cap in focus.

As Williams was giving his version on the *Footy Show*, Nasser was interviewed for a rugby website in New Zealand and delivering a slightly different message. 'He has made a statement and if an [NZRU] offer was to come he would definitely consider it,' Nasser said. 'He was basically saying he has achieved what is there to be achieved in league. You have to remember, I'm also associated with Anthony [Mundine], and with a lot of great athletes and sportsmen these days [they] want to test the boundaries. We will see what unfolds.'

Nasser spoke with a certainty unusual for the situation. Was he daring the Bulldogs?

Regardless, they were filthy at his comments.

'These things are all going to come to a head soon,' Nasser said. 'I am waiting for Anthony's fight to finish, then I am going to have a big chat with him. We will have to work out what will happen, we are going to have to meet up with the club in the next two to three weeks.'

Few knew it at the time, but Nasser was already negotiating. Just nobody knew where.

NZRU chief executive Steve Tew was surprised and cautious of Nasser's enthusiasm, saying, 'We are not interested in being part of a contract negotiation.'

Six days later Mundine defended his title against Soliman over twelve. It meant Nasser was flying back to Sydney.

IN the meantime, with all this going on, Williams went out and reminded everybody just what this was all about. He was a hell of a footballer. He practically destroyed Cronulla in Monday night football. The Sharks were on their way to finishing the season equal first and would have been the big story of the season if not for Williams.

This night, though, Williams came up with a performance few in the world were capable of. He scored a try and went after the more fancied Cronulla pack with a zest that seemed personal. Right on halftime he came together with Cronulla's representative five-eighth Greg Bird. They collided and a brawl threatened to erupt. Then midway through the second half he came together with big Cronulla prop Ben Ross and this time referee Tony Archer called him out.

'I gave you the benefit before halftime,' he said, before threatening to put him in the sin-bin. 'Go on with any rubbish one more time and I'll sit you down. Calm down.'

Later, Cronulla coach Ricky Stuart came as close as anybody did to describe the quality of Williams' performance. 'He beat us on his own.'

WHAT happened next is just about the most important part of this whole tale. It certainly goes a long way to explain many things that happened in the days and years since.

Peponis finally booked that meeting with Nasser. By now he was aware of all Sonny's concerns, not just the belief he was being underpaid but of Sonny's desire to be a greater voice at the club, to be a stronger voice in the Polynesian community. Demands they believed they had already agreed to meet. Peponis and Greenberg had no idea exactly what Williams' new demands would be, but prepared for the meeting with an open mind and an acknowledgment to do as much as possible to convince Williams the relationship could be repaired.

A day before the meeting Williams' contract was leaked to the *Sydney Morning Herald*. It was a wonderful piece of strong-arm negotiation, designed to the minute. There were several concerns, apparently. The first was that the annual payment of $400,000 did not increase from year to year, 'regardless of inflation, form or his status in the game'. It also included an amount 'in lieu of leave entitlements, superannuation and fringe benefits tax'.

What, no holiday pay for an athlete who works four hours a day, five days a week?

Reading the *Herald* that morning the Bulldogs were convinced that Nasser was preparing to challenge the validity of the contract. The *Herald* also produced a 'leading agent' who was prepared to support the view that the contract, a standard NRL contract, was unfair. The leading agent did not want to be named, which was understandable, preferring to remain anonymous for fear of being revealed as an idiot.

'You would think that his money would go up over that amount of time otherwise, in real terms, he is getting less and less each year,' he said.

Of course he is right about that: the annual fee should have risen each season. But the fact Williams and his previous management did not believe it was necessary to include this in the deal at the time they negotiated it did not make the contract invalid.

The leak angered the NRL. They believed it was designed to embarrass them. For one, it was timed to cause maximum damage. Secondly, the benefits spoken of actually were there. I called the League the morning the story broke to ask how they could make standard contracts without basic workplace rights and a standard contract soon came my way.

There it was, in Schedule 1, Clause 3 (b), paragraphs (i), (ii) and (iii) of the contract: annual leave, superannuation and fringe benefit entitlements built into every player's annual salary. It was standard across the game.

Peponis spoke to Nasser and a meeting was set for 4 June. He was not prepared for what happened. Given the importance of the meeting Canterbury Leagues Club chief executive John Ballesty joined them along with Bulldogs sponsor Arthur Coorey. Expecting a dinner meeting with Williams and Nasser, they arrived at Le Sands Restaurant in Sydney's Brighton Le Sands, a suburb on Botany Bay, under a howling rain, and looked at the assembled posse. There was Nasser, Mundine, Solomon Haumono (another former NRL player now boxing), Williams' father John and his brother John Arthur. No Sonny.

Now, the Bulldogs officials were all successful people in their own right. And it is fair to say they have attended the odd business meeting in their time. So it was only natural to assume that at some stage early in proceedings they expected an explanation or at the very least an apology to be made for why Williams, the guest of honour, was not at a meeting he spent months urging for.

When no explanation was forthcoming, confusion consumed the Bulldogs. No, Nasser explained, Haumono and Mundine were there because Haumono was an ex-Bulldogs player and from a Polynesian background, while Mundine was close to Sonny.

The Bulldogs officials were polite enough not to roll their eyes.

Asked later where Williams was, Greenberg said, 'I've no idea.'

No meals were ordered, just coffee and water and hot chocolate. This was news. It was the first time, and perhaps the last, any Bulldog official attended a meeting where the beverage of choice was hot chocolate. Greenberg sat at the end of the table between Mundine and Williams' father, and opened it up.

'We thank you for agreeing to meet with us,' he said. 'It's a shame Sonny is not here. I want to make it clear that the club needs and wants Sonny to honour his contract with the club. We have been hearing rumours for some time that he is looking to leave. He has a contract which we believe is lucrative and makes him one of the highest paid players in the League. If he is not happy about certain things then please let us know what we can do to help him. You must understand that there is a salary cap which we have to honour. We keep reading in the newspapers that Sonny has issues. We would like to hear what those issues are.'

Greenberg looked to Nasser. 'Khoder, you're his manager, what's this about?'

Nasser was brief. 'Those reports are bullshit,' he said. 'They are not coming from us. He is going to stay with the Bulldogs but you should be doing more to get him third-party deals. He needs to feel the love.'

Williams' father agreed. 'Just treat him right,' he said. 'All he wants is to be treated right.'

Peponis, sitting opposite Nasser, stepped in. The smartest man at the table, he knew they could drink hot chocolate until they got spots on their chin but nothing said that day was going to matter until they spoke to Williams.

Here you had to feel for the good doctor. Peponis had no clue he was playing Sonny Ball at the time and what a tremendous waste of time the whole meeting was. He certainly had no idea the Bulldogs were being kept off balance as Nasser negotiated elsewhere.

'We will do whatever we can to get him third-party deals,' Peponis said. 'We have been doing our best. However I would like to meet with him.'

Nasser massaged the Bulldogs officials. The contract, he told them, was 'better than Fort Knox . . . You can get out of Fort Knox, you can't get out of this'.

He said it, but he didn't believe it.

'The whole time,' he would say later, 'I was thinking, "You arrogant fucks, I am going to fuck you right up."'

Greenberg was somewhat evasive in the next morning's press, unprepared to reveal all the details to the media and let it play out publicly.

'We just talked about some of his concerns and we're not going to get into the details of his concerns but they're all things that we'll work on in the coming weeks and they're all achievable. Again, both parties agree that Sonny is a big part of the Bulldogs' future.'

Nasser echoed his sentiment.

'We have broken the ice and now we're just trying to find some common ground. They were pretty positive talks – but it's just the first step.'

Before the dinner meeting ended they agreed to meet again.

Three days later, on 7 June, Greenberg was in his office with Peponis waiting for Williams and Nasser. In front of him was the *Sydney Morning Herald*. Peter FitzSimons, the columnist, was going against trend. Greenberg saw he had support in FitzSimons, whose message was the same as many believed. A contract was a contract, a 'legal and honourable commitment'.

As Greenberg folded the newspaper Nasser turned up alone.

'Look,' he said, 'I have spoken to Sonny, we would like to catch up for dinner with you and George on Tuesday [10 June]. He is not going anywhere. Don't believe what you read. Just make him feel important. He wants to hear it from you. How are you going with the third-party deals? I assume if we can negotiate something that will also make him happy.'

Nasser was in luck.

'Someone has contacted me interested in talking to Sonny about a third-party sponsorship,' Peponis told Nasser. He mentioned a six-figure amount.

Williams finally turned up to his own dinner on the Tuesday. It was held at Pinocchio's in Randwick, and not one person there gave a thought to the great irony of that.

'I want to see myself as a leader and I want to be a leader of the Polynesian people,' Williams told them.

'I also want some guarantees about third-party deals,' Nasser added.

Peponis listened. 'As Todd would agree,' he said, 'there is no doubt that you are one of the leaders of the club. Whether you will be a captain is a matter which will play itself out in time. However, being a captain does not happen overnight, it's something that you achieve by proving yourself as a leader.'

'Sonny,' said Greenberg, 'you have a big future at this club. You're one of our stars. We need to help you become a leader and equip you with the right skills.'

'We can't guarantee third-party deals. That's against salary-cap rules,' Peponis said. 'What I can do is introduce you to people and then it is a matter for you to sort out direct with that party regarding any third-party deals. The club cannot be involved in these discussions.'

Everyone could see what was happening.

To pave the way, Peponis then told Williams he had met with a sponsor willing to sponsor him.

'I hear you. I'm happy with this,' Williams said.

For three hours they spoke, their conversation strictly private until they turned up in a court affidavit, word by word, two months later. Greenberg and Peponis revealed their plans for the future, for Williams to become captain of the club and a leader in the Polynesian community. All the things he wanted.

It looked like their business was done. Greenberg took it to the conclusion.

'Well, I would like to put out a press release which talks about the club and Sonny moving forward,' he said. 'As you know, Khoder, there has been a lot of media speculation about Sonny leaving. It has upset a lot of our supporters, particularly young kids and our supporters.'

'I don't have a problem with that,' Nasser said. 'Let me know what you are going to issue so I can approve it on Sonny's behalf. Sonny, is that okay?'

'Sure,' Williams said.

'Would the third-party deals be under the present contract or something new?' Nasser then asked.

'These deals will be over and above your current contractual entitlements,' Greenberg said.

What was said next explains everything.

'Looks like the only person who is not going to make any money is me,' Nasser said. 'Sonny's previous agents are the only ones who are laughing.'

While Williams had sacked Gavin Orr earlier in the year, Orr still held the legally binding contract.

The next morning Greenberg was relieved. 'It's about giving him leadership opportunities, opportunities to meet people,' he said to every reporter who called. 'Sonny has very strong views on football. He's very intelligent and articulate. I think he's grown up a lot in the past twelve months.'

Greenberg called Nasser to read him the press release about to be sent out, reaffirming Williams' commitment to the club.

'That's fine, my man,' said Nasser.

So out it went: 'Sonny Bill Williams has moved to end speculation about his future with the Bulldogs, confirming his commitment to the Club for the duration of his contract at a meeting . . .'

It included a quote from Williams, no doubt made up in the office but endorsed by Nasser: 'I now have a better understanding of the direction the Club is heading and there's no question it's something I want to be part of.'

Not one step in all this was easy. And just as the Bulldogs thought they were moving forward, it changed again. Now Williams was unhappy about something else.

In an interview aired on TVNZ in New Zealand in early June, Williams revealed his unhappiness with the Bulldogs was not just about wanting more money, or a greater leadership role. He was also unhappy he was forced to admit he had a drinking problem a year earlier when he was fined for urinating in public. It was the third time in three months Williams had found himself in the headlines for alcohol-related incidents, after a driving-under-the-influence charge and a tryst with ironwoman Candice Falzon.

'I feel like I was hung out to dry,' Williams said in the interview. 'I didn't want to go and speak to the media. I'm a frigging twenty-year-old kid and the CEO says stand here and say that. What are you supposed to do? It's like you've been naughty and that's just the fastest way to make it right. I was very pissed off that I had to say I had a drinking problem because the only problem I had was being naïve.'

Why this was not brought up in private when they could have addressed it puzzled the club. For that reason the Bulldogs were not too concerned. The constantly moving goalposts appeared, to them, an attempt at leverage and with the problem almost sorted they figured it would soon disappear. The CEO Williams referred to was former CEO Malcolm Noad. It was far enough removed that they could declare a new regime was running the club now.

Not every Bulldog was happy with Williams, though. Built on toughness, with a little steel in their soul, the Bulldogs' clubmen came out with one strong voice. All were committed to an ideal. The club was bigger than the player. To them it was club first, player second, the only way it would ever be.

Matt Ryan played centre in the Bulldogs' 1995 premiership. 'The hard part is he is still a kid and it comes back to the advice you are getting. If someone keeps on telling you something, you will eventually believe it. I think he is very confused. I don't think his new manager is doing the right thing,' he said.

Again, the conversation was going on around Williams.

'I stayed at Canterbury because I loved the club,' Ryan added, 'not because of money. If [then chief executive] Peter Moore said I was worth $70,000, that's what I took. I didn't have a manager until Bullfrog retired. Sonny Bill is on fantastic money. They are not rockstars, they are athletes. Sonny Bill should just knuckle down and play football.'

Another former player, Darren Britt, was of similar mind. 'I don't like seeing the Bulldogs in the papers like this. Sonny Bill has been on good money all his career and at the end of this contract he can get even more. If he wants money he just has to stay dedicated. He signed a contract, he should stick to it.'

Joe Thomas, hooker in the Bulldogs' 1988 premiership, said, 'The longer this issue drags on, the worse it will get for the Bulldogs. It is tarnishing the jersey with the bad publicity and we don't need it.'

By now Steve Mortimer, the club's greatest player, had already seen too much. 'I wish Sonny Bill the best of luck.'

'How many games has he played compared to the cash he gets?' said Paul Langmack. 'Who does he think he is, Harry Kewell? He comes across as a humble bloke. I like the kid but he should just worry about football. His manager is ruining his image. That meeting the other night was outrageous. The only thing missing was Don King.'

Under the new rules of Sonny Ball, being played here, the balance of power shifts from club to player. Where once the club held the balance of power, able to work closely with other clubs in a gentleman's agreement, and later a salary cap, to ensure payments stayed down and players stayed in order, power was shifting to the player. There are many good reasons to explain why. Changes in poker machine laws, membership structures, increasingly made clubs answerable to their own success, or lack of. The upshot was clubs needed to pay more attention to on-field success to drive profits across their business. At the same time, players had the choice now of not only joining other clubs but, if they did not like what they were seeing, other codes, in other countries.

But not every player.

Only the very best could play Sonny Ball.

FOR a while everything returned to normal, or as normal as normal as it got nowadays. Days after Nasser gave Greenberg the go-ahead for the press release, reports surfaced that Williams was unhappy about his quote in the press release. He told those close to him he was still far from happy.

The only bright news was that his knee injury was recovering and a week after the Bulldogs conceded their most points in forty-nine years in a 58–18 thumping to Canberra, Williams was ready to return.

'The medical staff told him if he can get through all the footy stuff this week he'll be right to play,' said hooker Corey Hughes. 'There's a couple of others we're missing at the moment that are key for us – and Sonny is certainly one of them so it will be good to have him back.'

The Bulldogs were playing the Sydney Roosters but Mason was missing, stood down to prepare for the State of Origin representative clash. He was playing for NSW.

Even with no Mason, former Bulldog Mark O'Meley taunted them the week of the game. 'They have lost their aura a bit,' he said. 'And they are not the family club anymore. They're about business now and they don't put the players or the families first.'

O'Meley then went out and destroyed the Bulldogs, leading the Roosters to a 24–14 victory.

Williams was strong in his first game back in a month, laying on both his team's tries with flick passes.

Maybe Nasser saw it as an opportunity. Who knows, but after the game Williams received no points in the Dally M judging for the game's best players. Judge Laurie Daley allocated all three-, two- and one-point votes to the winning Roosters players.

Nasser was not particularly happy with the judging and included it as part of a larger agenda.

'To judge that Sonny Bill wasn't one of the three best in that game shows how out of touch with reality he is. I know Laurie is an expert, but he also helped picked the Blues team and look how they went. I agree with my man Anthony Mundine that Laurie is a person created by the same people who created

Super League. Laurie, eyes don't deceive most people, why did they deceive you? Or didn't you see just how good Sonny is?'

Former Australian player Geoff Gerard, a NSW selector with Daley, thought it an odd comment.

'Fancy him questioning Laurie over football.'

Williams was named man-of-the-match the following week when he led the Bulldogs to a 26–18 win over Brisbane.

'He was outstanding,' said Brisbane coach Wayne Bennett. 'Certainly no one tried harder than him out there today. He was on the right-hand side, then the left . . . he was everywhere. I thought he played himself into the ground.'

It was a typical Williams performance. For all the improbable skills, his greatest asset, according to a teammate, was his attitude to what they call 'the one-percenters'. The small jobs, often the dirty ones that, done right, contribute greatly to the victory. Few had attention to detail like Williams.

'People talk about his ball skills and the stuff he does in attack but . . . those sorts of things where he is covering up kicks in behind and pushing up in support – they aren't easy, pretty things in the game, but that's what we all want to do,' skipper Andrew Ryan said.

He was never more valuable to the club.

The Bulldogs had won just once all season without him. They averaged twenty-five points a game when Williams played and just ten when he wasn't: on his own, he was worth fifteen points a game. On top of that Williams led the club in tackle breaks, offloads and line-break assists. These mean nothing to those who do not know the game but everything to those with even a little understanding about what makes a player worth the emblem on his chest.

Williams led the club even though he had missed six games through injury. It went without saying he also led the club in average metres per game, meaning he ran further than anybody else.

For a moment things were back to normal. Williams was back playing football, playing well, and all the talk was what he liked most, about what he could do on the footy field. For all the soap opera around him, Williams always struggled with that part of it. So it was good to finally be back in the newspapers for all the right reasons.

Until the following week, when it got crazier. You would be disappointed if it didn't.

In their bid to appease Williams and his Polynesian voice, Canterbury announced a promotion they believed would be received with unanimous support across the rugby league community or, at the very least, please Williams. They announced free entry for Saturday's home game at ANZ Stadium between the Bulldogs and New Zealand for anyone who turned up with a New Zealand, Fijian, Tongan or Samoan passport. Polynesians in for free.

Given a large part of the club's supporter base was Lebanese, and the largest group by far was still of Anglo-Saxon heritage, many of those fans wondered what they had done wrong. For years the club had maximised the extreme popularity of Muslim winger Hazem El Masri to promote itself as a multicultural club with a clear majority over other clubs when it came to Lebanese and Middle Eastern fans.

The club's website went into meltdown, all citing reverse discrimination.

'Just because I don't live in the Island I have to pay. Discrimination if ever I have seen one,' wrote David of Sydney.

Nobody had any doubt the move was to appease Williams. Yet Greenberg was quick to address the anger.

'This is the first of different initiatives we are doing with different parts of the community . . . We might have Australia Day, who knows?' he said. 'I want to be a leader of a club that tries different things and if we get criticised, shoot us down.'

There was never an Australia Day, a Lebanese Day or even a Middle Eastern Day. The idea backfired enormously. Not because 2893 Polynesian fans turned up, but because Sonny Bill didn't.

He pulled out with a back injury the day before the game.

5

FLYING HIGH

TODD Greenberg was at home the day his world changed. It was one of those late winter afternoons, not really winter at all, and he was in the backyard doing what his job rarely allows him to do. Be a father.

It was 26 July and it started like it usually starts in this game, quietly with a phone call. At the other end was broadcaster Ray Hadley in an ad break from his 2GB radio show, the 'Continuous Call'.

A caller had lit up the radio box.

'You know anything about Sonny Bill being spotted going through Customs to get on a flight?' Hadley said to Greenberg.

Greenberg had been Bulldogs chief executive for only six months but already he knew the story would take some beating.

'Sometimes you're close to the mark,' he said to Hadley, 'but geez, you've really missed it on this one. You probably need to check your sources.'

Greenberg knew Canterbury was playing Monday night, just two days away. More than that, he spoke to Sonny the previous day at a kids' coaching clinic and not a word suggested he was doing anything other than getting ready for this game, which was necessary because the Bulldogs were not travelling all that flash.

Sonny at the airport?

Hadley laughed, 'Fair enough, just thought I'd check with you.'

Still, Greenberg hung up and felt an itch. On Thursday he sat in a meeting with Williams and incoming coach Kevin Moore and captain Andrew Ryan discussing next season's plans. A reporter called to check out a rumour that Williams was weeks away from walking out on Canterbury for a rugby union deal overseas. While the gossip columns had alluded to it for months it was at odds with the Sonny in the meeting, so Greenberg quietly put it to bed and not a peep made it into the press.

Yet it was not as absurd as it seemed, not in the newspaper offices where everybody knew the Orrs' contract ran four more years and not in the Canterbury football office either, where they knew the same thing.

Greenberg called George Peponis and they agreed Arthur Coorey would meet Nasser the following day, the Friday. The next morning Nasser cancelled and rescheduled it for the next day. Saturday morning, Peponis called Greenberg to tell him the meeting had gone ahead and Nasser had assured him Williams was going nowhere.

Yet after Hadley's call Greenberg thought it was all a bit convenient, so he went through his phone until he found Nasser's name.

'Hey mate,' Greenberg said.

'What's happening?' Nasser said.

It seemed very cordial.

'Look Khoder,' Greenberg said, tired of games. 'Enough nonsense. Just tell me, are the reports true that Sonny has left the country? Yes or no?'

'Yep,' said Nasser. 'Sonny's had enough.'

'Right. I don't want to talk to you any further,' Greenberg said, hanging up.

As simple as that, it all changed.

It was late afternoon, after 5 pm, and Greenberg sat down and let it wash over him. It was true. For five whole minutes he sat there, gathering himself, knowing his world was about to change. It was the last five minutes of peace he would have for some time. Soon, reports Williams was spotted travelling through Customs will be all over Hadley's show. More than one witness saw him at the airport.

Anthony Mundine drove him, with his Canterbury teammate Willie Tonga. Tonga's presence was kept quiet. Mundine noticed Williams was 'jittery' in the car, though he maintained he was doing the right thing. There were a few laughs, a few quiet moments, some serious talk.

'He genuinely feels in his heart and in his mind that he's done the right thing,' Mundine said the following day. Mundine was three days from a title defence in Newcastle on 30 July, against Japan's Crazy Kim, and so happy to speak. He needed every chance he could get to sell the fight against the Japanese fighter, unrecognisable on his own street.

'The only thing that was really bugging him was that he didn't have the opportunity to explain to his boys – and I don't know if that was boys as in teammates or boys as in his mates close in the team – and his hardcore fans at the Dogs and in rugby league in general how he felt.'

HIS small window of peace over, Greenberg called Peponis.

'Do me a favour,' he said at the end. 'Ring each of the board members and tell them to turn their phones off. It's really important we don't get found out here. We need to all be on the same page. And when you've done all that, turn your phone off, too.'

Greenberg then called coach Steve Folkes. The Dogs had a training run the following morning.

'First thing you need to figure out is who's playing in the jersey on Monday night,' he said. 'I don't have much other info but do me a favour and don't talk to anybody until you get to training tomorrow.'

'You know me, I don't answer my phone anyway,' Folkes said.

Then Greenberg called the captain, Andrew Ryan. Where Peponis and Folkes were stunned, Ryan's pain went beyond. He kept asking questions. Sonny had walked out on them? Greenberg had no answers.

'It's really important that you talk to some of the senior boys and tell them that we'll talk about this tomorrow at training,' Greenberg said. 'You need to tell them not to talk to anybody. We need to be really tight in our messaging.'

Greenberg stressed silence again to Ryan, afraid what the players might say. He was not afraid that the players would criticise Sonny but the opposite. Greenberg was afraid that in their confusion the players would fall back to default mode and defend Williams' walkout: he's not a bad guy, we're going to miss him, all that. And all of which, when the reality set in that Williams was truly gone, would be far more catastrophic on the club and player morale. Williams was not coming back. The sooner the players realised, the better.

By now, Sonny was sitting in seat 14D with his cap pulled low. His travel companion was Nasser's brother, Ahmed. He had no clue a Customs officer tipped off Hadley. Even before the plane reached cruising altitude Hadley was airing reports Williams had walked out on the club. Disbelief was starting to register. Sonny stepped to the counter using his newly acquired Samoan passport, not his New Zealand passport, and told the officer he would be out of Australia for eight months. The Customs officer read all about Sonny Bill. He knew what that meant.

★

SONNY BALL

LIKE every good newsroom the *Sunday Telegraph* had the radio on and, at Ray Hadley's report, heads popped up. As quick as that, the room was alive. An energy runs through the newsroom when a story is breaking and, as confirmation arrived that Williams was gone, the paper gutted its news pages to make room. Pages were redrawn, stories thrown out to make room for this, the one they would all be talking about.

Nobody had heard of anything like this before. Rumours surfaced quickly that Williams was going to French rugby club Toulon. The figure was a two-year deal worth three million dollars. Some reporters began defending him, saying he was finally getting market value. What would happen to Williams' current contract with Canterbury was uncertain. He was in the first year of a $400,000-a-year deal with the Bulldogs, far less than the Toulon deal, but it was signed and registered, with four more years to run. It was 26 July 2008, a week before Sonny Bill Williams turned twenty-three.

The *Sunday Telegraph* ran the story on page one, reporting Williams had signed a two-year, three-million-dollar deal with Toulon. 'Sonny Bill Flees To France,' said the headline. 'NRL Bombshell: Superstar Quits'.

For reasons never explained the *Sun-Herald*, which had broken much of the news on Williams' complaints through-out the year, was slower off the mark. It had no mention of Sonny's walkout and flight to France until the fifth print run. Even then, the story ran five pages inside its sport section at the *back* of the newspaper where you would need a miner's hat to find it, under the headline 'Sonny Flees League'. Even more oddly, the first paragraph of the *Sun-Herald* coverage barely dealt with Williams' flight at all: 'Sydney Roosters forward Willie Mason revealed he knocked back a possible multi-million dollar deal to join renegade Sonny Bill Williams in French rugby.'

Here is one cost of Sonny Ball. All of us in the business were being played in different ways. Most of us knew it, as we often do, and went about getting the job done anyway.

So when the newspapers hit the stands the following morning the *Sunday Telegraph* remained deliriously happy. It was all anybody wanted to talk about and they had it, page one. The *Sun-Herald* was paying the price for trying too hard to stay sweet with Williams and Nasser. It splashed with ABC correspondent Peter Lloyd on bail in Singapore declaring he would not run from drug charges. Lloyd's arrest was already nine days old.

If the *Sun-Herald* was looking to do a story on a runner, they needed to chase the other guy. But the *Sunday Telegraph* was miles ahead. Two more full pages were devoted in the sports liftout. Teammates were sought for reaction, prop Jarrad Hickey relaying how his mum called and immediately when he heard the tone in her voice he thought there had been a death.

'Then she told me Sonny Bill Williams was on his way to France,' he said.

Fullback Luke Patten, among the club's leadership group, was strong and defiant, and his resilience filled the air with a warmth the Bulldogs fans needed to hear. 'If he doesn't want to be here, then perhaps it's a good thing because we only want guys that want to be here,' he said.

Immediately the TAB, the government betting agency, suspended betting on the Monday-night game against St George Illawarra, such was the impact. At NRL headquarters boss David Gallop was angry, trying his best to sound civil as he urged Williams to return in a doorstep press conference.

'It is obviously unacceptable to walk out on a contract,' he said. 'If he has personal issues we are happy to discuss them with him. But we will support the Bulldogs in any legal action to prevent him playing for anyone else other than the club he is contracted to. I am sure his teammates and fans would like an explanation.'

Greenberg told the *Telegraph* he already had advice from a Queen's Counsel. The Bulldogs' contract was watertight. Then the reporter, David Riccio, found French agent Pierre Vandome, who brokered Luke Rooney's move from the NRL to Toulon. Vandome confirmed the French club's interest. Not only that, Toulon wanted to buy out the final four years of Williams' contract worth $1.6 million.

'I know Toulon is interested to buy Sonny Bill Williams, not just to put up the money, but to buy out his Bulldogs contract.'

Vandome might have had the best of intentions, but not a word of what he said was true. Toulon had no intention of buying out the contract.

The *Telegraph* asked Andrew Johns to write a column. His column started: 'Disbelief. That was my initial reaction to hearing Sonny Bill Williams was on a plane on his way to France yesterday. I'm staggered by it to be honest. At the very least, it is poor form on Sonny's part. He has turned his back on his club, his fans and most importantly, his teammates. They'd be devastated and no doubt looking for answers. They're also entitled to be filthy that he has cleared out.'

And there, in essence, is why it was such a big deal. There is nothing new in a parting of the ways. Players leave clubs all the time, about as often as clubs sack players. But there is a bond between teammates, a trust that was severed in the most dramatic way. In looking after himself, Williams left his team-mates worse off. It is a sentiment that spreads across the National Rugby League and nobody can quite explain why he did it.

Wallabies coach John Connolly echoed Johns' sentiments. Connolly's nickname is Knuckles, which gives a small indication of his approach to life.

'My first reaction was that it can't be true,' he told the *Sun-Herald*. 'Contractually it can't happen unless someone at the club told him yes, you can go or unless he hasn't been paid third-party money or something like that, it just can't happen.

I think it's pretty bad form from Sonny Bill. These guys, these highly paid young guys, just seem to have a different set of loyalties and values. It's all about the dollar. Every manager worth his salt will be trying to get his player over there now.'

Phil Gould, a *Sun-Herald* columnist and a critic of the NRL administration, texted one quote to his paper: 'I told you so.'

ON the plane, Williams felt a tremendous sense of relief. He had finally done it – the bad marriage over. There was nothing to do but sit back and let the relief filter through. His plane landed late in Singapore and he missed his connecting flight to London. He had nothing to do except wait.

He turned on his phone and among the messages that came in was one from Folkes: 'Sonny this is the worst decision of yr life. You hav allowed others to run yr life. This will lose u the respect of everyone. I feel betrayed personally. I cannot stick up for u on this one. I am lost for words. I hope u no wat yr doing. Money is not worth yr integrity. U alone r accountable for this.'

It registered not a bleep with Williams. We can all figure that out by now. He lost respect for Folkes months ago. Who cares what he thought?

It did not take Williams long to learn of the furore back in Australia. In his white T-shirt, a black cap and backpack, he was just another traveller wandering Changi Airport. The time delay gave chasing media the chance to find him, though. Already reporters in England were being hustled and told to get to Heathrow to catch Williams before he connected to France.

The *Daily Telegraph*'s Lisa Davies was at Changi, returning from holidays when, in a gift from heaven, she saw Williams walk by. Doing what any good reporter would do, she approached him. Williams quickly made for the toilets. Soon the whole scene became comedy, a B-grade fugitive chase. Williams strode through the airport carrying his ticket and passport and refused to be diverted or even slowed as a small blonde, weighing about as much as six dollars worth of chopped liver, stayed hard on his heels. Soon after, the first pictures of Sonny Bill Williams were beamed back to Australia. The magnitude of what he was doing was starting to hit.

Soon there was another problem. Williams was travelling on his Samoan passport but was told he needed a visa when he landed in France. It was vital he entered the country as a Samoan, not a Kiwi. French rugby had a three-import rule, under what was called the Kolpak ruling, handed down in the European Court of Justice five years earlier. Under the agreement European Union countries and others with EU trade agreements, of which Samoa was one, were exempt from any import quota.

New Zealand was not. Toulon's three imports were taken by former All Blacks Jerry Collins and Tana Umaga, and former Penrith NRL player Luke Rooney. But by travelling on his Samoan passport Williams entered France as a Samoan and so was exempt from the rule. Before the week was over the French newspaper *L'Equipe* was likening the drama surrounding Williams' defection to an episode from *Dallas*. Who watched *Dallas* anymore?

While a Samoan passport allowed Williams entry into French rugby, Eddie Jones couldn't swing it the same way in England. Nobody figured Williams might need a visa. So, instead of transferring from Heathrow to Nice as planned, Williams needed to go to the French Embassy in London for his visa once he arrived in England.

And he knew what that meant. More reporters.

As Sunday morning dawned in Australia, Williams was flying to London. For a moment there was once again calm in his world. Nobody could get to him here on the plane.

Back in Australia it was only getting hotter. Confusion still dominated any discussion about Williams, and every discussion was about him.

On Sunday morning a Channel Nine producer called Danny Weidler to appear on the morning rugby league show, the *Sunday Roast*. Nobody knew for sure where Williams was. But the debate about to take place on air goes a long way to defining the odyssey of Sonny Bill Williams.

Sitting beside host Andrew Voss was Matt Johns, the former Newcastle star and international. Mark Geyer, a former Penrith player and also an international, was on Voss' right. Geyer was so angry he was shuffling in his seat. Across from him, to Johns' left, sat Weidler. He might have been shuffling in his seat for different reasons if he had noticed Geyer.

Sitting in the chair, Johns' mind went back more than ten years to the Super League war, when News Limited attempted a hostile takeover of the Australian Rugby League. It made many young men rich and brought such pain to the sport that people emerged convinced that if this didn't kill the game, it would never die.

In its early hours, when both the ARL and News Limited were signing players, Newcastle loomed as crucial. The Knights were not an initial priority but, as honours appeared shared in the frantic early rush the club emerged vital to both sides and at one point held what appeared to be the balance of power. News Limited sent two delegates to talk to the club and they were wholly unimpressive. As the players sat listening to rich promises, some among them, those who could be kindly described as not being top tier, sent the hearing into comedy. Players, reserves for reserve grade, started saying they might go . . . for a million dollars.

After the meeting, News made its trump play. The company knew it did not need the Knights as such. It just needed its two most popular players, Andrew and Matthew Johns. The only other player to match their popularity was captain Paul Harragon, but he was already signed and committed to the ARL, and News was prepared to take him on. They quietly made their offer and the brothers' eyes spun in dollar signs.

The Johns brothers knew how serious News was. Panicked, Harragon became the highest paid bus driver in Australia as he drove the Newcastle players to ARL headquarters in Sydney to negotiate directly with Phil Gould who, along with Australian coach Bob Fulton, was running the ARL fightback. Training was cancelled.

The ARL offered the entire playing group loyalty contracts to stay with them. Every player would be on more money than if they went to News Limited except two, Matthew and Andrew.

The Knights told Gould they wanted to make a decision as a group. They got on the bus and headed back to Newcastle for training. Before they hit the field in Newcastle, Matthew received a call from News. They were doubling the offer to him and Andrew. With the new figures rattling around in his head Matthew approached Harragon at training and told him, 'I don't know how we can knock it back'.

Hold on, Harragon said. Gould was already on the freeway to Newcastle.

Gould called the players into a room and filled it with ghosts. He spoke about traditions and rolled off old names and the current players' place among them and what it meant to be part of something bigger than where they were now. In their small dressing room, the sound echoing off painted brick walls, he spoke of qualities and character and all those things that make a young man's blood pump and then he ended his speech by saying, Now put your hand up if you're going to sign with the ARL. All hands went up bar two: Matthew and Andrew.

Now, sitting on set this morning with Sonny Bill Williams on a plane to a game where they will pay him top dollar, Johns remembered what kept him at Newcastle.

'Gus signed us,' Johns told Voss. 'He signed us to a good deal but he knew the Super League one was worth a lot more and he said, "Look boys, I'm going to give you a twenty-four-hour clause to get out." So we took it away and after we signed a lot of the Newcastle boys, my closest mates, some of the boys I went to school with, went in and signed with the ARL. When Super League found out that we had a clause to get out they offered us huge amounts of money and, in the last couple of hours of that clause, said "Money is no object." We didn't go back to Super League. We kept our deal with the ARL, which was a lot less, because of teammate loyalty.'

Johns' opinion reflected the overwhelming sentiment in the game. 'What disappoints me is what he has done to his club and his teammates, and the game, by walking out,' he said of Sonny. 'I really believe if the offer was so good and he was really that disillusioned, surely he should have given the Bulldogs the opportunity to say, OK, that's it.'

Here Johns was, getting to the heart of it without agenda. Whatever was said after, nothing spoke more to the truth of what happened more than what was just said.

Geyer seemed to understand as much. He was anxious to get off his opinion too and couldn't stay still. Voss put him through an unusual agony, though, first crossing live to NRL boss David Gallop outside NRL headquarters.

Gallop was forty-three on this day but there, standing in the morning sunlight, didn't look a day over sixty-five. You could lay pipe in his worry frowns.

'I think we have to start with something pretty fundamental and it goes way beyond contracts and money,' Gallop said. 'What we're talking about here is someone walking out on his teammates mid-season. It flies in the face of everything that kids are taught about team sport and that's the most disappointing aspect of it.'

Voss was doing a first-class job. If for no other reason than the whole time through the Gallop interview he could see what was happening to his right. Geyer was shuffling like a prize-fighter before the first bell.

Finally, Voss turned to him and, somewhere, Geyer heard a bell ring. 'To get out in the middle of the night, and back door it like he did, it's a dog act,' he said. 'I don't care what you say . . . I would never have done it to my teammates. That's the one rule you don't break.'

Geyer believed the $1.5 million a year was money Williams would have made anyway.

'He walked out on his mates,' he said again. 'He had a contract. The kid's not a star in my eyes – far from it.'

There seemed little doubt Weidler knew before Williams got on the plane that he was going to leave. Nobody was closer to the Khoder camp than him, and he had hinted at it in his *Sun-Herald* column for at least some weeks. If so, Williams' runner put him in a delicate position. While he no doubt supported Williams' actions, he also had confidences to keep.

'He had to go,' Weidler said, indicating at least some planning had gone into Williams' escape. This was no spur-of-the-moment decision.

Even if it was, as expected, as Geyer asked, 'why did he go out the back door'?

'There are legal reasons he had to do it this way. I'm not a lawyer, I can't go into it all but Sonny Bill had to go and he had to go in the best possible way for himself. He had to look after himself and his family by going this way.'

Voss asked why he could not have waited seven more weeks, at least until the season was over. He would still have had four more years on contract but at least he would not have deserted his teammates, and it would have given him and the Bulldogs a proper chance to see if their differences could be settled.

Weidler conceded he could have, but said little would have changed. 'Again, he would have had to go the way he went, without telling his teammates, without telling the club, because he just had to go. He had to cut, as simple as that.'

'I can't let this statement go,' Voss said. 'You're saying he *had* to go? What? He had a gun to his head saying he had to go?'

'If you're being threatened with injunctions, right, you've got to go,' Weidler said. 'If you're being threatened with worldwide injunctions, on your sport, or an injunction in Australia, and they're going to start throwing every legal mind in the country at you, you've got to make a move. You've got to make a move before they get an opportunity.'

Until now, Williams had been threatened with nothing because outside Williams' inner sanctum, nobody knew he was going anywhere. Had he sought legal advice that raised the prospect of injunctions?

Reading between the lines it became clear Williams had planned this for a while, or at least long enough to explore a legal strategy to escape his Canterbury contract – or, in the event there was none, the legal ramifications if he went anyway. The story was happening so quickly few had the time to consider that, but how long had he been planning it, and what was the whole Pinocchio's meeting about if he had?

Weidler then said something else widely overlooked in all the days that followed. He suggested that Williams was coerced into signing the five-year deal. 'Something which is a very important point,' he said, 'when Sonny went to sign that last contract he was told by medical officers with the Canterbury club that "your knee is dodgy". I heard Gavin Orr, his manager, saying it on air. "So you better sign up and sign up good." Now, this is a twenty-one-year-old kid. We're older than twenty-one, we can make better decisions in our lives. Now a twenty-one-year-old kid listens to a doctor, listens to a manager and says, "Okay, well I've got to do this now". Now, maybe somebody has opened his eyes. Maybe Khoder Nasser has opened his eyes.'

In any of the meetings or discussions between Nasser, Williams and the club none of this was mentioned. The chief reason for going, reported in the papers, was that Williams' two-year three-million-dollar deal at Toulon was finally delivering him market value. No other argument had been raised, save for Sonny briefly saying in New Zealand that he was unhappy being told to say he had a drinking problem a year earlier, among whispers of a falling out with coach Steve Folkes, all unconfirmed.

Geyer asked Weidler to 'tell me honestly' if Nasser was a bad influence on those he managed.

'Absolutely not,' Weidler said. 'His priority here is the footballer. It's not the club. It's not the game. It's the footballer.'

'So it's to break contracts then?' Voss asked.

'To make money for his client,' Weidler said.

'And in so doing,' said Voss, 'to break contracts then.'

'But that's his business,' Weidler said.

As the *Sunday Roast* was airing the Bulldogs assembled at Belmore Oval for training. It was a tough time for the club. They had won just one of their previous seven games and, nobody knew it yet, but they would finish the season in last place.

Andrew Ryan was still coming to terms with it. He revealed he met Williams on Thursday to discuss his future role at the club, long term, as part of the ongoing concerns about Sonny's role at the club.

'We are very shocked and disappointed,' he said. 'To give us no indication at all and to walk out on us while we're trying to prepare for a game is quite difficult to take.'

He talked quietly, the depth of his hurt poured into every syllable. 'He has hurt a lot of us, yeah.'

Ryan did not know where Williams was heading. 'It was on everyone's minds this morning and all of us are extremely disappointed with Sonny leaving us with the way the season is going. I had no idea. I got a phone call at 5.30 pm on Saturday. As far as I can tell no one here knew about it. For him to do that to the club which has given him a lot is disappointing.'

There was no doubt where Folkes stood.

'He has been here since he was sixteen,' he said. 'We have supported him in every way possible, sometimes above and beyond.'

Folkes spent much of the previous night wondering where it went wrong. 'I am thinking it is a decision he is going to regret. It is all a bit unbelievable,' he said.

Folkes was asked if he thought Sonny's new management had anything to do with his decision. 'It's just a coincidence, don't you think?' he said.

But he knew it was serious and permanent.

'I certainly noticed the change in his behaviour and his demeanour over the last three months or so. He was a lot more withdrawn and not as open and not as friendly. But the fact is he's responsible for his own decisions. Regardless of how much or how little he has been influenced by Khoder in a negative fashion, he's twenty-two years of age and he's responsible for the decisions he makes.'

Ryan agreed. 'Sonny is a big boy, he's a man and he makes his own decisions. Your manager only gives you options on things, but obviously Sonny makes those decisions as a man.'

Later that afternoon Gallop walked outside NRL headquarters at Fox Studios and stood in the entertainment quarter. For good news, announcements and press conferences were inside, with sponsored signage as the backdrop. Bad news got done out front. Gallop spoke slowly, deliberately and forcefully. He tried to get everything he was earlier briefed on out in the right order.

He called on the International Rugby Board (IRB) to refuse to register Williams' contract.

'On an urgent basis,' he added. 'Certainly we will be making an approach to them formally. They will know of this and they will know it is condoning international piracy to allow a player of either code to just walk out on a contract. If they condone this they are condoning a form of international piracy. If Sonny Bill were to play overseas, certainly the door would be closed for his return to the NRL at any stage in the future.'

It was big news. Gallop's stance had hardened overnight and Williams now faced a life ban from the game. Come back now or there was no coming back was Gallop's ultimatum. It was a gamble that depended entirely on Williams doubting his decision.

Gallop could have saved his breath with a quick call to the Australian Rugby Union. There was nothing the IRB could do to stop Williams taking up a French rugby contract. The IRB held no jurisdiction over the privately owned French clubs.

'The club is entitled to take on whatever player they see fit,' IRB spokeswoman Alison Hughes said. 'Our jurisdiction is a player must make sure he is fit to play international rugby. The club contract is a very different animal.'

The IRB believed it was a legal matter, not jurisdictional. If nothing else, that meant the contract would be registered in France. Who cared about Gallop and his NRL? The news sent Greenberg back to the lawyers with a migraine that would pull a train.

Meanwhile, and predictably, the place was going mad. No game in the world likes to drag the storm cloud over itself like rugby league. Player agent Steve Gillis revealed another player had a French rugby contract waiting to be signed while two more were in secret negotiations. Then Willie Mason, just months after playing against Williams in April's Trans-Tasman Test, confirmed the *Sun-Herald* story, claiming he still might go. 'Never say never,' he said.

At the Sydney Football Stadium the Sydney Roosters beat Manly and former teammates Mason and Mark O'Meley refused to comment on Williams' walkout.

Roosters coach Brad Fittler, a man of principle, knew it couldn't be ignored. 'He's walked out on a lot of people. I find it quite disappointing,' he said. 'I'd be quite disappointed if one of our players did it for whatever reason. I couldn't find a strong enough reason for his actions. His talent and his drawcard, everything about it is a big loss to rugby league, no doubt in the world.'

6

THE GAMES MEN PLAY

THE place was different now. For the first time you could see the hurt at Belmore, where for so long the Bulldogs were so defiant in the wake of whatever trouble you might want to throw their way, as if it might reveal weakness. Now, staff openly cried, though they had it together enough to keep it within the offices.

Gear steward Fred Ciraldo, a man who tries hard to present a tough image to the world, wept. Ciraldo was among those staff who had invited Williams into his home over the years, providing him with home-cooked meals and, more importantly, company. They could not believe Williams had walked out on their club without even bothering to say goodbye.

Folkes returned home from training and sat quietly trying to piece together where it went wrong. Apart from the obvious, when Williams signed with Nasser. That's when Sonny, as he said, went quiet and became more removed.

He thought back to when the Bulldogs agreed to provide free entry for Polynesians at the New Zealand Warriors game and Williams volunteered to be used in a midweek promotion. He volunteered because the whole promotion was set up to accelerate his role as a community leader. It all looked good. Then, the day before the game, Williams called him after their final training run and said he had a back problem. Folkes didn't think any more of it. The next morning Williams called again, withdrawing from the game.

They all seemed reasonably normal health worries, Folkes thought, except for those who know. He thought about the small details around Sonny's behaviour.

Football clubs are high on routine. If a player is unfit to play, he returns slowly through the rehabilitation group until he is fit enough to resume full training with the playing squad. The day after the Bulldogs lost to the Warriors, a 40–22 flogging without their best player, Williams turned up at the recovery session and said he wanted to train with the playing squad. There was no sign of a back problem.

Two days later the Bulldogs were flogged at training and Williams completed the whole session without any signs of discomfort, as you might expect if you were carrying even the remnants of an old injury. Williams looked fine, Folkes thought, and had no trouble proving his fitness for the St George Illawarra game the following Monday. But then he rang club doctor Hugh Hazard on Friday to say he was up all night with vomiting and diarrhoea. Dr Hazard told him he probably caught a virus and to stay at home to avoid passing it on to teammates.

'That was the last we heard of him,' Folkes said later.

HOURS after watching Danny Weidler defend Williams on the *Sunday Roast* the network did what any good network should do and continued to press its advantage. Sonny Ball works both ways. *National Nine News* prepared to interview Khoder Nasser in Newcastle while he was overseeing the final stages of Mundine's fight on Wednesday.

Nine News host Mike Munro protested. One of Australia's most respected newsmen, Munro feared it could descend into an embarrassing fight promotion and shed no great light on why

Williams walked. He believed Nasser might hijack the interview and use it to promote Mundine's fight. Finally Nine news director Ian Cook stepped in and told Weidler the interview could not contain Mundine and could not be a promotion for the fight but, as later reported, 'a proper look at the story'.

With that understood, Nine agreed to lead its bulletin with the story. A wonderful exclusive. From the top, Munro led with a report on Williams' walkout before crossing live to Weidler in Newcastle.

'Danny, you're with Sonny Bill's manager Khoder Nasser, what's he got to say about Sonny Bill taking off overseas?' said Munro.

'Well, Mike,' said Weidler, 'hopefully a lot. I'm about to have a chat with him now. Khoder, first of all, Anthony Mundine fights on Wednesday night here in Newcastle. That's why we're here. Why aren't you on a plane with Sonny Bill Williams looking after him with all this drama going on?'

'First,' Nasser said, 'I'd like to say that I'm up here for Anthony Mundine's fight night and that's a priority to me and I've got to be here for that. Why aren't I with Sonny Bill? I'd like to make this point strongly, I do not, I am not, authorised at any stage to speak on behalf of Sonny Bill Williams.'

'So you are saying you are not Sonny Bill Williams' manager?' Weidler asked.

'That's correct.'

The interview was not a minute old and already the fight was plugged twice and Nasser denied he was Williams' manager, the entire reason for the interview. Things didn't improve.

'So, can you speak to me then as a friend of Sonny Bill Williams and say, look, he has walked out on his teammates, a lot of people want to know why he went the way he went. As a friend of his, can you tell us why?' said Weidler.

'As a friend of his, I mean, what he's done, he's done, and we won't know until we hear from him.'

'But you've talked to him. I mean, you know what's going on through his mind. Give us an insight.'

'Well, there's a lot of things running through his mind and he must have, obviously, thought that was the best thing to do at the time.'

'Okay, look, it's been called a dog act,' said Weidler. 'Mark Geyer said that today. That's a strong description of what he has done.'

'Well, when we refer to a man like Mark Geyer who went from Penrith to the Tigers to Perth and, you know, everybody knows that he was on dope as well. So I don't take much of a comment from a man like that seriously. And for him to refer to Sonny Bill as a dog says a lot about him being the dog that he is.'

'Well, obviously this criticism is getting to you,' said Weidler. 'Obviously you're feeling it. As a friend, you know, Sonny wouldn't know about the criticism. Have you been able to contact him at all?'

'Well, that's the beauty. That Sonny doesn't even know about the criticism and I haven't contacted him. I know that Anthony Mundine has spoken to Sonny and that he said the only regret that Sonny had was that he couldn't tell all the fans, all the young kids that really look up to him, the reasons why he had to do what he did. But in time he'll be able to tell that.'

'So can you tell us why he went the way he did without telling his mates?'

'Well, at the end of the day everybody is sitting here and thinking about their own selfish needs, about "why hadn't he told us". I mean, nobody is thinking about Sonny and why Sonny did what he did. Everybody's thinking about themselves. I think in time we'll see why.'

'Khoder, thank you for joining us. I know it's been a difficult time. Mike, I hope that answered some of the questions.'

On the plus side, it was a tremendous plug for the fight.

The interview only deepened those concerned for Williams. And despite all that had happened, there still were some who were. Folkes' wife Karen had already called Sonny's girlfriend Genna Shaw to check she was okay. Williams had gambled everything to walk out on a contract and, live on television, the man orchestrating it was distancing himself.

Should the rest of us be concerned here?

Never.

As Weidler alluded earlier, Williams had gone through all his legal options well before getting on the plane. Nasser knew where they were legally vulnerable; Gallop and Greenberg's legal threat was completely expected. If it all went bad for Williams, and even Nasser, their assets could be seized. Unless . . . Nasser was not really his manager, but a friend. And if Sonny could not be found, papers could not be served.

For reasons nobody can quite explain, and certainly won't admit to now, some within Nine headquarters thought the interview was simply brilliant television. Oh, they will all be talking about this one forever, they thought. Others, with even a little experience in a newsroom, put their heads in their hands and thought exactly the same thing.

The following day Munro resigned. When 2GB's Chris Smith interviewed him hours later, Munro said of the Nasser interview, 'I wasn't pleased at all. And I said to the powers-that-be at the time, "I'm worried this is going to be one big plug for the Mundine fight. And it's not the story. Sonny's the story."'

As the Bulldogs prepared for St George Illawarra on Monday 28 July, Williams landed in London. It was 5 am and, as expected, his visa was a problem. Immigration refused to allow him to connect to France without a visa in his Samoan passport. Williams believed Toulon had already organised the visa in France but, after five hours, the officials did not change their minds. He needed a visa. Williams had to spend the night in London. A contingency plan was made to keep him out of sight.

Instead of heading to the usual tourist haunts, Williams and Ahmed headed to Wimbledon, for no other reason than they believed nobody would look there. Williams still took no chances and pulled his hoodie down tight when he and Ahmed went out that night.

The following morning fifteen reporters staked out the French Embassy, waiting for Williams to arrive to get his French visa. Not one of them had a clue. You can say this with great certainty as they all stood at the front entrance of the embassy, failing to even consider there might be a back door. This was a man, remember, who did not want to be seen.

But the visa was not ready, and Williams was told it would take at least 48 hours to clear. Williams now had to lay low in London for a couple more days until his visa could be issued.

Within hours of Williams landing in London that Monday morning the NSW Supreme Court issued a subpoena giving the Bulldogs a day to serve Nasser. The subpoena ordered him to provide documentation on where Williams was staying in Europe within twenty-four hours. Aware Nasser was in Newcastle for Mundine's fight, a process server travelled up the F3 freeway to serve the papers. He had good luck and bad luck. The good luck was that Newcastle is not a big city, so if some-thing as important as a world title fight was in town then only a few hotels would be deemed up to standard. The process server had no trouble finding the hotel where Nasser was staying.

'We've been able to locate him, but we haven't been able to eyeball him,' Bulldogs lawyer John Carmody said, which was the bad luck. 'We knew what hotel he was staying in at Newcastle, but he wouldn't accept service. He just stayed in his room and, of course, under privacy laws we're not allowed to find out from the hotel proprietor what room he's in.'

*

FOR all these reasons that night's game between Canterbury and St George Illawarra was some big deal. Nothing makes a game shine like a soap opera.

Before the game radio broadcaster Triple M asked Gallop to the box to talk about the NRL's position. Gallop knew how important it was that the game appeared united and strong on this. He was clear on the NRL's strategy. It was all about the sanctity of the contract. It was the only defence the game had.

Gallop walked into the small radio box and there, taking up a lot of the glass, was Phil Gould in his role as a Triple M commentator. So much had happened it was hard to believe it was still only a day after Gould's 'told you so' text message to the NRL. When Gallop walked in and Gould failed to turn and acknowledge him, Gallop knew it was on.

'David, David, can I just ask,' Gould began the interview, 'because I've heard you interviewed all weekend and I hear the same statements coming out time and time. Every time there's a question answered you repeat yourself every time, so you've got your little patter down pat there. Why would you make a state-ment that you're going to get the IRB to do this, or look into that, without having first having contacted the IRB and got their reaction to your problem? Because what you're doing is giving the IRB a chance to say "NRL who? What do you mean? We can't do anything about it". It makes us look like a second-rate sport.'

'I don't think you need to call what I've said "patter",' Gallop said, 'but what I've indicated . . .'

'Well, I'll go through every interview you've made this week,' Gould said, interrupting. 'It's the same language every time.'

'Give me a chance to answer,' Gallop said. 'What I indicated yesterday, on a Sunday morning, was that we'd be calling on rugby union and the IRB to get involved, because I do believe this has ramifications for both codes. If French rugby is an attractive option, it's surely going to be an attractive option to rugby union players, as well as elite rugby league players. I think they do have an interest in this. The club involved is part of their member nations and they must have jurisdiction to make sure this sort of thing doesn't happen for either code ... it's important that a contract is a contract. And ...'

'Please, please, please,' said Gould.

'Just let me finish, just let me finish,' Gallop said.

'Why has the sanctity of the contract suddenly raised its ugly head like this, when we've treated contracts like confetti for fifteen years? Why suddenly now are we going to make an example of Sonny Bill Williams?'

'I don't agree we've treated them like confetti.'

'Well, let's go back to Super League.' Gallop was heading into dangerous territory here. If Gould is not the smartest man in rugby league he is in the grand final, and, while Gallop was Super League's lawyer during the war, Gould emerged as one of the Australian Rugby League's most formidable soldiers. He knew his territory.

'Okay, let's go back to Super League,' Gallop said. 'What happened in Super League was players and clubs were party to a contract.'

'Yep,' said Gould.

'Clubs agreed with players that they could go. In this case the Bulldogs have not agreed that he could go.'

'See, now you're wrong. You're wrong. That's a very narrow description of what happened in Super League, because you challenged contracts everywhere.'

'Just let me finish.'

'You challenged contracts everywhere,' Gould said.

'Yes,' said Gallop.

'And broke contracts everywhere.'

'No, just let me finish,' said Gallop. 'In cases where clubs didn't release players to go to either competition, there were long protracted court battles over whether those agreements were enforceable.'

'When News Limited challenged the validity of the contracts. And even players we signed to the ARL,' said Gould, 'did you not induce them out of their contracts, and challenged their contracts in court? So don't say the sanctity of the contract has been upheld in our game, or in any walk of life, and suddenly Sonny Bill Williams is going to be the shining-light example of who can or who can't walk out on a contract. I want to know why Sonny Bill Williams has left our game. Why our most elite player has been driven out of the game. Why does he feel as though this is the only step he can take?'

'I would like to know that as well. But just going back to the point . . .'

'Well, can we stop making threats until we know that?' said Gould.

'Just let me go back to the point and let me answer you. There have been many cases over the years including during the Super League period where when clubs didn't want to release players, they went through a very long court [battle]. In many respects a very simple situation. There needs to be contractual certainty. All codes need that, all sports need it.

'Look, I think it's highly unusual that a player is going to walk out mid-season without telling anyone in his club he's going to go. I can't see very many players doing that.'

'Jamie Lyon did it.'

'No. He went to his club and said "I want to go." He didn't slip away secretly.'

'But he walked out on his contract.'

'And they let him go eventually.'

'Eventually. They didn't want to.'

'Very different circumstances.'

'And he was welcomed back three years later to play for Australia. You said that Sonny Bill Williams will never play in the NRL again. You can't enforce that threat.'

'He has never given any indication why he has gone, except . . . that he'd "had enough", whatever that means.'

'Sonny Bill Williams is like many players in this competition. See, Sonny Bill Williams is a great player, so he's got the opportunity to go to other employment. He can go to another code and get a contract. Ninety per cent of our players in the game can't do that – they're not attractive to rugby or they haven't got that sort of status. Sonny Bill can do it, but every player in the League is looking at the administration and the direction of our game and saying, "we have no plan, what is going on?"

'Everyone keeps telling us the game doesn't rate, we're playing in big stadiums in front of very small crowds. No one is telling us whether that's right or wrong. Earlier this year we went out and watched the Tigers and the Titans in front of 17,000 at Leichhardt Oval, and you said, David, "It was great nostalgia, great feel – but you'll go broke if you keep playing there."

'What are players led to believe with that? We hear about the poker machine tax, and the nine clubs in Sydney are struggling and players might not get paid. And we hear that the AFL is worth more than us in broadcast rights. We see Gasnier and [Jason] Ryles and these fellas are going to France and now Sonny Bill Williams has walked out. He's playing for a club that's got fifteen years here at ANZ Stadium. He's playing in front of 5000 and because he's Polynesian, he can't play State of Origin. He's got to watch those big games that he's not in. His team isn't going to make the finals this year and don't look like they'll make the finals for the next two years. "Where's my future, I've only got so much time, no one's giving me answers, there's no plan to this game." And all you're doing is giving him rhetoric. He said, "bugger this, I'm off."'

By now Gallop was frustrated. 'And all you're doing is outlining the game's problems and challenges, without giving solutions.'

'Well, give us answers to the problems. Let's not beat up on Sonny Bill Williams. Let's give us solutions to the problems. We've got no plan, David.'

'Of course we've got a plan.'

'You haven't got a plan.'

'Of course we've got a plan.'

'You can't answer the issues of the game.'

'What I'm telling [you] is the game has done some very significant things strategically. The game will go into a period of growth over the next few years. We will put ourselves in a position where we can do a great broadcasting deal.'

'On what research are you saying the game is going to grow? On what research?'

'The game's growing every year. The crowds are actually up four per cent this year.'

'Oh please.'

'Membership is up twenty-five per cent.'

'Please, please, please.'

'Well, where am I wrong?'

'I'm at the games. I'm at the games. The crowds are not growing, David.'

'The crowds are growing. Up four per cent this year.'

It was an exchange that went back thirteen years with barely a kind day in between, back to the Super League war, and every time Gallop and Gould found themselves together it invariably went the same way once again. It meant nothing because they were two men with different agendas and they could share that small radio box until it snowed in February and they would never resolve it.

It meant everything because Sonny Bill Williams was currently waiting in London for a visa for all those reasons spoken about.

7

VIVE LE SONNY

SONNY never struck anybody as the type to hide. That was him, just a month earlier, aiming to be a spokesman for Polynesian people. He spoke the language of someone bigger then, almost noble.

Now? Not so much. The great game of cat and mouse was underway.

Here in Australia the debate was on. An overwhelming majority believed Williams acted wrongly. The conversation was in every corner shop. Even NSW Premier Morris Iemma acknowledged the anger, saying, 'He has walked out on his mates. It's a five-year contract and he is one year into a new contract and he has walked away.'

While Sonny had slowly withdrawn from public as much as he could in the months before he shot through, he or someone close to him had slowly began leaking his version of events increasingly to the Fairfax media. And while it was a lightly worn path, the footprints in front of him were all Anthony Mundine's. Mundine began doing it successfully years earlier and Sonny looked to be copping the tip. By hiding and then selecting sections of the media to speak to Williams added to his troubles. Sonny Ball was killing him right here. The trick to manufacturing consent is to reach a broad media stream, not a narrow-cast stream. Any story like this cannot be ignored and the coverage soon split into separate storylines. The *Daily Telegraph* and the *Australian* and much of the electronic media focused mostly on the outrage and moral debate over Williams' walkout. Here Sonny earned several nicknames, all on a similar theme: Money Bill Williams, $onny Bill Williams or sometimes just $BW.

The *Herald* continued treating it as a sports story, a player leaving his club like many had done before, because who wouldn't swap a job that paid $400,000 for one that paid $1.5 million? His teammates left bleeding behind were largely ignored.

By Wednesday David Gallop was refusing to appear on Thursday's *Footy Show* if Phil Gould was going to interview him. Gallop did not believe he was able to properly explain his point without being constantly attacked over Super League. Gould assured everybody he was not scheduled to appear, anyway.

The rush for news was in every conversation in the newsroom. With Williams still not found, focus spread. Mundine's fight was on the Wednesday night and the one place Nasser was guaranteed to be. While the way Williams walked out on the club was unusual, such dispute was not uncommon in the game. Terry Hill challenged the draft in 1991 when he wanted to play for Western Suburbs but, in the very first draft, Eastern Suburbs Roosters drafted him.

'Mine wasn't a money issue,' Hill told the *Herald,* 'I chose to play for a certain club and they tried to force me to play for another club. Looking back now, I should never have left the Roosters. There were a lot of very good people at Easts and, in a nutshell, I believe I was wrongly advised. I look back now and it's a regret.'

Before Hill, though, the original industrial relations case was Dennis Tutty, and some were comparing Williams favourably to him. Tutty was an international player at Balmain but sat out the 1969 and 1970 seasons to challenge the game's player transfer system.

'It hurts me if there have been comparisons to me,' Tutty told Andrew Webster at the *Herald*, speaking of Williams. 'Mine's completely different to his. I didn't have a contract with my club and I had clean hands when I went to court. His hands are unclean. Because he signed a contract.

'If he was happy to sign a contract he's only got himself to blame. Or he should have gone to the club and said he wanted more. I thought he should have worked a way out before he went by offering to pay his contract out. I don't think he or his management put a lot of thought into what he did.'

Like Tutty, there were already whispers that Williams was preparing to negate his contract with the Bulldogs by taking it to the industrial relations court to challenge the salary cap as a restraint of trade. In Williams' favour was the courts were naturally reluctant to force players to honour their contracts under such circumstances. It had nothing to do with players being in the right but more to do with the reality that while the courts could order a player to return to his club, it could still not order him to play well. Invariably it ended in tears.

But first, the courts had to find him.

ANTHONY Mundine weighed in a day before his fight against Crazy Kim and used his press conference to support Williams. It was 29 July, a Tuesday. He turned the criticism back on those critical of Williams and sounded a lot like Nasser.

'I'm one hundred percent behind my brother and what he wants to achieve and what he wants to do as far as his new goals and new dreams in life,' he said. 'I think that all of us people – some of us are selfish. I'm going to miss him playing rugby league, I'm going to miss him being out there because he is one of the best, probably one of the greatest ever to lace a boot on.

We are going to miss him but it's our selfish need that is making us talk the way we talk and think the way we think.'

This was all delivered with a straight face. What the Bulldogs players back at Canterbury were thinking, wondering how they were going to save their season, was anyone's guess. And *they* were being selfish?

Mundine wasn't finished. 'Men change their mind from time to time – and I aspire [sic] any kid out there who wants new goals and new dreams to go for it and everybody should support them. There's a lot of haters and a lot of people that want to bring you down and tear you down. Then you have people talking about he's going to ban you from this and ban you from that.'

It is important to understand here that Mundine was not talking only about Williams here. He might as well have been talking about himself. As Australia's most polarising athlete he had felt the sharp blade of criticism much of his public life, mostly self-inflicted.

Mundine then turned on the salary cap.

'There is no salary cap on the workers – as far as a plumber, as a carpenter, as far as a builder. The worker should get what he's worth. There should be no salary cap. There should be privacy [sic] owned. They should get what they're worth. And yet all the game is making millions off their names. Where is the loyalty from the NRL to the players?'

It was a nonsense argument but it caused many without time to properly think it through to ponder. Plumbing companies and builders might not have a salary cap, but you can be sure they had another little device called a budget that performs a similar role. And plenty went bankrupt. On top of that all but a few NRL clubs ran at a loss and needed NRL funding to survive. The NRL simply applied a 'salary cap', which could also be called a budget, to stop clubs spending themselves broke in an attempt to buy all the talent and win the premiership.

As Williams' supporters sought to dilute the criticism through red herrings in the media, it took the purity of a child to find clarity.

The day before Williams left the country the Uralla Tigers under-10s travelled to Sydney. They had not won a game all season and had not scored even a try. Their sole victory for the season was to win a competition on the *Footy Show* to have Sonny coach them and this was their day.

Williams had sound advice for them as the Tigers struggled to find their first victory. 'You've got to stick with your team and work as a team,' he told them.

With that still strong in their minds, few understood what he did the following day.

'He signed a five-year contract with the Bulldogs and then he walked out for the money. He told us we should stick together as a team and do the right thing by your teammates and now he's done this,' said Scott McGann of the Uralla Tigers. Scott was nine.

'I think most players play league for the love of the game but I guess they've got to make money too. Maybe Sonny forgot why he was playing. I really thought he was a nice guy – I thought he was really committed to his team . . . I've been a Roosters fan my whole life – I was ready to give that up.'

The game is sold on heroes. This is what the game was losing.

The same day Mundine gave his press conference Toulon owner Mourad Boudjellal was tracked down and interviewed by New Zealand radio. Just so he would not disappoint the image anybody had of him Boudjellal, who made his money in comic books, was holidaying in Miami, Florida. Boudjellal seemed almost a comic figure himself. He always wore black, as often happens when successful men see one too many Al Pacino movies, and he owned no home but was often seen driving around France in his Maserati Gran Turismo or his Ferrari Enzo. The guy had a certain style.

By now he had owned Toulon for two seasons and in that time lured Tana Umaga as coach and former Wallabies captain George Gregan to the club to raise them from French second division.

'I know that Sonny Bill, he want to play rugby, he want to play for the All Blacks,' Boudjellal said, his English broken, like his interpretation of the law book.

'He don't want to play . . . in France we say *jeu à trieze* [game of 13], I don't know how you say in England. I know from his agent he want to play just rugby, rugby, rugby now.'

Boudjellal seemed to be under the impression Williams was free to join his club as rugby union was not rugby league, and Williams' contract with Canterbury was to play rugby league. He was concerned at the threat of legal action.

'I don't want to do something outside,' he said, but he did confirm he was aware of legal threats from the Bulldogs.

'I know and I want to see this problem with the FFR [French Rugby Federation]. Yes, he has a contract but rugby is not the same thing.'

Yet Boudjellal remained adamant Williams had not signed. Rumours suggested Williams had signed with the club the previous night. FFR laws required all contracts to be signed by 9 July, which was weeks earlier, and really makes you wonder what, in any of it, was true.

Referring to the Bulldogs as the 'Bulls', he indicated there were still hurdles, 'I need to speak to the agent, I need to see if it's possible with the problem with the Bulls and I need to see if it's possible with the money that he wants. Afterwards, we see. I think it's possible. I am not sure.'

Boudjellal only added to the confusion. He said he would be in Florida fifteen more days and Sonny Bill's whereabouts were anybody's guess.

'We don't know where is he, we don't know nothing. I do not know if he wants to speak to Tana Umaga. It's not a problem. I don't know how much money he wants to play. I don't speak with Sonny Bill Williams. We have no news. We are waiting.'

What was lost in the noise of all this coverage was Boudjel-lal's trashing of one of the chief reasons Williams' supporters were citing for his leaving. Money.

'Today I think that Sonny Bill Williams, should he sign with Toulon, it would be for the equivalent conditions to what he's currently getting,' Boudjellal told the ABC in another radio interview. 'But it's not at all a question of money. If Sonny Bill Williams wants to play rugby today, he no longer wants to play league.'

With those words Boudjellal threatened Williams' whole defence. Further doubt was created when Roy Masters wrote in the *Herald* the $1.5 million on offer might not be quite the $1.5 million that everybody was talking about.

It was supported again several days later when Masters spoke to Greg Willett. Willett negotiated Craig Gower's deal to join French rugby the season before. Talk that Williams was going to be the second highest paid player in French rugby, as put forward by several small voices, was fanciful. Willett told Masters the top players at France's Top 14 club Bayonne, the level above Toulon at the time, were paid about €350,000 a year.

But there were ways to maximise that money. Under French law, the first twenty-five per cent of a player's contract was allowed to be paid in image rights. The first €38,000 of those image rights was tax-free, and the remainder was taxed at twenty per cent.

'Say €80,000 of the €350,000 goes to image rights,' Willett said. 'At the current rate and tax, that can turn into $112,000, while the remaining €270,000 is taxed at 30 per cent, leaving him with around €190,000, which equals $306,000.'

Add the $112,000 to the $306,000 and Williams would clear, in cash, approximately $418,000. Willett then told Masters that when you add expenses, such as a car and free home rental, it pushes the net income towards $750,000 a year.

The figures were somewhat rubbery. It would take a house and car worthy of the Packer family to push the figure that high. But you could see how the money was still substantially higher than what he was being paid in Australia. Given a little licence to justify the switch, it wasn't all that far wrong.

Significantly, it meant the Orr brothers would no longer receive their commission. Where the commission went, we can only guess.

Yet Boudjellal indicated the figure being thrown around was smaller than $1.5 million, and that the real figure was 'for the equivalent conditions to what he's currently getting'.

Still, it was money the NRL would struggle to compete with if it ever got to a serious head-to-head battle.

AFTER two days hiding in London Williams went to the French Embassy to pick up his visa. He walked in the back door, as if there was any doubt. The only addition to the fifteen media or so gathered around the front of the embassy was the most important of all the uninvited guests – another private investigator with Williams' court injunction.

This is where it gets a little troubling for those trying to defend Williams. If what he was doing was so justifiable, then why the back door? Forget the media. By now Williams would almost certainly have known a process server was in London to serve him with an injunction to prevent him playing in France. If he failed to acknowledge it he ran the danger of having assets in Australia stripped. And if he did not know that, he should have. His legal advice had already anticipated it.

Inside, he met the Consul-General of France in London, who was not alone. Embassy staff asked for photos. Some were from Toulon and knew all about this hot young footballer about to light up their town. They were quite excited and processed his visa application in quick time. Here was Sonny Ball again: visas normally take weeks to process but for Sonny Bill Williams, the kid making all the big headlines back in Australia, it took just three days. Williams was good to fly to France.

Now all Williams needed to do was get to France. But, ridiculous as things were getting, they were about to get worse.

WHILE Sonny was being feted in London Mundine was getting ready to fight in Newcastle. Not just Mundine was suffering nerves on this night.

When they couldn't find Nasser at his hotel in Newcastle the Bulldogs hired a private investigator to serve him with court papers at the fight. When he turned up somebody started following him. They knew who he was, and it is fair to say this guy was no Philip Marlowe. Rather than turn around and growl, like the movies taught us these guys do, he squawked. The investigator waited until Mundine was about to enter the ring and tried to enter the VIP area in a bid to locate Nasser and serve the papers. Inside, the papers compelled Nasser to hand over his phone records and what knowledge he had of Williams' whereabouts. Yet as soon as he tried to enter the VIP area Nasser's supporters surrounded him and became threatening.

'When you get him outside you know what to do with him,' one said. 'Stick to him like shit to a blanket.'

Hostility filled the auditorium, a vipers' nest of young men driven by mob mentality. These were not fight supporters but young men spoiling. After the events of the previous five days their emotions were high, filled with misguided purpose, as they believed they had finally found somewhere to fight back against all the criticism and anger directed towards Williams, Nasser and Mundine. Soon they gathered ringside, threatening reporters there to cover the fight. As it threatened to bubble out of control the investigator sought the help of Sergeant

Lindsay McDonald and Senior Constable Maurice Geerlof The police officers recommended he leave before the main event. A reporter from the *Daily Telegraph* was also advised to leave.

As the investigator got to his car a carload of young men, recognisable from inside, drove past. A highway patrol car was called to escort him out of Newcastle. Later, the investigator told the *Telegraph*, 'I was only trying to do my job but, at the end of the day, it was just too dangerous.'

Mundine could have been fighting Lil' Kim instead of Crazy Kim and few ringside would have been able to tell the difference. He lost just two of the ten rounds. Mundine's fights never had what you would call your typical fight crowd in attendance. Instead they were Mundine fans, the best explanation for why they were more often there for a coronation than a fight.

It seems only proper that, after all that, Khoder Nasser failed to attend the fight. It gave the Bulldogs until 10 am the following day before the injunction expired. That was okay. All week the whisper was Nasser would join Williams in France the moment Mundine's fight was over. The club planned to catch him at the airport.

BY now it was hard to believe Williams did not know authorities in Australia were looking to serve him an injunction to stop him playing in France. Five minutes in any internet cafe would have revealed whispers that papers had already been faxed to London.

Williams' actions also indicated a man not keen on being discovered. Lots of effort went into not being detected. As word emerged that Williams had secured his visa and was heading to France, reporters rushed to Heathrow. Sonny and Ahmed Nasser headed to Gatwick. His French agent, Nicolas Pironneau, tipped them it was the best way to get out of London unseen. Instead of flying in to Toulon and risk walking off the tarmac into the hands of a process server Williams and Ahmed flew into Biarritz, seven hours from Toulon, and spent the night at a resort in Pau.

Williams headed down to the gym that night where a couple of locals recognised him. He denied being who he was. They printed a page from the internet on the gym computer and took it to him. He left the resort the following morning.

Ahmed and Williams moved to a small town and stayed in the house of Pironneau's friend.

'I stayed in a little town and did training out in the fields there,' Williams said. 'It had that beautiful feel like one of those *Rocky* films, training in the wilderness surrounded by beautiful fields. I did boxing, core work, played volleyball and tennis and swam.'

Sonny turned twenty-three that Sunday, while he was hiding out with the family. They bought him a rugby diary and celebrated with two cakes. 'They cooked for me, cleaned up and looked after me. I'm really grateful for everything they did,' he said.

Weidler was missing from the *Sun-Herald* the following Sunday. 'On leave', his *Last Word* column said. It was top secret, but he was flying to France for an exclusive interview with Williams that would run during the following Thursday's episode of the *Footy Show* and then more in print the following Sunday. The courts could not find him, but Weidler knew exactly where he was.

In his place Adrian Proszenko and Will Swanton filled the column and led on Williams.

'These three words could explain everything. *Last Word* recently interviewed Sonny Bill Williams after being tipped off that he was considering following Anthony Mundine into a professional boxing career. At the time Khoder Nasser freely admitted he was the manager of both. We were reliably informed Williams was serious about getting into the ring. The man mooted as his first opponent? His friend-turned-foe Willie Mason. Asked if a boxing career really was on the horizon, Williams replied, "Whatever Khoder wants."'

8

CODE BREAKER

SONNY Bill was about to take on the greatest education of his life. He was in France, away from the bonds of life that kept him feeling safe.

And as process servers staked out Sydney airport after the Mundine fight, hoping to catch Nasser, who flew out of Brisbane, Mundine also got on a flight. All parties were planning to come together in Toulon.

Even Boudjellal teased them. 'Williams will be in Toulon on Monday or Tuesday,' he said. 'We have discussed things with his agents and we are going to try and complete the move. If everything goes well he will have his medical on Tuesday and could make his debut in a friendly match on Friday.'

Boudjellal wanted Williams to play the friendly against rivals Hyères-Carqueiranne–La Crau.

'I'm obviously disappointed to learn of this through the media reports,' Greenberg said. 'It's not a setback. He's over there and getting ready so it's obviously all part of the plan.'

David Gallop remained strong on his original threat that Williams was not welcome back in the NRL unless an apology, followed by a return, came quickly.

'I am really clear on this,' Gallop said. 'If Sonny was to play rugby union in France in defiance of his contract then, like many people, I believe the door should be closed on him returning.'

The Bulldogs went back to the NSW Supreme Court that day hoping to get substituted service papers. In lieu of locating Williams and Nasser the substitute papers could be served on others connected to them. The papers were sent to Toulon Rugby Club as well as Williams' home and business addresses. Boudjellal and Nasser were also added to the Bulldogs lawsuit. They were allowed to send Williams a message via SMS, surely the first time this had happened, telling him court orders had been made and a case was proceeding against him on Friday.

At the same time lawyers were sending text messages to Williams and Nasser, arrows in the dark, Williams fronted a press conference in Toulon, holding up the club jersey. He confirmed he had signed a two-year deal with the club.

'Our problem is: is Williams under contract with another rugby union side? The answer is no,' Boudjellal said. 'Therefore he's free to join whoever he wants, he doesn't need a letter to leave.'

Not quite.

The Bulldogs also tendered Williams' contract, which revealed once and for all that no matter how often Boudjellal or Williams' supporters claimed the footballer was doing nothing wrong, he was, indeed, breaking contract.

Under section 3.1 (t), Williams had agreed to not 'participate in any football match of any code other than matches approved by the club and the NRL'. Clause 3.1 (s) stated he agreed to 'not play the Game with any person, team or organisation save for the club or in a Representative Match or matches in the Related Competitions except with the prior written consent of the Club'.

In court we saw, for the first time, a hint of the cost to the Bulldogs of losing Williams. Their submission revealed fears of

significant financial losses in ticketing, merchandise, sponsorship and the club's image. Greenberg's affidavit said the club's
recruitment and marketing were centred around Williams. The
club revealed almost $2 million in sponsorship was due to expire
at season's end and, without Williams as the star player, it would
be harder getting sponsors to recommit.

'It's difficult to quantify what loss will be suffered by the
loss of the first plaintiff [Canterbury] in respect of the above,'
Greenberg's affidavit said.

Greenberg even conceded he was considering a move to
Gosford, on the Central Coast, to escape the financial squeeze
in Sydney. The Bulldogs were one of nine Sydney clubs.

'It has not been discussed at board level – ever,' he said.
'I reckon every Sydney NRL chief executive should be looking
at Gosford. If you don't look at it you haven't done your job.
You would be silly not to look at it.'

Manly chief executive Grant Mayer saw an opportunity.

'I'll put my hand up. I'll happily be called silly because we're
not looking at the Central Coast. But we wish the Bulldogs the
best at the Central Coast. The Central Coast Bulldogs has a ring
to it,' he said.

Before Mundine, but after Nasser, Weidler arrived in Toulon
for an interview. It was fast getting to the stage of who didn't
know where Williams was.

The answer: the courts.

Nasser emerged after a late-night meeting with Weidler
and a producer from the *Footy Show*. A photographer for News
Limited snapped him at the Holiday Inn.

'Don't flash me. I'll smash your fucking camera,' he snapped.

Nasser, who looks to be no more than about nine stone in the
old scale, in his shoes, could be somewhat fiery. He went nose
to nose with the photographer, then seemed affronted at the
photographer's lack of etiquette.

'Get out of my personal space. Fuck off.'

Williams greeted Weidler with a hug when they met.

'I'm in a beautiful city about to start a new adventure,' Sonny said.

Former All Black and now Toulon teammate Jerry Collins knocked on Williams' door as the interview was about to start. Williams was keen to get on with it.

'I've been looking forward to this, let's start it up. Bruz, I have been copping it for days, my name has been disgraced, that's why I am so keen to say what really happened.'

At times he rambled. At times he looked like a naïve young man clearly confused.

'Do you think that before I left I didn't think my name was going to get slammed, that I wasn't going to get vilified, that my family weren't going to get harassed, that I wasn't going to be made up to be some rapist, some killer, some murderer?'

He saved the heavy artillery for Folkes, saying he 'got to me so much that I went to see my old man. He said, "People like that try and give you advice – but not only give you advice, make you take that advice and use it." He said, "He's a tyrant."'

More than ever, you could see Nasser and Mundine's influence. Not only in his views but the structure of his sentences. The absurd hyperbole. A murderer? A tyrant? Somewhere, a movie was playing in his head and Williams was imagining himself a great statesman.

'Who is he to come and question my friends and their values and their religion?' he said of Folkes. 'Who does he think he is? Does he think he is God? Is he God or something? Yeah, whatever comes out of his mouth, is that right?'

He remained determined to be offended that Folkes approached him at training in what seemed almost a lifetime ago now. He spoke of being let down by the club and not supported by the coach, all selective memories of what happened.

The Polynesian day was a lost memory. The meeting with Coorey long faded. Folkes' approach, he suggested, was close to the moment that convinced him to leave. If true, we can assume everything else after was a charade. An act.

'I rock up at training and Folkesy, Steve Folkes, someone that, to be honest, has never paid any interest in my personal life, he comes up to me and starts saying, "You're not turning Muslim, are you?" I just laughed.'

He thought he acted bravely walking out on Canterbury the way he did. 'I'm no coward, you know. I stood up for myself and I stood up for player rights. What I took, it's not a coward act, it's a ballsy act, you know what I mean? For those people, or that person, or whoever people that called me a dog – dogs take orders, I don't take orders.

'I'm one of those kids that used to love watching everything about rugby league but . . . I see that it is just a business. They don't care about me, they treat us like cattle. It is about the boys getting a fair go – you know, it's about them standing up and having the balls to get what they should be getting because if we're going to be treated like that, why can't we treat the clubs like that?'

That much is true. But what could never be justified was his way of demonstrating it, and Williams still seemed to miss that entirely.

By accident he seemed to hit on the one bit of common-sense in his whole argument: the tremendous double standard of the professional contract. Clubs sacked players more often than players wanted to leave. Yes, it was a business, and for that reason any man who does not get all he can is a fool, which might include accepting a rival offer. But whichever way they fell there was always a contract, and contracts were put in place to protect both parties in an agreement. If one party no longer wants to honour their end they can't simply walk away. A negotiation must take place and, often, compensation must be paid.

Weidler went through it all, even repeating allegations Williams was a 'greedy bastard'.

Williams bristled at the description but, later, stretched out on one of the two beds in his room, Nasser on the other, he said he understood. 'I know that a lot of people think I am. And I can't change what they think.'

Though he gave it an honest try.

With the interview in the can the next job was to get the biggest audience possible. Straightaway Channel Nine boss David Gyngell knew what that meant. Forget about Sonny Ball, this was the big boys now, so Gyngell ignored the cosy little relationship between Williams, Nasser, Mundine and the *Herald* and sent transcripts of the interview to the *Daily Telegraph* and its greater readership, to be run the day Nine aired the full interview on the *Footy Show*. You can bet it upset several at Fairfax, who thought their loyalty had not been repaid, but it spoke to the truth of the business.

The day before the interview was to be aired on the *Footy Show* I sat in the *Telegraph* office going through the transcript. The belief of many was that it would finally contain the apology. Certainly the population was led to believe that Williams would apologise to teammates while explaining his reasons for abandoning them.

I read through it all, hearing Williams' voice and wondering what had become of him. It was sad, in a way.

I called Folkes at home. 'In light of what has happened,' he said, 'my advice about him not putting too much credence into what Anthony Mundine says was probably good advice.'

Folkes agreed with little of Williams' version of events. 'If you asked Hazem [El Masri, a fellow Muslim at the Bulldogs] about how I perceive Muslims you'll find I've often asked him questions about the religion because I don't fully understand it. If something comes up that I heard, I ask him,' he said.

Folkes took the chance to put it straight. 'It's certainly not right of him to say that we took no interest in his home life or personal life. I supported him through the Clovelly Hotel

100

thing [when Williams was photographed having sex with iron-woman Candice Falzon], his drink-driving thing, through his public-urinating thing. We stood up for him and did our best to try and get him through that so I think it is a pretty naïve statement to make.

'In light of some of the decisions he has made recently he probably does need some help. And at the club we certainly tried to give him that help. And not just us, but professionally.'

Folkes was adamant it was Williams who began to withdraw from the Bulldogs, not the Bulldogs turning their back on him. 'Sonny hasn't been willing to talk to anybody for the last three or four months,' he said. 'It's like getting blood out of a stone. That doesn't make me happy to hear him think that, but that's life. I only know him and his mates . . . he has withdrawn himself from a lot of stuff that he used to do with them. We have supported him through a lot of incidents.'

It's a view with independent support. Andrew Johns, with no vested interest, had also noticed Williams withdrawing at training before he disappeared.

Right to the end, and beyond, the Bulldogs cared.

Folkes remained convinced Williams was getting bad advice from Nasser and Mundine. 'It wasn't that long ago that he signed a five-year deal, so I assumed to commit to somewhere for five years he was happy to commit to that. I know Sonny has been going around crying poormouth about only earning $500,000 a year; can't survive on that.

'I don't know if it is just this generation, whether it is young footballers or Generation Y in general but they expect everything and don't want to cough up for it. They expect that everything is going to be given to them on a platter and the fact he can't survive on $500,000 a year is a bit sad, really. He will do anything now to try and justify this decision, regardless. It is indefensible. I was in the room last year when he agreed, shook hands and signed a deal to stay with us for five years. So regardless of what he says now, it's all piss in the wind, really.'

Reading through the transcript, Williams missed nobody. He found time for a crack at NRL boss Gallop for pursuing him through the courts. Again he banged on about Mundine earning $600,000 a season nine years earlier at the Dragons compared to his $400,000 at the Bulldogs, with no mention of the unusual circumstances of Super League.

He left Nasser's assertion that he was not his manager dead on the floor: 'A lot of people don't realise that I, SBW, employed Khoder.'

'When I think about it,' Williams said, 'David Gallop, you know, he has got a lot of problems, rather than me. He shouldn't be worrying about me, he should be worried about looking after these new boys. All the rest of the boys in the NRL, because I'm telling you, things are not going too well over there at the moment.

'Like I said, he's got bigger things to worry about than Sonny Bill because Sonny Bill is not worrying about David Gallop.'

Confusion and anger were all over the pages. And now he was talking about himself in the third person.

'Who does that sound like?' Folkes said.

I read the transcript and read it again. It contained no apology.

'Say sorry for what, man? Have I like murdered someone? Have I?'

We did not have the entire interview but took out pages with what we had. Sonny in his own words, for the first time since he left.

Later that night, many hours after the paper was on the streets and just an hour before the interview was due to air on the *Footy Show*, Bulldogs captain Andrew Ryan sat on a hard chair in a TAFE building working on his marketing diploma.

Ryan did not have the natural talent of Sonny Bill Williams but had it where it counts most, what a horse trainer once described as 'the great tick of the heart'. This night, looking to get an answer he still hoped was coming, Ryan had no idea of the small bomb about to go off.

By the time he got home the interview was being aired.

'Andrew Ryan,' said Weidler, 'the day after you walked out, was very critical . . .'

Williams, still fighting the ghosts in his soul, put the proud footballer that is Ryan in his sights. 'I'm just hurt that some of the players have come out and bagged me straightaway without knowing the facts,' he said.

'Because I thought with them knowing the kind of bloke I was, there would have been a legitimate reason for doing what I've done. Those players that have stood up and hammered me straightaway probably weren't my friends in the first place.'

Here was Sonny Bill, lost in a world of his own creation, critical of a man for not giving him the same consideration he was not giving him.

Ryan went to bed that night unable to sleep. He kept thinking of old plays, football things, things the team could do better to give them a chance of winning. He knew Sonny wasn't coming back but they still had games to win.

The Bulldogs had mostly aired their disappointment at the situation, not at Sonny personally. A day earlier Luke Patten was promoting the Bulldogs–North Queensland Reconciliation Cup game in Brisbane.

'I think Sonny might be thinking he hasn't got that much longer to go and he needs to get out of it what he can,' Patten said. 'Looking at it that way, I can see his point of view, but I think the way he went about it and not letting us know wasn't the right way to go about it. It hurts. I'm not about to start slagging Sonny – I did have a fair bit to say when Willie left. The whole time Sonny's played for the Bulldogs I've been there with him. It's disappointing and totally out of character for him.'

Everywhere it was the same.

The morning after Williams' interview the Bulldogs were back in court to get an injunction to stop him playing the friendly game against Hyères-Carqueiranne-La Crau. Now he risked having his Australian assets stripped if he defied the order.

His interview the previous night was the winner Nine hoped it would be, but not quite so positive for Williams. Far and wide the rugby league nation supported Folkes and the Bulldogs.

'He sounds like he is confused,' said Darren Lockyer, the Brisbane, Queensland and Australian captain. 'He is a man now but he still seems like a kid. He just seems confused and whether these people around him are misdirecting him or not, I don't know.'

Sydney Roosters captain Craig Fitzgibbon saw where Williams was trying to place himself, even if he was not quite able to get himself there. 'In some respects he has got a point but I wouldn't do that to my teammates, to the fans. We're not trying to say we're doing it tough or we've got money or we're broke, everyone is trying to say they want their worth in a rough comparison to what other codes are getting. But what he has missed is, I love my club, I love the colours I wear, and I wouldn't do that that to my teammates, I wouldn't do it to the fans and I wouldn't do it to the game that has given me so much.'

His former Bulldogs captain Steve Price, now captaining the New Zealand Warriors, found it hard to match the Sonny he played with against the Sonny of now. 'From the Sonny that I know, the thing that disappoints me is it doesn't seem like a decision that Sonny would make, just from the morals that I know he has got. If you asked me ten weeks ago, "How will Sonny Bill Williams leave the game of rugby league?", most would have said as a superstar . . . I don't know whether that's the case now.'

MUNDINE landed in France on the Thursday, 7 August, and greeted Williams as he arrived for his first training session with

Toulon. Williams turned up in a grey tracksuit with the hood on, shielding his face, skipping out of a four-wheel drive into a rear door to the clubhouse. An hour later he emerged, stripped down to a white T-shirt and black shorts, with number forty-three over the thigh. It was a Puma T-shirt.

All the way back in Australia, something as simple as that struck the Bulldogs. For years Nike had invested in Williams, one of his personal sponsors. Now, without a second thought, that too was forgotten on his bold adventure.

He ignored questions. Asked specifically if he had anything to say to his Canterbury teammates as he walked on the field, he said nothing.

There was nothing remarkable about the training session. The usual warm-ups, speed and agility drills. A crowd of Toulon supporters turned up to see the man hailed on their website as 'Toulon – *qui d'autre?*', which translated as 'In Toulon – who else?' under his picture.

For nearly two hours he trained, the only unusual part being when it was over and several players, with coach Tana Umaga, took him to the far corner for personal instructions on tackling and rucking.

'Tana just asked a couple of us in the backs to help him out,' said fullback Orene Ai'i, a Kiwi. 'Being the player he is and the sort of guy he is, he's always willing to ask questions. Sonny will be the first one to say that he's got a lot of ground to make up. He's got to learn but he'll pick it up real quick. It will be amazing how much he improves over the next week. We're all going to pitch in and help him out as much as we can.'

The next day in Australia the NSW Supreme Court granted the Bulldogs their injunction to prevent Williams playing. He now risked losing his Caringbah home if he played.

But this was SBW, what did he care?

Not even twelve hours later Williams, who had spent the day out of sight, travelled to the game in a private car instead of the team bus with his teammates. When the players went to warm up, Williams was unspotted. It wasn't until the team ran out of the dressing room that Williams appeared wearing the bright-red Toulon jersey with number fourteen on his back.

He headed to the left wing and almost immediately reminded everybody how good he was, and what the Bulldogs had lost. After some nice touches early he sat out the second quarter and returned at inside centre in the third, where the legend began.

French schoolteacher Laussucq Arnaud took the ball and Williams hit him with a shoulder charge that the Frenchman, when he finally recovered, said felt like he had been 'electrocuted'.

Now, shoulder charges are illegal in rugby union, so Williams was sin-binned, sent to the sideline for ten minutes as penalty, but it only added to the awe round him. Arnaud later joked that he was officially Williams' 'first victim'.

'I want his socks and his shorts and then I'll forgive him,' he said.

Williams did not return from the sin-bin. Instead, after the game a man walked towards him, papers in his hands.

'You have been served,' he said, thrusting the papers at Williams.

Williams threw his hands in the air, refusing to take them. The papers were dropped at his feet.

'I don't give a fuck, I'm still playing,' he said.

The Bulldogs had finally found their man and, while Williams remained defiant, he and Nasser finally began to see the gravity of what was transpiring.

'It's one thing not to comply with an obligation you have in a contract,' NRL lawyer Tony O'Reilly said, 'it's another thing altogether to defy an order of the court.'

Clearly concerned, Nasser spoke to a friend in Australia, lawyer Jack Jakova. Jakova recommended he speak to Mark O'Brien. As well as being a top-flight lawyer O'Brien had represented the Australian Rugby League more than a decade earlier during the Super League war. It was clear the Bulldogs remained sincere in their intent, never wavering that Williams had a contract that prevented him playing anywhere else in the world. Supreme Court injunctions changed the magnitude of it all. O'Brien knew the quickest way for a resolution was for Williams to reach settlement and buy out his contract.

That Tuesday, O'Brien called a close friend.

By Wednesday, former senator and Labor Party powerbroker Graham Richardson was finishing a round of golf at Concord before meeting Peponis at a Chinese restaurant. O'Brien had called Richardson and told him he needed settlement. Along with Todd Greenberg, Peponis agreed to meet Richardson the following day, a Wednesday, at a Burwood café.

'I'm going to offer you a number,' Richardson said. 'It's a number I'm authorised to offer and it's a very reasonable offer and it's the only number I'll offer.'

He gave a small pause. 'It's a hundred thousand dollars.'

Greenberg and Peponis looked at each other. Without a word they stood from their chairs and walked out. Richardson caught them at their car. The Bulldogs were thinking more like a million dollars.

Richardson later claimed it was two hundred thousand. What did it matter?

More meetings took place that Friday. By Saturday they were in the final stages of agreeing on a deal. They were about to agree on a payout of $750,000.

Then Greenberg insisted on one more non-negotiable that nearly blew the deal. He wanted a clause inserted that prevented Williams returning to the NRL until after his deal would have expired.

Nasser refused. Greenberg was worried how Bulldogs fans would feel if the Bulldogs took a settlement and a year later Williams was back in the NRL, playing against them, as he believed was strongly possible.

Richardson argued that once the release was granted the Bulldogs had no right to say where Williams should be able to play. Greenberg refused to budge. Richardson argued that once the financial settlement was paid Williams should be free to do what he likes. Greenberg told him he could, just not in the NRL.

Richardson countered that Williams had no intention of returning to the NRL anyway, he wanted to play rugby union.

Greenberg then asked what the problem was.

Finally, the clause was inserted on Williams' deed of release.

'I've had people asking me what I got for doing the deal,' Richardson said. 'Nothing is the answer. And I paid for the Chinese lunch, so I'm out of pocket.'

That Monday, Mundine walked into the Bulldogs football office with three separate cheques drawn from his companies totalling $750,000.

And just like that, Sonny Bill Williams was a free man. Nobody was quite comfortable with the resolution. If nothing else, the game seemed smaller.

PART II

9

GAME CHANGERS

IN 1974 Bill Hamilton walked into the Manly dressing room clutching a *Rugby League Week*. Hamilton was a big man, so big his nickname was Herman in a nod to the striking resemblance he bore to Herman Munster from *The Munsters*. This is not something you covet. At this stage of his life Hamilton had put that big head to tremendous use and played more than one hundred and fifty games at front row for the Sea Eagles, including the club's twin premierships the two previous seasons, 1972 and 1973, and it guaranteed him nothing. Hamilton was trying to save his job at the club.

And so this day in the Sea Eagles dressing room, while getting ready for training, he opened *Rugby League Week* to the match report which carried the crucial player ratings and, after a quick scan, he held it out for teammate Peter Peters to see.

'Look at this prick. Who is he?' he said.

He was referring to the writer. Harry Jacobs covered the game for *Rugby League Week* and he rated Hamilton's performance a very average two out of five. Peters rated a handsome four out of five. That was bad news for Hamilton, given Peters was battling to take his starting position.

'I've had one of my best games,' Hamilton said, 'and he's given me a two.'

In any dressing room around the world nobody would be much surprised by this. It was not the first time a sportswriter got it wrong, and rumour has it that it wasn't the last. Players are always questioning the knowledge of those who cover the game and it only gets worse when they rate poorly in something as public as a performance rating. Rating lower than a teammate in competition for the same position only exacerbated it. Understandably Hamilton was aware of the power of the press and soon had it confirmed when Ron Willey, the coach who had overheard the conversation, spoke up.

'You can trust *Rugby League Week*, Herman,' he said. 'You're not playing as well as you think you are.'

The early 1970s were days when players worked full-time jobs and whatever they earned in match payments was regarded a supplement to their working wage. Peters, as everyone in the team except Hamilton knew, and most certainly Willey knew, was a young journalist trying to keep a distance between his football career and his job at *Rugby League Week* where he wrote under the pen name Harry Jacobs.

Hamilton was playing at North Sydney the following season.

While Bill Hamilton would have made a poor witness, relations between the media and players were almost always cordial before the game got big. Things changed, though, as did the world.

Rugby league was perfect for Sydney in the days Harry Jacobs plied his trade. They were tabloid days. The rule in Sydney was that just three sports sold your newspaper: cricket, racing and rugby league. After that there was nothing. Aussie Rules could not sell one newspaper in Sydney. Rugby league grew in the 1950s and 1960s on the back of the Match of the Day, every Saturday, at the Sydney Cricket Ground. The newspapers sent their best league writers to the SCG to cover the best game, names like Ernie Christensen, Ian Heads and Bill Mordey, as the rest got sent to places like Belmore and Parramatta.

Mordey spent Saturday afternoons in the SCG's Members' Bar, a little Coke with his bourbon, writing news tips on his cigarette packet. That way, when he awoke the next morning and the rest of the bar was shaking off their hangover and fumbling for memory he began the day with half a dozen good news leads.

Mordey is probably the only rugby league writer who came in and beat the game.

It didn't always appear that way. He once bet several thousand pounds, a year's wages at the time, on St George winning the premiership during the Dragons' run of eleven straight premierships from 1956 to 1966. He felt wonderful the night before the grand final sitting in a pub, aware the Dragons had qualified and were now red-hot favourites in what was now a two-horse race and that he, too clever for the bookmakers this year, had got them at much bigger odds before the season started. That's when Johnny Raper burst through the door of the main bar, as drunk as ten men, leading champion halfback Billy Smith and several others behind him. It is a fair bet they were in song. Raper was always a happy drunk.

Mordey turned at the commotion and saw his riches disappearing with each step Raper took through the bar. An entire year's salary, for heaven's sake. This was not good for anybody, let alone a compulsive gambler. What would he have to bet with?

He got straight on to his bookie to cancel the bet, which did not take as much convincing as you might imagine. Mordey did not let on to the scenes he had just witnessed inside the bar, which was to his advantage, and the bookmaker knew he was laying the Dragons for a fortune at fat odds. The phone call was a godsend. Of course he let him off the bet.

Naturally, the Dragons won the grand final the following afternoon and, naturally, Johnny Raper was the man of the match.

It was one of a thousand stories I could tell you about Mordey and the punt, most of which he would recall over a Jack Daniels and Coke while waiting for some fight to start, or a race to jump. We were sitting in a sportsbar at Wests Leagues Club in Newcastle one afternoon betting on Scone, of all places, when a horse broke the barrier and galloped several furlongs before the clerk reined him in.

'What number is it?' Bill kept saying to his son Craig.

'I can't see,' Craig kept saying, walking closer to the television.

'Is it four? I bet it's bloody four,' Bill kept saying.

'It's the four,' Craig said.

'Cancel it!'

Craig took Bill's ticket and got in line as the four horse was led back to the barriers and they took an eternity to reload him. With each false start at the barrier the line got shorter by one and it looked like it was going to be a photo whether the ticket got cancelled or not.

Just as they jumped Craig turned and smiled. The bet was off.

The four horse never stopped running. He finished several lengths in front and looked like he could have done another lap if requested.

Bill shrugged and downed his Jack Daniels, which is all he drank, dropped a couple of hundred dollars on the table and said he was going. Kostya Tszyu was fighting Roger Mayweather in several hours and Bill wanted to get to the venue to check everything was okay.

After leaving the newspaper game he eventually landed on fight promoting and finally won big when Tszyu walked out on him and the Supreme Court regarded it a breach of contract and awarded Bill more than seven million dollars in lost earnings. He retired to a farm near Scone and invested in several slow horses.

In the meantime, Bill became regarded as Australia's greatest fight promoter.

To understand Sonny Ball and why, even today, there are such varying opinions on Sonny Bill Williams, we need to step back to an era when the newspaper business and the media industry was starting to come under pressure from the internet age, then still in its infancy. The two afternoon tabloids, the *Sun* and the *Mirror*, where they had the most fun, had long ago shut down. *Rugby League Week*'s circulation had fallen heavily.

When Sonny walked out on the Bulldogs, Sydney was essentially a two-newspaper town. The paper that you bought in the morning mattered.

Events were often reported differently from paper to paper. Up to now, Fairfax's *Sydney Morning Herald* had virtually an open line to Williams and his manager Khoder Nasser. This gave the paper a tremendous advantage over their rivals, News Limited's *Daily Telegraph* and the *Australian*, and allowed their reporters an inside run on Williams' next step or latest complaint.

The divide was even greater among the rugby league writers. Any sense of a healthy rivalry between the papers got fried during the Super League war of the mid-1990s, a battle over broadcasting rights and the fight for supremacy between Australia's two moguls, Rupert Murdoch and Kerry Packer, for control of Australian rugby league. The rivalry between the papers was intense. Clubs that had been in the NRL were threatened, and some even died. The North Sydney Bears disappeared forever. The Western Suburbs Magpies and Balmain Tigers were forced to merge and become the Wests Tigers, to forever be loved like a stepchild.

Officials who spent their whole lives working for their clubs were fighting for a future that might not be there. Coaches were also in on that battle, as were some of the media.

That it was Rupert Murdoch's News Corporation that launched the war intensified the bitterness between papers.

The war broke on April Fool's Day 1995. News Corporation had ambushed the Australian Rugby League (ARL) to start a rival 'Super League' and launched legal action in the courts at the same time it signed several dozen of the game's best players, and even some of its clubs, in a weekend blitzkrieg.

After months of speculation the news broke in the *Telegraph Mirror*. It was a Saturday, page one, the headline: 'Stars Rush to Superleague'. It was still one word then. Superleague. Written by chief league writer Peter Frilingos, this story on this day had a tone of finality to it that was missing in everything else previously written. It worried the hell out of us at the *Sun-Herald*, where I worked.

Speculation of a Superleague had been around for weeks. Everybody knew something until you wanted it on the record and then they knew nothing. I was twenty-four and light on contacts and spent that Saturday hitting brick walls trying to confirm whether Frilingos was finally breaking it or whether this was another red herring.

Later we found out later News Corporation kicked it off the night before and went into Saturday, sweeping players into top-secret meetings to sign them. The strategy was to have all the signatures done by the time the ARL found out about it.

When the early edition of the *Sunday Telegraph* arrived at our office that Saturday evening a sick feeling overtook everybody at Fairfax. We stood on the fourth floor of the old building, the *Sydney Morning Herald* floor, around the sports editor's desk for several long minutes. Page one carried breaking news that Canterbury chief executive Peter Moore had resigned from the board of the Australian Rugby League because he was taking his club to Super League. The story confirmed all the speculation.

The sports liftout carried pen pics of the biggest names in the game over a headline 'Signed, Sealed and Delivered'. One by one we checked them off: Allan Langer, Steve Renouf, Brad Mackay, Laurie Daley, Brad Clyde, Ricky Stuart, Steve Walters. . .

After a while the sports editor, Ian McKinnon, looked my way. 'Oh well, better go ring Quayle,' he said quietly. John Quayle was the ARL general manager and for weeks they denied to him that a Super League was planned, even as he read it in the papers.

It could not have come at a worse time in the game's eighty-eight-year history. Just a month earlier the ARL had launched a brand-new twenty-team competition. Clubs from Auckland, Perth, South Queensland and Townsville joined the League. The game was never better placed, launching teams across the country and into New Zealand. A hundred years of goodwill was about to evaporate.

Most of the good players went with Super League. Many promises were made about the quality of the new Super League, including the famous line from the man soon to be appointed Super League's chief executive, John Ribot, that Australian players like Ian Roberts would 'soon be recognisable in China'. In those early days Ribot spoke long and often about Super League's 'vision'. Of brilliant plans to take the game to the world to finally realise its potential. He spoke so long and so often his 'vision' became a punchline. There soon was no dirtier noun in sport, so much it was soon banned from use within Super League headquarters.

The entire war was about finding pay television content. Pay-TV was just starting in Australia. News Corporation was about to buy into Telstra's Foxtel against rival Optus and knew that the key to subscriptions was in two areas: sport and movies. Given Murdoch had bought US giant 20th Century Fox in 1985, the movie content was covered.

The need for sport did not surprise Murdoch. As Roy Masters wrote in the *Herald*, Kerry Packer had planted the seed for him some years before at a meeting in London.

'You know everything about newspapers. You thumb through the world's leading papers every day. I don't read them – but I do watch TV. The one thing that works on TV is sport. If you want to get out of trouble you've got to tie up sport and convert it to pay-TV,' Packer told Murdoch.

Murdoch copped the tip. He paid $530 million for the rights to British soccer in 1992 and turned Britain's BSkyB into a profit-maker.

There were three obvious sports in Australia: cricket, rugby league and the AFL. This was a problem for Murdoch. Kerry Packer had secured the rights in 1991 to televise rugby league, paying $24 million for a deal that he extended for another seven years in 1993 for another $70 million, and that also included first rights on pay television.

In the end, lawyers for News found a way around Packer's stronghold. It was quite simple, really. They realised that the players were contracted to the clubs, not directly to the ARL, and that the clubs' sole obligation under their own agreement with the ARL was to provide a team each week in the ARL competition.

The other thing the contracts did not say, Super League realised, was who had to be in those teams. In other words, Super League's proposal was for clubs, besides their contracts with the ARL, to also sign contracts with them but to provide the best players for their competition. They could still fill the team for the ARL competition with whomever they liked – a second-grade side, so to speak – but the best players would be reserved for Super League.

All Super League needed to do was sign the clubs it recognised as strategically crucial and the ARL would be crippled.

Then they blew it.

The night before the *Sunday Telegraph* landed on the sports desk, Super League officials began signing players. It was so strategic they hoped to have them all signed by the time the paper hit the streets on Sunday morning.

But there was a hold-up signing the Brisbane players, which meant there was a hold-up moving from the Broncos to Newcastle, also seen as a crucial signing. The hold-up was also just enough lag for the Australian Rugby League to salvage enough clubs, along with those Super League had no interest in, to keep the battle evenly poised.

The Australian Rugby League had twelve clubs: South Sydney, Manly, St George, Sydney City (formerly Eastern Suburbs), Newcastle, Parramatta, Balmain, Western Suburbs, North Sydney, Illawarra, Gold Coast and the newly formed South Queensland Crushers. Super League had ten: Brisbane, North Queensland, Adelaide, Auckland, Canberra, Cronulla, Penrith, Sydney Bulldogs (formerly Canterbury), Perth's Western Reds and later the Hunter Mariners. Auckland, North Queensland and Perth were not even a month old in the new competition before bailing out.

By the time the war ended in 1998 it would cost Murdoch $560 million, according to figures the *Australian Financial Review* obtained in 2005, half a billion dollars more than the $60 million estimated. More than $400 million was spent in the first four months. His rival, Packer, paid less than half that. Packer had not only convinced Optus of the need to take on Murdoch, but to use their money. When Super League won in court the right to run its competition in 1997, Packer did a deal to televise the rival competition on Channel Nine.

The only true winners were the players.

Brad Fittler stayed loyal to the ARL for $300,000. Tim Brasher, the same. Laurie Daley signed with Super League for $100,000 sign-on and $600,000 a year for five years. Brad Clyde took the same terms as Daley, but for seven years. In many cases contracts were tripling and quadrupling and it went that way right across the League. Anybody who did not get a healthy pay rise had a limp.

Steve Walters, the Canberra and Australian hooker, had so much trouble believing the good times would last he deposited his cheque in the bank first thing Monday morning and paid fifteen dollars for a fast clearance.

Yet, as the war was playing out, a small conversation took place, overlooked at the time. They were the butterfly wings that set in motion what would be a significant piece of this story.

Gorden Tallis was playing at St George when the Super League war broke. This, you might remember, was only a couple of years after Nathan Brown saw enough of him to later describe him as one of the greatest young players he had seen and the benchmark for a young Sonny Bill Williams.

St George was one of the great clubs in the League and quickly aligned itself with the ARL. On the day the war broke the ARL quickly rallied and many players walked into ARL headquarters – it would have seemed rude to run – to sign loyalty contracts. Why wouldn't they have been in a great rush? They were about to get upgraded for a job they had already agreed to do. Events like this come along only once in your life, and only if you're lucky.

Keen to see what he would be offered, Tallis headed into the NSW Rugby League Club with his manager George Mimis and was immediately taken into an office with Gould. In most cases the negotiations were remarkably simple. In some cases it was as simple as asking players how much they wanted. Few heard the word no.

This is what makes what happened next to Tallis even more difficult to understand. Tallis was emerging as one of the game's great impact players. His coach, Brian Smith, chose to not start him in games but to introduce him later when fatigue had set in on his opponents and a fresh Tallis could come on and explode in what was hardly a fair fight. This was the very early days, before bench players became specialised.

Who knows what Tallis asked for; the amount has been lost in the dust of time. I know he is a great friend now and has told me the story forty times with barely a misplaced syllable.

And Gould's answer will never be forgotten. He told Tallis he was not worth near that much. He was only a bench player. At that Tallis, a proud man, got up and walked out.

James Packer saw him leaving and asked how he went.

Not good, said Tallis. He was going to see what Super League had to offer.

Packer tried to turn him around, telling him if St George didn't want him he would do a deal for him to join Sydney City. He was on the club board, it would not be a hard sell.

'How can you say that when your coach just told me I was a bench player?' Tallis said.

Tallis signed with Super League and announced he would be playing for the Super League-aligned Brisbane Broncos. A lot happened in the Super League war after that and you could not tell it all in a thousand pages.

But the war headed to court and players were left in a strange kind of limbo as the 1996 season rolled around. With no peace made, the Australian Rugby League-aligned clubs and Super League-aligned clubs were forced into an uneasy peace, forced to remain playing in the ARL competition as they waited for the Supreme Court to sort it out.

There was plenty of player movement as players aligned themselves to the competition they had pledged loyalty to. Canterbury, for example, released Dean Pay, Jason Smith, Jim Dymock and Jarrod McCracken to the ARL-aligned Parramatta after claiming they signed their Super League contracts under duress, later signing loyalty contracts with the ARL.

But St George was in no mood to release Tallis from the final year of his contract, even though he had pledged loyalty to Super League. If he wanted to play football, they said, he was going to play at St George.

This is why you never corner Tallis. Rather than go back on his contract with Brisbane he chose to sit out the 1996 season for the Dragons and remain in Brisbane. The Broncos, frustrated to see a perfectly good athlete train alongside them every day but unable to play, stayed angry that St George refused to release him.

Then in May 1996 the Broncos called a press conference in Brisbane. They announced Tallis' St George teammate, Anthony Mundine, would be joining Super League and the Brisbane Broncos the following season. It was the belief of more than one that his poaching was revenge for St George not releasing Tallis.

10

DRY RUN

ANTHONY Mundine played unhappily at Brisbane in 1997. From the start he was a poor fit, complaining to coach Wayne Bennett before his first competition game that he did not see enough of the football in the opening two trial games.

His manager Daryl Mather reinforced the message in the *Telegraph*: 'Anthony has been having trouble fitting in at the Broncos and was concerned at his lack of involvement in the club's two trial games. He is a very forthright person and feels he is not in the game as much as he should be now he has moved to the centres. Anthony was very disappointed with his last performance against the Rams and said he only touched the ball a handful of times all game. He and Wayne talked the matter through and I believe it has been resolved.'

Already Bennett was showing his hand to the season ahead, playing down the problem and managing it. 'Anthony came to me because he was homesick more than anything else. It is the first time he has been away from Sydney for any length of time and he is missing his friends and relatives. But at no stage did he ask for a release and we want him to be in the team.'

Bennett would later say, privately, that winning the premiership with Mundine in the side was one of his greatest coaching achievements.

All season Mundine wanted to play five-eighth, a position occupied by Kevin Walters, the Queensland and Australian five-eighth. Mundine's second positional choice, fullback, was taken by Darren Lockyer, the Queensland and Australian fullback.

Mundine believed he was better than both. In May, he upped the stakes and went public with his desire to oust Walters from the five-eighth position.

'I would rather play there, but that is out of my hands,' Mundine told Danny Weidler at the *Sun-Herald*. 'If I was five-eighth the side would be a lot stronger and more creative. I've had a heart-to-heart with Benny [Wayne Bennett] about my role. He has given me a free rein to do what I want. I just feel I need to be where the action is. I can't be caged in the centres. By giving me that freedom I feel the Broncos will be a better team.'

Bennett was doing all he could to keep Mundine happy and stop him disrupting team harmony. His great advantage was the maturity of his players. They were able to see Mundine for what he was and play around it. So nobody really cared too much one Sunday afternoon when Walters, with the Broncos behind the posts after being scored against, told Mundine to 'fuck off back out to the centres'.

Mundine did not fit at the Broncos. The team was built around halfback Allan Langer, who they should write songs about, and his combination with childhood friend Walters. Walters' twin Kerrod was the hooker. All three grew up playing backyard football in the same street. You could run out several dozen players and they would not bring to the performance what these three did. Langer was voted one of the game's greatest hundred players in the League's centenary season. Kevin Walters won six premierships at the club and would finish his career playing more finals games than any player in history. They complemented each other on and off the field and they made the Broncos great. They brought something to the club that could not be measured in statistics.

Mundine did get a chance at five-eighth though. In June Bennett rested Langer and Walters and centre Steve Renouf in the World Club Challenge. The game is interesting for only one reason. Not the Broncos' 76–0 win, or even any outstanding performance from Mundine, but his comments after the game to the *Courier-Mail*'s Paul Malone.

'I love performing because I know it rubs off on a lot of Aboriginal people,' he said. 'I can help people by performing at my best. It's about more than the fame and the money. I represent disabled kids and my [Aboriginal] people and being a role model.'

All season long the Broncos managed Mundine, nursing him so he would not disrupt team harmony and detonate their premiership chances. Bennett allowed him to fly home when he felt like it, even missing training sessions, to avoid homesickness and keep him happy.

Mundine was never for the long haul, though.

Towards the end of the season St George chief executive Brian Johnston took a phone call. It was from a fellow called Khoder Nasser, a Dragons supporter Johnston knew was close to Mundine. Johnston thought they might have even been school friends.

Nasser had something for Johnston. He told him he believed Mundine might be interested in returning to Sydney.

Johnston was sceptical. Mundine still had two more seasons to run at the Broncos and had denied rumours he wanted to leave, but Johnston did not want to be discouraging.

'Well, if he comes back to Sydney he needs to come home,' Johnston said.

Nasser gave Johnston Mundine's mobile number. Not long after Johnston travelled to Brisbane for an ARL chief executive conference and, taking a punt, called Mundine from his hotel room.

'I probably had the longest conversation I've had with Choc, which is not easy . . . he was genuine. He wanted to get out of Brisbane,' Johnston told me.

Johnston knew Mundine had to finish the season and he did it the best way, being part of Brisbane's grand final win over Cronulla. Throughout, Johnston negotiated with Nasser to bring Mundine back. Fortune fell Mundine's way. By now it was 1997, two years into the Super League war, and in that time numerous court cases were fought. And only recently the Industrial Commission ruled that the loyalty contracts the ARL offered early in the battle were legal and binding. In other words, the loyalty contract Mundine signed with St George before he walked out to join Brisbane was binding, which opened the way for him to rejoin the ARL-aligned Dragons.

None of this was known when Nasser began negotiating Mundine's return to the Dragons. It was just pure luck.

If there was anything odd about it, it was that Nasser was virtually unknown around rugby league but here he was, negotiating Mundine's deal to return while Mundine's manager remained Daryl Mather.

'When the contract was negotiated for Choc to come back, Khoder was front and centre,' Johnston said.

While Mather still remained his manager, on paper, Nasser handled all the negotiations with Johnston.

'Most of those early meetings, I will say, Choc was in attendance,' Johnston said. 'With Choc, those early days, he was the majority of time in attendance. Choc would just make those broad statements that he does at the end of a conversation. "Yeah, that's what I want brother," that type of thing. But Khoder is the negotiator.'

With both the ARL and Super League deep into peace talks, St George called a press conference for 8 October. There, they announced Mundine was returning to Sydney.

And here the legend was born. And Sonny Ball got its first true foothold. Be very sure here; it began with Mundine, who did all the early lifting for Sonny Ball. He paved the way, made the early mistakes, took the early bruises. He refined it so by the time Sonny came along they were walking into familiar territory.

Mundine arrived at the press conference with an all-day sucker that flipped from one side of his mouth to the other and had Dragons chairman Doug McClelland looking around for hidden cameras. Until now Mundine was still very much one of many good footballers in the game, with little to genuinely distinguish him from others around him.

Mundine reached into that rich imagery playing in his brain and saw Denzel Washington playing him in the telemovie, returning to St George as saviour. Even though he was still contracted to Brisbane and there was a semifinal for the World Club Challenge in two days Mundine, in doubt with a thumb injury, had already moved on from the Broncos.

Brisbane knew the press conference was going ahead but, given they had first paraded Mundine in a Brisbane jersey while he was still playing for St George, it would seem a bit rich to protest now positions had flipped. Besides, Mundine assured the Broncos he would be available.

Then, Brisbane chief executive Shane Edwards got a phone call from Mather. 'I got a phone call from his manager fifteen minutes before the press conference started saying he wouldn't be playing and it wasn't on the basis of a thumb injury,' Edwards said. 'We're disappointed with him and it's very disappointing for the people of Brisbane. There are a lot of people up here who took him into their hearts and he's let them down.'

Mather confirmed it was Mundine's decision not to play. Mundine also told Brisbane coach Wayne Bennett the day before that he wanted to play.

And then he couldn't. Clearly the thumb injury had worsened overnight.

'I might need to get it pinned,' Mundine said.

Then the camera lights flicked on and we got a glimpse into the future.

Mundine looked out into the small gathered crowd of reporters with their empty notepads and asked who was he not to accommodate them and help fill all those blank pages. The early blueprint was in place: talk himself up, cry foul, then disrespect.

What followed was no humility, no gratitude. In the space of one afternoon, Mundine was about to transform himself from Anthony Mundine, footballer, into The Man.

'It was frustrating. I felt caged. I like to be "The Man" on the field,' he said of his time in Brisbane. 'That's when I perform at my best. I feel I'm the best five-eighth in the world and I really want to come back and start flying with St George and prove it.'

He kept going. 'I've made this place my home. I'll be honest with you guys, I was homesick up there all year. I couldn't wait for the day I came back. I feel so privileged to get the biggest contract this club has ever offered an athlete. It's just good to be back home and smelling the air. You saw a good Anthony Mundine this year. Next year you'll see a brilliant one.'

Mundine repeatedly referred to himself as The Man. He did it at this press conference and in several interviews around it. It got so over the top, so blatantly stolen from the worst of American hip-hop, it was used as a punchline to deride him. Whenever somebody talked about Mundine in the days and weeks after they were immediately corrected: 'You mean The Man?'

And then a funny thing happened. It caught on.

Mundine, with no antennae for irony, quickly adopted The Man and later, when he took up boxing, believed it only natural that it should follow him into the ring, stitched onto his robe.

Mundine's press conference upset the Broncos, the reigning premiers after beating Cronulla in the Super League grand final.

The following morning Bennett spoke to his players about Mundine's decision. 'We had a brief discussion and I gave them the details of what happened. I thought they deserved to know. We were all disappointed,' Bennett said.

'We've made another final and we have done it without the world's best five-eighth,' a player, identified only as a 'senior Broncos figure' said after the game.

The smart money was on Kevin Walters. The Broncos felt slighted by Mundine's press conference, and Edwards conceded some players were upset, others angry.

'The players should be congratulated on their courageous win, and the last thing I want to talk about is Anthony Mundine,' Edwards said. 'I have spoken to a couple of the boys about it and they are disappointed in a personal and a professional sense that this has happened. They made him part of the team.'

Weeks later Mundine responded in an interview with Weidler. 'Brisbane didn't treat me like royalty like St George did,' he said. 'That's how I was used to being treated. They treated me a lot worse than that and I really wasn't looked after by the club. They failed to deliver in a few areas that I asked them to. Just rent matters and things like that.

'I signed up too early. They were not paying me what I was worth and they backed away from a few things. The vibe wasn't right at Brisbane. You know when it's right. Shane Edwards painted me as the bad man, saying I just left the club without trying to contact him. The truth is we rang him fifteen minutes before I held my press conference to tell him I wasn't going to play because of my thumb injury which gets operated on this Tuesday. No one believes me about that. Shane Edwards refused to talk to me and kept saying that I just left the place.'

Mundine saw the world differently from others. 'I got on very well with Gorden Tallis and Wendell Sailor up there, but I knew I had some enemies among the players. I don't want to name names. They didn't like me because I'm confident and brash and I speak my mind.'

A week earlier Steve Crawley, speaking for the rugby league community, wrote a column in the same newspaper, the *Sun-Herald*, urging Mundine to put a sock in it.

'I'm not going to put a sock in it, as Steve Crawley said I should in last week's paper,' Mundine told Weidler. 'I want to speak my feelings like no other athlete has done in Australia. People don't know how to take it. Especially being Aboriginal and saying things, it's more of a freaky thing. I've got the confidence and the ability to back up what I say. I don't mind the pressure being on me because the fear of failure will just increase and that will push me along. My family is right behind me and they have told me to tell the guys who are bagging me to get stuffed.

'The people who know me know that I am humble and a genuine guy who will speak to anyone. Talking things up in the press just revs me up. The best athletes in the world express their feelings and I want kids out there to know that it is OK to say what you feel and to be themselves. I hope I can help them be confident in themselves. I really want to help inspire kids, especially sick kids or those who haven't been blessed with natural gifts. I want to help inspire them in the battles they are facing. I want people to know it's OK to be confident and proud.'

Here is Mundine, still not fully formed, fumbling for identity. He knows what he wants to be and with a little confidence he might get there. In many ways Mundine is a timid man.

I got that the bold declarations were about challenging himself. By saying it, he gives himself no choice but to do it. It was the old Muhammad Ali line, 'Whatever I say I'm willing to back it up'. The bold statements are the commitment to challenge himself. So while the confidence is a con, the courage is not.

But as Mundine will unfortunately discover, when you create a big personality there is always pressure to be that big personality. Inevitably it resulted in Mundine unable to navigate the subtleties of what he said, which often was tremendously offensive. He crossed the line between acceptable banter and good taste and many times seemed confused when those he offended reacted. As an act it became tiring and, by default, he became tiring. After a while few bothered to even try to learn if there was anything behind the circus act.

His relationship with Weidler was perfect. It meant that nearly everything he said went straight to the masses, without filter. As I recall their relationship goes back to a Sydney night-club in the mid-1990s when Weidler ran into Mundine, then playing rugby league for St George. They were the only two non-drinkers in the club and so naturally they found each other.

I worked next to Weidler for a time, adjoining desks at the *Sun-Herald* and it was clear Mundine trusted Weidler like no other. By association, the relationship was extended to Nasser and then later Williams and, along the way, several others.

IN August 1998, the season Mundine returned from Brisbane, Weidler finished covering a game and called work, checking they had his copy, and packed his computer to go home. Canterbury just beat St George 20–12 in the elimination final. It was the last ever Dragons game as a club, St George merging shortly after with the Illawarra Steelers to form St George Illawarra Dragons.

Weidler's phone rang. It was Mundine. He told him a Canterbury player wearing number ten had racially vilified him. Weidler sat down and took out his computer and started filing a news lead.

'The Canterbury player's comments just blew my roof,' Mundine told him. 'I know that they will try to make me out to be the dumb one in all this, but why should I have to put up with being racially abused? The player could have said anything he liked. He could have said, 'We're kicking your arse', but instead he chose to call me a black c—. That's just not on, and

I don't want to stand for it and I don't want other people to have to stand for that.'

The story detonated.

The player, Barry Ward, never denied saying it, he just said it was directed at another player, Robbie Simpson, in retaliation for Simpson calling him a 'fat c—'.

A fairly large chunk of the rugby league population insisted that what was said on the field should stay on the field, as was the time-honoured tradition, unaware their world had changed. But Mundine held the line. He spoke to nobody but Weidler, who quoted him fully, and gave the NRL no room to wriggle away from Ward's comment.

In the end the NRL made the only decision any reputable organisation could make. What could not be disputed was that it was said and, in the end, it did not matter who it was directed toward. Ward was fined $10,000, reduced to $5000 on appeal.

You might think this was the craziest story to happen that season in the NRL, but that would be wrong. It was not even the craziest involving Mundine.

SOLOMON Haumono, a man with large talent, was late for training at the Bulldogs. Haumono was going to be anything as a footballer if he got himself right, but missing training wasn't the way to do it. The previous season, 1997, he represented Australia from the Super League competition after spending many of the early rounds putting the hurt on opponents. Few players could hit like Haumono in defence. Canterbury coach Chris Anderson was asked about Haumono's potential and whether he had the ability to be as good as Gorden Tallis.

'He's way in front of Tallis,' Anderson said. 'As a runner he could be anything. He's just a tremendous athlete. He can belt a bloke in defence and he's simply devastating in attack.'

When Haumono was late for training this day Steve Folkes, who had replaced Anderson as coach for the 1998 season, dropped him. It was not the first time Haumono arrived late for training. Glen Hughes was also dropped for missing training.

'I don't want to make it sound more sinister than it is, but I'd rather keep things to myself. It is a club matter and we have handled it in-house,' Folkes said.

It was the Canterbury way. When asked if he was disappointed in Haumono and Hughes, Folkes said, 'Definitely. I'm sure the two players are disappointed. But it is very important we show everyone – no matter who they are or how well they're playing – they'll be penalised if there are indiscretions.'

What Folkes didn't say was that Haumono had rung the club when he realised he was late for training.

'I've just woken up,' he said. 'I'm in Manly. I can't remember how I got here.'

The club tried to be sympathetic but already Haumono had amassed $25,000 in fines that season for missing training or turning up late.

Then it began to get weird.

The easiest way to understand is to realise that the previous year Haumono was in England with Canterbury for the World Club Challenge. As any coach knows, put in a situation like this with young men away from home, players can tend to get a little carried away at times. In a bid to control behaviour then-coach Chris Anderson paired the players up. Players were not only responsible for themselves, he told them, but their partner as well. If one let the team down, both got fined.

Anderson paired Haumono with Steve Price, the future club captain. There was none more responsible. Unfortunately for Price, he had no idea that Haumono's girlfriend was based herself in London or that her nickname was 'The Pleasure Machine', which explained quite a bit.

Halfway through the trip Price called his wife at home. 'I think we're going to have to mortgage the house.'

He could not count how many sessions Haumono had missed, chasing his girlfriend, Gabrielle Richens, to London. He was sure the team manager could, though.

Haumono struggled with the responsibility of playing NRL football. But there was more to his struggle. He was naturally shy. The trick was to sit with him and let him talk at his own pace, let the words come when he wanted to say them. When I spoke to him at Belmore Oval in May 1998 after he was dropped, we sat on the blue bucket seats in the grandstand chatting softly. Occasionally, he intimated there might be more to his being dropped. More than just his struggle with responsibility.

It is amazing what stays in your brain all these years later.

He did not tell his parents why he got dropped. 'But they found out,' he said.

Haumono's dad Maile was a former Australian heavyweight champion and remained close friends with Tony Mundine. They fought three times in the mid-1970s and their sons grew up together.

Maile now worked the doors at some of Sydney's more blue-collar pubs, where they called him 'One Man Out'. In other words, he worked the door alone. If Maile wasn't rostered on, management needed three men on the door. His mum Lavinia is a wonderfully gentle woman who twice ran onto the field when Solomon was knocked out. She packed his football bag and went to watch every game and every time suffered through a terrible anxiety. Haumono was the most damaging hitter in the game, the most feared tackler playing, but he was still her boy. She promised to stop worrying but she loved her boy too much.

'The reaction was, obviously, that they were upset,' he said. He was trying to explain himself this afternoon, sitting on those blue bucket seats. 'What I'm trying to do is not get everyone involved because I know it's affecting everyone. Because I'm not doing what I'm supposed to be doing.'

He never told me outright what his other problem was.

Towards the end of our interview he admitted he had a problem with his memory. There was a recent incident that he did not want to talk about. Two recent knockouts on the football field, the ones that saw mum come running, had added to it.

'I do have medical problems and I don't want to use that as an excuse,' he said. 'There have been two incidents through football and through stuff that's happened when I was young and some of the training sessions I missed this year are with memory. I've seen a [brain] specialist and stuff like that. The club helped me out in that way, taking me to see a psychiatrist. And I've seen a specialist. The head, you know, I've got a bit of damage there. I realise I've got to change, and I know that change is going to happen. I think about it consistently. I say my problems will be over pretty soon, through everything that I plan and that I have planned with someone else. It shouldn't be long now that my problems will be over, one hundred per cent. I think everyone will notice.'

He was vulnerable that afternoon and had been for some time. 'I keep telling myself that I'm not going to do it, that I can't afford to do it but . . . I know all the stuff in my head will go and I will just have my thoughts on my true profession. I don't think I have been a real professional,' he said.

'I don't expect anyone to understand. Everyone has put their arm up to help me but I have got to deal with it.'

Three weeks later Haumono missed Friday's training session and also one the following day. After all that had happened, the Bulldogs had nowhere else to go but call him in and sack him.

Only they couldn't find him.

His mobile phone was disconnected, the bill unpaid, as was his home phone. The club sent a couple of players around to his house but he was not there. Mundine was contacted and said he saw him Thursday night, 28 May, before the missed training sessions.

'He seemed fine,' Mundine said. 'He was on the phone for ages talking with his girlfriend in England.'

And so it begins.

When Haumono failed to attend Sunday's game without explanation his career at the club was over. What the Bulldogs did not know was that it was impossible for Haumono to get to the game – on Friday he had boarded a plane for England.

He was lovesick.

The following weekend St George Illawarra, fighting for a share of the competition lead, went down 22–20 to Adelaide and the next afternoon Mundine boarded flight QF001 to London. He was going to bring his friend back. 'He needs someone close to him. His parents can't go, so I'm going over there to show him some support, just to talk to him,' Mundine said.

Dragons coach David Waite said he had no problem with Mundine going provided he was back for training by Thursday. And so began a 34,000-kilometre, forty-five-hour odyssey.

Mundine landed in London Monday morning and by Tuesday night was flying home, with Haumono beside him.

Naturally, the world went crazy when they arrived home.

And naturally, the painfully shy Haumono responded to the enormous attention the only way you would expect. He went on the *Footy Show* just hours after he returned, explaining it all away like this: 'I think a man should be with his woman.'

Then he produced his big surprise. Out walked The Pleasure Machine in a hot-pink shirt.

'I don't blame you, Solomon,' yelled a man from the audience.

Richens had flown in on a separate flight.

A Channel Nine spokesman declined to comment on industry whispers Haumono was paid $20,000 for the interview. 'We wanted to use this window of opportunity to do something to help him with his personal and professional difficulties,' executive producer Rory Callaghan said.

Of course.

It had nothing to do with ratings.

What nobody realised was that, with Mundine by his side, Haumono was playing an early draft of Sonny Ball. There was more than love at work here.

Two days after returning, dropped by Canterbury to the second-tier Metropolitan Cup team Moorebank Rams, Haumono declared he wanted to play with his 'soulmate' Mundine at St George Illawarra and that if he stayed at Canterbury his heart would not be in it.

That said, Haumono missed two more training sessions the following week while his girlfriend, Richens, went to the club to pick up his pay cheque.

Canterbury's chief executive at the time, Bob Hagan, spoke for the club with his frustration. It was clear the time was getting near.

'We've got to really start looking at his future,' Hagan said. 'You get a little bit tired of it all, don't you? It's an ongoing saga. All I'll say is that the yellow card has been issued and the red card is in the top pocket. That's about as clear as I can be.'

The Bulldogs refused to promote Haumono back to the NRL any time soon and after three weeks' loitering in the lower grades, Weidler questioned why the club had not reinstated Haumono, given 'He has been mixing training with both the Moorebank Rams and the Bulldogs and, according to sources, has been very good with his attendance'.

'Surely,' he wrote, 'he has done his time for disappearing and deserves another chance in the big time? If not, why don't the Dogs cut him with the other ten or so players they are axing so he can get on with his career at another club.'

The following week, having missed more training sessions, Weidler 'tracked down' the 'missing' Haumono at a Sydney coffee shop.

By now, true to Sonny Ball, the message had begun to change, with Haumono saying, 'a big reason I went was to get out of the environment at Canterbury. I'm not happy at the club. They have treated me without respect. When they said things like I couldn't remember to pay bills and things like that in a newspaper article, they humiliated me. What they said wasn't true. They have failed to show me respect for a long time.'

Weidler wrote that Haumono was sharing a coffee with Mundine and 'another close mate, known as "Abs"'.

Abs was Khoder Nasser.

'Instead of playing games in the media, why doesn't Bob Hagan give me the red card he says is sitting in his top pocket?' Haumono said. 'That way I could get on with my life.'

When Canterbury played Brisbane in the grand final six weeks later, Haumono watched at Canterbury Leagues Club. The day after daring Hagan to sack him he was told to find another club for the following season. He did not anticipate that the Dragons would have no room for him and he had to go to Balmain.

That season, when Haumono hoped to be playing alongside his 'soul brother', Mundine was leading St George Illawarra to the grand final. This was what he had been brought back for and in his second season back at the club the Dragons led Melbourne 14–2 when, eleven minutes into the second half, Mundine got the ball metres from Melbourne's line with a defender in front of him and two unmarked players outside him.

Instead of passing Mundine, who had dedicated the game to the 'stolen generation' in the *Sun-Herald*, elected to go himself. Melbourne winger Craig Smith knocked the ball loose as Mundine dived over the tryline.

Mundine's critics, happy to recall his errors, never let him forget the day he cost them the grand final because he made it all about him. Melbourne came back and won with a controversial penalty try in the seventy-sixth minute, 20–18.

This is one to give Mundine, though. I don't agree with the criticism of Mundine. Yes, a simple catch and pass and the player outside might have scored, and the Dragons possibly go on to win the premiership. But when Mundine gets the ball where he is, his first choice is whether he can reach the tryline himself.

How was he to know the ball would be knocked loose? His first decision at that moment was whether he could get to the tryline himself and he did. It is easy, in hindsight, to say if he passes they score. But if he had passed to Darren Treacy outside him and Treacy had dropped the ball, which in reality was more likely than Mundine having the ball knocked loose, then everybody would have asked why he didn't hang onto it. It is an argument he cannot win for as long as the result stays the same, which is forever.

Also in the *Sun-Herald* that grand final morning was a Weidler profile on Mundine. Making an appearance once again is 'Abs', this time identified as a 'key figure in Mundine's rescue mission of Solomon Haumono'.

Still no formal identification, though. Nasser likes to keep a low profile.

The similarities between Haumono's choices in 1998 and Sonny's walkout on Canterbury in 2008 are very similar and, put together, are loose strings in a story, nothing more. A conspiracy theory.

That is until many years later, in 2011 and well after Haumono eventually made it to St George Illawarra.

In a newspaper interview, Haumono revealed the whole ruse to fly to England in search of love was a con job. Done because Haumono wanted to get out of his Canterbury contract to join Mundine at St George Illawarra.

Here was Sonny Ball's dry run.

'I was under contract for the Bulldogs so it was decided to come up with a plan that would ultimately force the Bulldogs to rip up my contract,' Haumono told the *Herald*'s Jamie Pandaram in August 2011.

'So the plan was formed that I was going to chase after my girlfriend at the time in England. So off I went and before

I knew it, the paper got a hold of it and blew it up, making headline news and myself being chased by the media at home and even there in London.'

Intending to help his friend, Mundine's involvement stepped it up a notch.

'It was crazy, Choc [Mundine] added a twist by flying over to rescue me and that just created more of a stir,' Haumono said. 'We arrived back at Sydney and it was just chaos. All the media wanted to get in on the buzz so it literally didn't stop. We bypassed Customs to a room where family and management were waiting, hidden from all the mayhem of reporters, camera crews and general public wanting to see what all the fuss was. We had security escort us to a car that we quickly took off in.'

I read this and I think back to Haumono's comments to me that day at Belmore.

I say my problems will be over pretty soon through everything that I plan and that I have planned with someone else . . . It shouldn't be long now that my problems will be over, one hundred per cent . . . I think everyone will notice . . .

He knew what he was doing.

And Mundine was integral in the planning.

'We had to calculate it in a manner that we had to try to get him out of the deal with the Dogs because, by mouth, verbally, the deal was done,' Mundine told Pandaram, assuming the deal was done with St George Illawarra. 'We put on that little stage-play to try and get the Dogs to do what we wanted them to do.'

Mundine even said it later influenced how they orchestrated Williams' walkout on Canterbury.

'Yes, we had a bit of experience in that department,' he said. 'No one thought Sonny was going to get out, not even the Dogs, but we found a way.'

Haumono is married now, with four children. Not to Richens, who later returned to England. After converting to Islam with Mundine in February 1999 he has returned to Christianity with a strong faith in Jesus and is tinged with regret.

His career became a big what if. He left rugby league with Mundine and tried to make it in boxing.

For reasons that were good Haumono admitted to himself that he was playing only to please others and he could not find the motivation to continue playing for himself. After two-and-a-half years he quit boxing and tried to return to the NRL. He returned to Manly, his first club, but whatever was there once was now lost. He played two seasons at Manly and then headed overseas for two more seasons in England's Super League before retiring and having another crack at boxing. He fought around Australia, in New Zealand and Japan, and finally retired with a 21–2–2 record, with 19 knockouts.

What if.

'My whole sporting career has been in the spotlight for both good and bad reasons,' he told the *Herald* that day. 'I'm not above anyone else, but I thought I was an immature person. Having an older head on my shoulders helps me to live as an example to help the younger generation through the difficult times of growing up.'

11
ENTER THE MANAGER

IN early 2000 Sydney was prettying itself up to host the Olympic Games and Cathy Freeman, aware of the political lightning rod the Olympics can be, urged her fellow Aborigines not to turn the Games into a political statement. The Aboriginal community was more than two hundred years into a wait to hear one word from the Australian Government.

Sorry.

Nobody was going into these Games under more pressure than Freeman. She was the reigning world champion and Australia's highest profile track athlete and if the Olympics were to turn political Freeman would undoubtedly be caught up in it. She was asking her community to leave her alone so she could concentrate.

Elsewhere in this little world Mundine began writing a column each Monday for the *Australian*. In the history of great decisions, hiring Mundine was not one of them. The strange choice became obvious a day before just his second column when Mundine spoke to Danny Weidler about Freeman's statements. Mundine's comments appeared in the *Sun-Herald*. You could see who was getting the value here.

'Really, I don't believe they are her real views. I know Cathy. She is a friend of mine and I know what is in her heart. I think

she is being used by the powers that be. They realise it is important to keep their friends close and their enemies even closer.
They have got to her. I believe she is being used because they
know how much respect she has in the Aboriginal community
and they don't want trouble,' he told Weidler.

Mundine wanted the Aboriginal people to go the other way.

'I urge my people to ignore her comments and remember her
actions. She gained so much love and respect from the Aboriginal people in Australia and from other Australians when she
displayed her pride in her race [after carrying the Aboriginal
flag on a victory lap after winning Commonwealth Games gold
two years earlier]. She became a real role model for her people
and that is why they want to close her down. I know, and I'm
sure deep down she knows, that you shouldn't run and hide
from the truth. That is not progress.'

The next day Mundine wrote a column on Solomon Haumono,
but ended it by saying he hoped Freeman would understand the
Olympics are bigger than a sporting competition.

'The plight of our people should be our major concern and,
no matter how successful we become in our chosen sports, we
should never let our sport overshadow the problems our people
face,' he wrote.

Mundine was still creating his activist persona. Finally given a
voice, finally being listened to, he began separating himself from
the herd. He wanted to be seen as more than a footballer. He
was making himself the man he dreamed of being. The previous
March he had converted to Islam. He was moving himself closer
to Muhammad Ali and that movie playing in his mind.

Like Ali, he continued to question the system, telling the
Daily Telegraph's Tony Adams early in 2000 that when he finished
his rugby league career he wanted to go into politics because
'I can give the cause a louder voice.'

'The current political system is intent on keeping the
Aborigine at the bottom rung of Australian society. They want

to take away whatever prestige we have – to keep the image of us as petrol sniffers and alcoholics. I have had success, people know me now, and I feel they will listen to what I have to say. I want to make a difference . . . with housing, health, imprisonment. We are in the same position as two hundred years ago when the white man came here and tried to kill off our entire race. I want to show people what the white man did to us was wrong.'

He also said something largely ignored at the time, considered just another hollow boast.

He said he was considering following his father into a career in boxing. 'I want to win a world title and will weigh it all up at the end of the year.'

The Dragons started the season poorly, failing to find the form that took them through to the previous season's grand final. Before the grand final rematch three weeks later Mundine finished his training run on the Tuesday to tell all who would listen that Melbourne did not deserve to beat them the previous September, when he dropped the ball over the tryline.

'I see us as being champions and we're going down there to prove that – not just to ourselves but to everybody,' Mundine said.

He then followed up in his newspaper column with his views on current premiers Melbourne Storm. Calling them 'pretenders', and that 'as a team over the whole season last year, we were better than the Storm'.

'I'm not saying they can't play, obviously they can otherwise they wouldn't have been in the grand final. Many critics are saying that some of the statements I make do nothing but fire up the opposition. That's exactly what I want to do. I don't want Melbourne to come up with any excuses. I want them to be at their best, I want them to be fired up and I want St George Illawarra to crush them because nothing is sweeter than revenge.'

That Friday, Mundine got his wish. Melbourne had no excuses. They won 70–10.

Before the weekend was over senior players at the club told Mundine to zip it.

'I know that a couple of the senior players have actually talked to Anthony about the fact you don't give other teams ammunition,' teammate Mark Coyne told radio 2GB. 'The players don't mind him talking about himself but when he starts saying, "We're the best team, we should have been the champions", that's where he probably crosses that line. So there's a couple of guys who are disappointed and have talked to Anthony and he appreciates that.'

A month later Mundine got on a plane and left the country. Like Haumono did two seasons earlier and like no one since in the game. No one knew where he had gone. The Man became the Running Man in newspaper headlines and, after a few days, Nowhere Man. For days reports surfaced of Mundine being spotted in Hawaii, Vancouver and Grafton, where his family is originally from. Every media organisation in the country was trying to find him. Dread grew each day, since each morning meant Sunday was a day closer when you knew Weidler would have him. The race was on to find him first.

Weidler's relationship was about to pay off tremendously.

Without their outspoken teammate, Dragons players travelled to Townsville and that Saturday went down to North Queensland 50–4. Broken in defeat, Mundine's teammates turned on him. One of the sacred rules of sport is to be there for each other and Mundine had abandoned them. They didn't know where he was but they knew he could have been there if he cared enough to be. His teammates felt that abandonment deeply. The following morning the *Sun-Herald* hit the newsstands and there, front page, was Mundine, in San Francisco, holding an *Examiner* as proof of location. He said he was 'chilling out' and considering his future.

Mundine spent a week away before returning, saying little as he walked through Sydney airport but bizarrely holding up a copy of Muhammad Ali's autobiography *The Greatest*, a book that by then had been revealed as little more than a tale of semi-fiction, a propaganda tool for the Nation of Islam.

You can bet they were still angry at the Dragons.

The following day Mundine was ordered to St George Leagues Club to answer questions before the board. He was looking at a fine of around $100,000 for going AWOL and a reprimand. The meeting lasted no more than ten minutes. Mundine walked in and told the board he was quitting. He was taking up boxing. He walked out sucking a lollipop.

It is here Khoder Nasser finally makes his debut, at least in the form of proper noun. Initially, he was identified as Mundine's personal assistant while father Tony took the role as manager.

Mundine announced his professional debut was just two months later against former New Zealand middleweight champion Gerrard Zohs. It was certainly ambitious. The Sydney Entertainment Centre was booked and a date was confirmed with pay-per-view provider MainEvent.

Mundine was doing a brilliant job at selling himself. Some fighters had been toiling in Australia for a decade and if they offered to fight for free in your backyard you would draw the curtains. Mundine's professional debut generated mountains of copy.

All anybody wanted to know was how he would go. While Zohs looked formidable, certainly as a debut, stories had circulated for years about the gym wars between Tony and Anthony, and Tony, remember, was an all-time great in Australian boxing. He won national titles at middleweight, light-heavyweight and heavyweight, was never beaten by another Australian fighter, and fought the great Carlos Monzón in Argentina for the middleweight belt in 1974. Monzón stopped him in seven. If Anthony could hold his own in sparring and they were as good as they said they were, then he must be something more than a novice, despite his lack of experience on paper.

Nasser's part in the promotion was seen as minimal but, soon, his full influence over Mundine would be understood. He was an alternative thinker who had captivated Mundine.

None of this surprises anybody who knows Nasser. He is intensely loyal to those he represents, which causes all kinds of collateral damage. He and Mundine struck no formal deal, just a handshake. Their big asset right then just might have been Weidler. By now I had left the *Sun-Herald* and, after two years at the *Sydney Morning Herald*, shifted across the road to the *Daily Telegraph* and *Sunday Telegraph*. As Mundine's boxing career advanced, still powered by the blazing electricity of his football career, he remained good for one backpage splash every fight and often in between. With his close connection Weidler led the way on many stories. Naturally, he pressed this advantage. You would be disappointed if he didn't.

This caused some chatter at my paper. The problem was there were times when Mundine genuinely was newsworthy and at those times we had no contact at all with him, and little likelihood. The San Francisco excursion was the great example. Other times the lack of contact forced us to talk to people around him in a bid to cover the story. It wasn't always ideal.

A big part of the conversation was that often at times the talk around work progressed to whether Mundine was selling papers or driving readers away. Nobody could be really certain. At times approaches were made about establishing contact between our newspapers and Mundine and his camp. They always broke down.

In some ways he craved it. Some years later Nasser sits outside Bar Coluzzi, the inner-city coffee shop, reading an article that's more than somewhat critical of Mundine in the *Daily Telegraph*. There is not a kind word in the entire story about Nasser.

'I don't care. Look,' said Nasser, poking a small pointer at the end of the story: *Mundine fights tonight at 7.30pm on MainEvent.* 'That's all I care about.'

Maybe he did care and it was just bravado. Maybe he didn't. His wife, Tatum Maybir, had already seen it. She has no doubt what drives him.

'His ego,' she told Greg Bearup in a *Good Weekend* feature.

'He's got an enormous ego,' she said. 'My gosh, he'll probably kill me for saying that. He's got a lot to prove, to himself and other people. He thrives on the controversy, too. We never get the *Telegraph* but when he's in that Bec & Buzz column, someone will point it out to him – he loves it.'

He might, but anybody who dared criticise Nasser was nearly always quickly banned from covering Mundine fights. No explanation was ever given, and seldom requested, but again it had less to do with Nasser being truly upset about what was written than it being his way of conditioning the media. Sonny Ball.

Nasser was about taking on almost everybody. Because almost everybody lived within the system. He promoted fights like nobody had ever done before.

Nasser was soon promoting all Mundine's fights and for years I heard nothing but positive reports about him as a promoter, and from those in the fight game who should know. I struggled to see it. Many of the undercards assembled were terrible, nearly always one-way traffic and fights that really did not progress the fighter in any way, except on his record.

The opponent selection for Mundine was at times awful. Undercard fighters were not paid a purse but instead given tickets to sell. Nasser was learning on the run and doing things his way. Mundine was so successful as the main event he absorbed Nasser's mistakes.

The compliments from those within seemed at odds with what we saw. I asked Nader Hamdan about it one day, well after Hamdan fought Mundine. How could you train for a fight when part of the job required you to also sell tickets?

He gave two great reasons why it worked better than any promoter in Australia.

First, he said, you earn more with Nasser. He no longer needed to go on after that. It was the greatest reason of all. Nasser, he said, provided as many tickets as a fighter could sell and they were easy to move on a Mundine card. And because Mundine had no major sponsors there was no conflict of interest and Nasser did not care if they entered the ring sponsored like a race-car. Nasser did not care much for sponsors.

'Marketing is its own monster,' he told Bearup. 'Between you and me, I couldn't give two flying shits about it. Marketing means that you are licking the arse of some corporation. They paint you on a billboard, make all the kids look up to you, while they're rorting every son of a bitch $200 for a five-buck pair of shoes.'

Secondly, Nasser was honest. There isn't a fighter in Australia or anywhere else for that matter who can't tell you a story about a promoter ripping them off when the gate fell short, or the sponsors didn't come through, or that he got ripped off himself and was trying to make good of a bad situation. Such news is nearly always delivered to the fighter with a fast car waiting outside.

Not Nasser. He not only paid fighters every cent they agreed to, but quite often paid bonuses for a good fight. He was completely transparent.

I could see why fighters wanted to be on his card.

NASSER'S grandfather migrated to Sydney from Tripoli in 1950 and worked in a factory for eleven years to save money to bring out his family. His son Yasser, Khoder's father, studied electrical engineering at university but had to quit when his father was killed in an industrial accident. He began working at Australia

Post, sorting mail, and was forever thankful of the opportunity Australia afforded him.

Khoder followed his dad to university but failed to finish, only returning later to get his degree. Even as a young man he was an alternative thinker. He did not share his father's gratitude for opportunities. Despite being born in Australia Nasser told Bearup he 'always felt like an outsider'.

'I felt it from some of the teachers at school, too, but if I ever complained [to his father], I'd get shot down.'

It is in these early years that Nasser's personality takes shape. He felt a sense of injustice, one perpetrated by the system.

Nasser enjoyed an argument. He would argue in a phone box given the chance. His father spoke of him being in trouble often as a boy because he was argumentative and strongly independent. So he became a searcher until, like many displaced young men, direction came when he found a copy of Alex Haley's *The Autobiography of Malcolm X*. It is a powerful book, its over-riding philosophy a message of strength and personal growth. Don't accept the future offered to you, create your own. It is the most influential book in his library not including the Koran.

Nasser's way of looking at the world through a different filter revealed itself through his belief Mundine was not feted at Brisbane like he believed he should be – 'like royalty' – and like he could be if he returned to St George.

The message only got clearer. Everyone was making money, he believed. Clubs were making money. Television stations were making money. Even shoe companies were making money. But it was the athlete that was out there every week busting his gut, giving hope to the millions of people. And yet he wasn't making the money he should be making because they were all taking a cut of what should rightfully be his.

Mundine listened and saw the sense of it. Nasser believed clubs got the better of players by signing them to long-term deals at a reduced premium. And it *was* that way.

But overlooked was the flip-side. By accepting the club's lower offer the player gained long-term security: that was the trade-off. If a player were to injure his anterior cruciate ligament, for example, it could rule him out for as long as twelve months. Under the terms of a long-term contract his pay, an entire year's wages, was still guaranteed.

By the time Williams walked out on Canterbury, to pluck just one example, he had played just 73 games of a possible 120, or 61 per cent. Yet he still got paid one hundred per cent of his contract money. Indeed, he spent 53 weeks, more than a year, treating injuries. By the time he left he would have pocketed, according to reports, $1,243,265 for those 73 games.

For Nasser, his great delight was to work outside the system. So what if promoters traditionally promoted a certain way? Nasser knew in Mundine he had something different, so he could do it differently. And he was able to continue operating this way only, as I said, because he was incredibly honest.

A line almost overlooked in the *Good Weekend* feature came from Johnny Lewis, the fight trainer. Lewis trained Jeff Fenech, Jeff Harding and Kostya Tszyu, and goes back to the days of the old Sydney Stadium. He is Australia's greatest trainer.

'If I had a young fighter with big potential,' he said, 'I'd get down on my knees and beg Khoder to manage him. I think he's a genius.'

Lewis knew boxing and he knew the sport had a history of breaking men worse than a bad marriage. Joe Louis, considered by many to be the greatest heavyweight champion ever, died broke and a heroin addict. Mike Tyson won the heavyweight championship in 1986 and earned $300 million in purses and yet filed for bankruptcy in 2003.

When Nasser emerged beside Mundine so little was known about him nobody was sure what to make of him. Nasser, quite cleverly, refused to set their mind at ease. He understood the great power of silence and mystery. The imagination always adds ten per cent. Twenty in the case of Sonny Bill Williams.

And he exercised his power with considerable joy. When rumours circulated in May 2008 that Williams might appear on television's *Dancing with the Stars*, just a month or so before he walked out on the Bulldogs, Nasser refused to confirm or deny them. He could quite easily have done so. Instead he said as little as possible, and let the mystique build.

There were stories he slept in his car, or on the beach, that there were nights he booked himself into expensive hotels and slept on the floor, forgoing the comfortable bed for no other reason than to ward off becoming soft and losing his edge. Strength through sacrifice.

Told in small whispers, they add to Nasser's own mystique. He often wore a ratty sports coat, sometimes with track pants and thongs, and showed few trappings of success. He drove an old Toyota. He was nearly once removed from a Mundine press conference when security thought he was a bum wandering in off the street.

Before Williams began troubling them Nasser would occasionally meet with then NRL marketing director Paul Kind for an exchange of ideas. Just weeks before Williams walked out, I spoke to Kind and he was entirely complimentary about Nasser.

'He looks at the way the system works and he believes the system doesn't necessarily work in the best interests of the athlete,' he said. 'He believes that what he is doing is showing the guts to do things differently and everyone else conforms to the norm. It's bit of a personal crusade.'

IN some ways, Nasser is right.

The system does not always work in the best interests of the best athlete but it is not designed to. It is designed to work in the best interests of *all* the athletes. The salary cap is the perfect example. It keeps clubs sustainable, so more players are paid.

That, however, is not Nasser's concern. He does not manage all athletes.

He is able to do things differently only because everyone else, as Kind said, does conform. If even one more manager disregarded the system the way Nasser does everything would descend into chaos. That was the biggest irony for NRL officials to accept. He was able to operate his way only because of the control they maintained over the system, the one David Gallop was trying to protect.

Gallop understood better than most that while top-end talent like Williams might leave the code for a higher salary elsewhere and cause many to shriek it was the end of the world, his insistence that the cap retains its integrity is what was saving the game. He didn't have the luxury of picking and choosing.

Gallop was a calm head in times of small crisis, which he is rarely credited for.

The day after Sonny Bill flew out of Australia Matt Johns sat between Geyer and Weidler on the *Sunday Roast* and spoke of a fear many now felt. 'I've got real fears that our game, that we love so much, has had its best days. That's my fears at the moment.'

Such was the move Sonny Bill and Nasser had pulled, Johns was not seen as an alarmist, but a realist. Was this opening the NRL to raids from rugby codes around the world? Could the game, which clearly could not afford to compete against rich overseas rugby union clubs, survive them?

The NRL always believed it produced the best footballers of whatever rugby code you chose. Now the rest of the world was awake to it.

Former ARL boss John Quayle watched Williams leave and Gallop stand out the front of NRL headquarters preaching the sanctity of the contract, and his mind went back more than a decade.

'Put it this way,' Quayle told Andrew Webster at the *Herald*, 'David [Gallop] should have plenty of experience dealing with players breaking contracts. Now he has to handle it – like we had to. It is David's job now, as it was mine then, to make sure you do everything possible to protect your game. And if that means taking rugby on, take them on.'

With the Super League war fresher in his mind than it was with most, Quayle saw the irony. 'It's reminiscent of twelve years ago,' he said. 'The comment from Super League was that its players would be recognised as stars around the world. Well, they've got one.'

There is no guessing where rugby league could have been if not for the Super League war.

Quayle, a former Eastern Suburbs backrower, is still considered rugby league's greatest administrator. Quayle was so far ahead of the game that as early as 1989 he was talking about the business of pay-TV. The rights were first written into the broadcast deal three years earlier. He even dared dream that by 2000 rugby league might have its own pay-TV network showing every game live. It was some dream. This was years before Major League Baseball launched its own pay-TV network in the United States, before any other sport anywhere in the world had done so. Before pay-TV had even come to Australia.

If Quayle made a mistake, it was that he signed rugby league's pay-TV rights away too cheaply when he did his deal with Packer. If it was a mistake, and only a harsh judge would deem it so, it was understandable for several reasons. Nobody knew what the pay-TV rights' true value were, for one. Also, Channel Ten was the game's broadcaster in 1991 when the network suddenly found itself in massive financial trouble. At the time, the deal with Ten was the biggest in Australian television history. Yet with Ten in financial trouble it was not worth forty cents.

Quayle and ARL chairman Ken Arthurson looked for a way out. Channel Seven was in receivership, which left only Kerry Packer's Channel Nine. Packer genuinely loved rugby league, and did a deal that benefitted both parties: the ARL got itself out of Ten, and Packer got himself rugby league for a terrific price.

So when ESPN approached the ARL in 1993 about optioning its pay-TV rights locally and internationally Packer immediately exercised his right of first refusal and picked up the rights. Under Quayle and Arthurson, the game was heading in the right direction – until Super League shot it into small pieces.

Peace was achieved on 19 December 1997. The ARL and Super League agreed to come under the banner of one competition for 1998 and the new competition would be called the National Rugby League. They planned to bring the twenty-two teams down to a preferred fourteen-team competition (which became sixteen) by 2000. Super League immediately disbanded the Hunter Mariners and the ARL culled South Queensland Crushers for the 1998 season while other clubs were encouraged to merge.

Pay scales were now way beyond what the game was capable of sustaining.

So the NRL created a salary cap of $3.25 million for 1998 and clubs were ordered to slash rosters to get there, although everybody knew it was going to take some time. As players came off contract they were offered heavily reduced deals. Some were shipped to England's Super League to clear up salary-cap room.

St George Illawarra was given special dispensation as the new League's first merged club, picking the best players from two clubs, and swayed under a salary cap of just under $6 million, according to chief executive Brian Johnston. The salary cap dispensation was a sweetheart deal to encourage the St George Dragons to merge with the Illawarra Steelers for the 1999 season. They became the first merged team of the new competition. Under such terms, the Dragons were able to continue paying Mundine his $600,000-a-year deal.

Yet belts were being tightened.

From the moment peace was achieved pay cuts were foreshadowed and players knew their next deal would not be the same. Brad Fittler's Sydney Roosters salary was tipped to fall from

$700,000 a season to $400,000. Laurie Daley (Canberra) from $600,000 to $400,000. Gorden Tallis (Brisbane) from $500,000 to $400,000. Andrew Johns (Newcastle) from $500,000 to $400,000.

And Anthony Mundine, before he walked out, $600,000 to $420,000.

'The goose that laid the golden egg has died and players and managers need to realise this,' Cowboys manager Rabieh Krayem said.

It remained an uneasy time for the game which, for the moment, was happy to enjoy the peace.

Without anybody realising, a subtle lesson passed, though.

Packer was in the midst of his contract with the ARL when the Super League war erupted, in what was the third year of a $70 million, seven-year extension. Yet when the war was on he paid, for the first and only season of Super League and with only half the teams, $50 million for that season's rights.

Like it or not, it took an outside force to realise the game's true value.

It sounded a hell of a lot like Sonny Ball.

12

INTERNAL COMBUSTION

A month before Williams fled Australia Phil Gould wrote a heavy-calibre column in the *Sun-Herald* criticising David Gallop and News Limited. The game could no longer tolerate a media company owning the game, he wrote. It was a theme he came back to often. He was frustrated there never seemed to be any movement on ownership. He believed the game was being held back. He questioned David Gallop and his administration and asked why the game did not take the leap, and he wondered whether there might be more to it than was being revealed.

Gould had many legitimate questions. He might not have liked all the answers.

Gallop is a tall man, built more to be a lanky fast bowler than a front rower, which was not all bad news, since, when the weekends came and he was a young man not working as an associate for law firm Holman Webb, he was opening the bowling for the University of NSW in the Sydney grade competition. Over the summer of 1994–95 a friend put Gallop in contact with John Ribot, who was working on a secret plan. Ribot was planning Super League and, at twenty-nine, Gallop was employed as the company's Legal Affairs Manager.

Gallop survived the peace negotiations. He was employed as the NRL's Director of Legal and Business Affairs when peace was made in 1997, until he took over as the game's chief executive in 2002. The competition was still half owned by the Australian Rugby League and half owned by News Limited, an alliance that gave Gallop heartburn.

For his part, though, he gave the game what it needed. More than anything he gave it stability. Part of the peace deal meant foundation clubs like Balmain and Western Suburbs were forced to merge and become Wests Tigers, North Sydney merged with Manly to become the Northern Eagles, then went to the wall all alone when the joint venture fell over and the licence reverted back to Manly. South Sydney, the spirit of the league, was kicked out in 2000 when it couldn't find a suitable partner and failed to meet the 'criteria', a ranking system to determine who survived the cull to sixteen teams and who did not. There was blood everywhere as businessmen decided what was best for the game. St George, owner of perhaps the game's proudest history, was forced to merge with Illawarra to take its place in the new competition. The net effect was many fans walked away forever, and almost all the rest were left hurting.

The game needed nursing. The inoffensive Gallop was ideal for the job.

All this is necessary to hear in our story now, to understand where the game was the day Sonny Bill Williams left town. While Super League was totally unrelated to Williams, just a boy growing up in New Zealand when the war was being fought, albeit with tremendous biceps, many prejudices still survived, living and breathing, more than ten years later. It remained the backdrop to the ill-feeling between Gallop and Gould who, at various points, really had tried hard to like each other and at times had even pulled it off. It played a part in the wildly different coverage of Williams' departure in Fairfax and News Limited mastheads, and there was extra venom in the competition between league writers that dated back to the war.

As for the game, at some point it needed to move on. It was essential for survival.

During the Super League war the AFL made great inroads in NSW and Queensland. The relocated Sydney Swans made the grand final in 1996. The Brisbane Lions formed the same year and by 2001 would win the first of three successive premierships. The Swans would win their first Sydney-based premiership two years after. Sydney sports fans were quick to adopt the new toy despite there still being nine NRL teams based in Sydney.

In some ways, though, the AFL was still the quiet cousin in Sydney.

Rugby league's traditional rival, rugby union, caused quiet panic in the game when it won the right to host the 2003 Rugby World Cup in Australia. The NRL then got very nervous when three genuine stars – Wendell Sailor, Mat Rogers and Lote Tuqiri – all announced within twelve months they were leaving the NRL for rich contracts with the Australian Rugby Union (ARU).

All three were in Wallabies gold by the World Cup. By then a great realisation had fallen upon the NRL. The tables had turned. After nearly one hundred years pinching the best of rugby talent, rugby was now squaring up. The game did not have the money at the very top end to match the contracts being offered across town at the ARU. Rather than fight, the NRL chose a different strategy to explain their defections. Sailor and Rogers were considered past their best and by the time they left some rationalised they had paid their dues to the NRL, so who could resent them for picking up rich contracts, superannuation payments effectively, with rugby union?

The argument then and the argument now for the NRL was the salary cap. It was a powerful argument because it was emotive. Not one fan wanted to see their favourite player leave his club because the game could not afford to keep him. How could the NRL afford to pay less than the Wallabies? Wasn't there a rich television deal? How could the NRL argue against such logic, no matter how far from the truth it was?

Less than a fortnight before Sonny walked out, St George Illawarra's Mark Gasnier ended months of negotiations with his chief executive, Peter Doust, by walking into Doust's office with his jaw firmly set. Doust looked across the desk and knew he didn't need to say a word.

'I'm wasting my time, aren't I?'

'Yes,' said Gasnier.

Gasnier was $300,000 short in contract money after third-party deals were undelivered. He was two years into a five-year deal, and it is fair here to note the different circumstances to Williams'. Gasnier's contract included a get-out clause in his favour should the Dragons fail to come up with the third-party deals. It was an unusual clause to include in the contract and Doust was criticised hard for allowing it.

'Mark signed a contract in 2006 for five years based on those commitments,' Doust said. 'We couldn't contractualise those com-mitments because the NRL wouldn't let us and so we had to put in a clause to allow him to make a decision if they weren't honoured. We've done the best we can to put together a deal to keep Mark in the game.'

The NRL's anger came from the perception that the clause was included as an unstated guarantee that Gasnier would receive the extra money. Certainly Gasnier believed that. He later said he did not realise the third-party agreements were simply 'letters of intent', one where the club would do its best to secure deals but made no guarantees, and 'not as black and white as I expected'. Under NRL rules, as we have already seen with Canterbury's 'best efforts' for Williams, arm's length third-party deals could not be guaranteed by NRL clubs. The best clubs could do was put players in contact with interested sponsors and hope they could come to an agreement.

The reason, again, is simple. Guaranteeing third-party deals not under the salary cap would simply be a way of artificially inflating the cap. Scheming clubs, and there is good reason to believe there might be at least one or two in the NRL, would simply divert potential club sponsors into becoming personal sponsors for players knowing the money would not be included in the cap. With no guarantee player risked the money might not come through. Therefore, it stands to reason, the sanctity of the cap is protected.

When blame was directed at the NRL and the salary cap for Gasnier's exit Gallop was forthright. 'We certainly met with Mark and the Dragons to point out the opportunities in rugby league but there was no commitment from the NRL to guarantee income,' Gallop said.

'Ultimately, the club decides how much it will guarantee in a contract and how much may or may not be available in the market place through sponsorship to keep the player. Had there ever been such a guarantee then the club would not have devised a "get-out" clause each year. That clause was there in case opportunities did not eventuate.'

The man who handled it best was Gasnier.

'Would you work if you only got paid two-thirds of your wage?' he asked reporters at the press conference announcing his departure. 'Would you be happy to keep turning up to work for two years and for that to keep going on? I didn't want to risk that and I couldn't foresee the future so I had to react to it. I'm definitely not going to leave thinking I did the wrong thing by anyone.'

Gasnier signed to play rugby with Stade Français. He said he would leave when his season with the Dragons was over.

Ultimately, this was about the salary cap, and criticisms the salary cap was not high enough to keep the top-flight players in the game. This, of course, happened just three weeks after

Williams had moaned about the cap himself and a fortnight before he took a different path out of the game.

Almost immediately after Williams walked out a conversation started about the legality of the salary cap. Already there were threats that Williams would challenge the cap's legality to break his Bulldogs contract. On the Tuesday after he fled Roy Masters wrote in the *Herald* that Williams was preparing to challenge the cap on the grounds it was an unfair restraint of trade.

Weidler had already revealed Williams had examined his legal options. The one mistake here was involving lawyers in the first place. Pay lawyers enough and they will tell you anything. Hey, they'll say, there is always a chance — usually while picking out their new boat from the showroom floor.

The day Masters' story appeared all sixteen NRL chief executives met in Sydney. It was a regular meeting but everybody knew the business of the day. All sixteen club bosses managed to agree on something. This is much harder than it looks.

'Quite simply, we have received unequivocal support from the other clubs,' said Todd Greenberg.

'There is solidarity among the clubs,' said Gallop.

'This bloke walked out in the dark of night — he was advised to do that,' said South Sydney boss Shane Richardson. 'The issue of player contracts is one that has to be seen in its own right and it is something that the clubs know has to be enforced.'

Richardson dismissed any legal threat to the salary cap. 'I'm not overly concerned with that because the salary cap has been put in place because of the financial status of the game,' he said. 'Players sign freely knowing there's a cap in place. They have a choice not to sign. The restraint of trade argument is a bit of a tawdry one under the circumstances.'

They agreed to support the Bulldogs' legal action against Williams and, if Williams did play rugby union and decide to return to the NRL, nobody would sign him.

'Once he laces up the boots to play rugby I can't imagine anyone would want Sonny Bill back in the NRL,' said Manly boss Grant Mayer.

Parramatta boss Denis Fitzgerald, the most experienced official in the room, put it in perspective. 'We don't want clubs going in a different direction on this issue and, if Sonny Bill Williams does come back, have to sign him,' he said.

Throughout, Gallop's stance never wavered. The sanctity of the salary cap was paramount. The fight was on his turf.

Why was it so important?

Because the game was not flush with funds. While the game's crowds might have been up four per cent in 2008, as Gallop told Gould, it was a skinny claim to suggest the game was in good shape based solely on that. For one, crowd figures lived and died by the success of certain teams. The most successful season in the NRL based on crowd figures was 2005 when, not by coincidence, the top four teams were the most broadly supported. Naturally the crowds followed. You only needed to look a little deeper to see the game was growing organically, not strategically, its growth tied to crowd figures and television ratings, which were influenced by a thousand different things beyond the NRL's control. And that's if they were doing a good job.

After the chief executives' meeting Fitzgerald warned clubs could be dead in as little as five years without the discipline of the salary cap. 'We've said before that it is a restraint of trade, however it is not an unreasonable restraint of trade so there's a significant difference there,' he said. 'Everyone is behind the salary cap. I would guess most of the Sydney clubs [would die without one] within five years under the current situation. It's most important with so many pressures on all clubs and especially the NSW clubs that are funded to a degree by the licensed clubs. We've got so much pressure on licensed clubs, primarily the increase in poker machine tax that has come into play in the last four years.'

Against this weight of experience and reason, Sonny Bill's claim of being underpaid because of an unfair salary cap was absurd. His yardstick remained Mundine's $600,000-a-year contract in 1999 against his $400,000-a-year deal in 2008.

While it gained him some public sympathy, it was also ill-informed. It paid no regard to history.

But none of that mattered in Sonny Ball. While Sonny Ball spoke of something bigger, the truth of Sonny Ball was that it was about something smaller.

It spoke of being limitless, yet its focus was the *individual*.

WITH Super League money now a memory, with poker machine taxes killing the club industry and the anti-smoking laws adding to the pain, the great saviour for the game was the broadcast deal. And that needed help.

When Williams walked out in 2008 the NRL got $89 million from broadcast rights with Channel Nine and Fox Sports. The deal was in its second year. Against that the AFL was taking in $156 million through its broadcast deal with Channel Seven, Channel Ten and Fox Sports. Now there are a dozen different ways to interpret television ratings and, in the hands of somebody who properly understands them, they can be manipulated to suit whatever argument you care to make. But it was generally considered that AFL rated slightly higher than the NRL although most would argue that the difference was not proportionate to the difference in rights cost.

The NRL was paying for a poor negotiation. While the deal was not making the game broke but it was not growing it, either. It was treading water. Right now its growth was tied entirely to the value of its broadcast rights, and little was being done to increase that value. The $89 million was about $20 million a year short of what it should have been. The greatest strain was the broadcast money was unable to fully cover the salary cap for all sixteen clubs.

Not that the clubs could help themselves. Many were fighting for survival but for reasons no-one can explain they operated no differently than they had a decade earlier when they were backed by highly profitable Leagues clubs.

Now, if you want to be kind, you can say it was understandable, if not acceptable. They weren't businessmen. In many cases they were former players gifted a job after they retired, or former committee men with a particular spark who hung around long enough until they eventually worked their way into the top job. It often came through nothing more than attrition. Their credentials were their passion for the club, not their business acumen. And their lack of credentials were disguised by the Leagues clubs, which for years profited millions through poker machines and who subsidised the football clubs with enough cash to camouflage their failures.

Where they got caught was the introduction of anti-smoking laws in 2000 and, more importantly, increased poker machine taxes in 2002. Both changes in legislation had a dramatic impact on club revenue. It left many Leagues clubs struggling for their survival and meant they certainly didn't have pots of money around to subsidise football clubs like they had and which was, indeed, their charter.

The game simply failed to move with the times, unable to find different revenue streams to supplement money lost from Leagues club grants. In that way, the broadcast deal signed in 2005 was a godsend. It saved some clubs.

But there was not enough left to grow the game. A great handicap for Gallop was the how the new board was set up. While the News Limited balance of power was businessmen who worked towards a clear bottom line, the Australian Rugby League side of the partnership still worked as a committee. So before any decision could be rubber-stamped in NRL boardrooms, with Gallop then sent out to get it done, the ARL first had to go and present the deal to the NSW Rugby League and Queensland Rugby League boards, which in some cases then had to go and present the information to the board of, say, the Country Rugby League. Only when a decision was debated and finalised would it then work its way back along the chain to NRL headquarters.

You bet it was clumsy. But it was what they needed to agree upon to make peace.

By the time all these meetings were convened, weeks or even months had burned, even for the most basic decisions. And this says nothing of the self-interest involved along the way. The last thing you pry from a dead committeeman's hand was his blazer. Such men were at the same time the game's great strength and its great weakness. Their doggedness is why many clubs survived and why the millions of fans still felt an affiliation with the game. They grew up watching the same teams that were playing now. It's why thousands marched on Town Hall in 1999 demanding South Sydney's reinstatement, the Rabbitohs finally brought back in 2002. Beyond everything, fans believed in the clubs.

Yet clubs were also part of the problem. Not all, but some were terribly run and inhibited the game's growth. Almost all the money clubs received from the NRL through the broadcast deal was put straight into the football operation. Little if any went to marketing or advertising or other areas of the business that would safely, but slowly, grow the business. A disproportionate amount from total revenue is dedicated to the football program. In any normal business this is an unsound business strategy. And it stifled the long-term growth of the game.

Clubs, in essence, were gambling. And it was a gamble that maintained the financial strain. Nothing if not optimists, clubs overspent on their football operation hoping it would end in better prepared players and more success on-field and more wins. They hoped that brought more free-to-air television games and media exposure, and therefore more sponsorships, memberships and crowd receipts. And money.

Where all this comes unstuck is simple logic. If all sixteen clubs think this same way, not all can find that necessary success on the playing field. Every week there are eight winners but also eight losers.

Only a long-term plan could break the cycle. This is where the AFL made great ground since forming its commission in 1985. It planned for the game's growth, economically and geographically, and was prepared to ride out whatever short-term bumps it encountered for long-term success.

The Australian Rugby League commission wouldn't come until years later, when News Limited turned over its fifty per cent ownership to the newly formed ARL commission in 2012. Within months Gallop resigned, after it became clear he had fallen out of favour with the new commissioners.

Many months later, former Lloyds Bank boss Dave Smith was appointed the game's new chief executive, marking a sharp change in direction for the game. Smith's focus was completely different. He immediately starting setting the game up for where it would be in ten years and beyond, rather than dealing with the spotfires continually erupting.

Smith focused on running the game as a business. For example, he bought Touch Football Australia and brought it in under the rugby league banner. He encouraged clubs to add business experience to their boards, breaking from the 'chook raffle' mentality. He set about investing in the game's lower levels, such as junior development.

The theory was simple. More participation meant more eyeballs, and more eyeballs would make the broadcast rights worth more. At the same time, once the broadcast rights were where they needed to be, they could cover the salaries at the clubs and leave enough behind for further investment in growing the game.

In the business world, they called it internal combustion.

Understandably none of this meant anything to Sonny Bill or any other NRL player, except for what was spat out at the end. And right now they believed they could make more money playing other sports. The only question then was whether they could transfer their skills.

With rugby union, of course they could. And Williams planned to show how easy that would be.

13

A HUNDRED THOUSAND WELCOMES

LIKE all legends, they heard about him before they saw him.

Everybody except Brad Clyde, the former Canberra great now working as Canterbury's marketing manager who, the first time he saw Sonny Bill Williams, had to rub his eyes twice. This was 2002, and sixteen-year-old Sonny had just arrived at Canterbury from New Zealand with a reputation as broad as the sea he just crossed.

'He had the big Poison haircut,' Clyde remembered. 'It was like the big Van Halen piece of work and then he had to run the comb through that to keep it out of his eyes. I thought, "He must want a tough time playing footy because everyone is just going to pull on that hair of his." It took two games for me to realise he had something special.'

And not just the haircut.

Sonny toiled away in lower grades for two seasons, learning the great lesson of being an elite footballer. He had no idea the benefit he was receiving in the Bulldogs' system. He was meant to play under-17s that first year but ended up spending most of the season in the Jersey Flegg under-20s competition. Clyde, also the trainer for the Flegg team, said he was hard to miss.

'There are a lot of young players that people say may develop into great players but with Sonny Bill I don't think there's too much of a question mark,' he said.

Sonny missed most of his second season at the club with injury and spent the time working at Belmore Oval, the old ground tired and weary. The Bulldogs trained there but no longer played there, since the ground was unable to handle even a small crowd. Sonny's job that year was to scrape the bird shit off the seats in the grandstand. It should not surprise anybody that he spoke about the job with an odd pride, like it kept him grounded, kept him humble.

Despite the injuries, he played enough football to be chosen for the NSW under-20s side and for coach Steve Folkes to name him in the full-time squad for 2004. Williams looked around at the likes of NRL legends Steve Price and Braith Anasta training beside him and felt a little out of place.

'A few years ago I wouldn't have dreamed of it,' he said. 'It's just a big buzz.'

All kinds of stories drifted up through the grades about Williams. The all-in brawl against South Sydney where Williams, his back to the sideline, threw three short ones and knocked out three opponents. Who knew if it was true? A dozen people claimed it was one hundred per cent correct but nobody wanted to ask Williams in case it ruined a good fairytale.

He had an offload like the great Arthur Beetson, they said.

'He's just got that ability to drag three blokes with him,' said Steve Mortimer, by then the club's chief executive.

He was described as being similar to anybody with talent. Beetson, Rod Reddy, Willie Mason – there was not a comparison that could not be made. They saw a little of all of them in him. The big right footstep and the offload that was found in two, maybe three, in the world at the time.

Already, a mythology was developing around Sonny. The Bulldogs set about giving him a first-class education. They poured the work into him like a trainer would raising a three-year old with an eye to next year's Melbourne Cup.

The Bulldogs were one of the best at it. Wherever players eventually moved on to, those who left always took with them a first-class work ethic that benefitted their new teammates.

As for Sonny, the best bit was that at least half the stories about him were true.

The story about the three knockouts was better than you could invent.

Late in that first season I asked Williams about the sideline fight, the three right hands and the three knockouts. Naturally he was modest.

'Just a bit of a scuffle, eh,' he said, smiling as he said it, almost embarrassed.

So I asked teammate Jarrad Hickey, who knew all about it.

'One of the Souths blokes said something to one of our blokes and pushed him a bit. They didn't target Sonny, he just stood up for his teammate and put one on him. The ref called him out and sent him off and Sonny was already off and, as the Souths guy started walking off, he started running for Sonny. It was right next to the Souths bench. He put him on his arse straightaway. Then he had the Souths bench to deal with, there was four or five of them . . . I don't think he had a bruise on him.'

This was wonderful news not because junior-rep football is any place to advocate violence but for a very simple reason: the physical gifts were true. A new star was being born, and everybody knew early enough to watch the development.

He made his debut in the first round of the 2004 season against Parramatta.

Before the game his family flew over, mum Lee and sisters Denise and Niall, the twins. Niall played touch for New Zealand. Sonny's father and brother were already living in Australia, brother John Arthur playing for the Sydney Bulls.

He was picked to play centre, a testament to his versatility, and to mark Parramatta and Australian centre Jamie Lyon.

As Sonny began to get dressed before the game he opened his bag and realised he had forgotten to pack his football boots. He rushed outside, looking for his brother. John Arthur had played earlier, in a preliminary game with the Bulls.

'Can you go home and pick them up?' Sonny asked.

John Arthur didn't think so, 'It will take too long. You'll have to use mine instead.'

'So Sonny went out there wearing his brother's boots,' Lee told the *Sun-Herald* later. 'It was unbelievable and just as well they wear the same-sized boots.'

It took only twenty minutes to announce Sonny's talent. He busted through the middle of Parramatta's defence and put Luke Patten away to make it 16–0. Already he had headed off on a fifty-metre break that ended with his support player, Corey Hughes, brought down in the Parramatta twenty-metre zone. Canterbury led 36–0 at halftime. They won 48–14 and, along with putting Patten away for a try, he set up another and scored one himself.

Afterwards he was described as the 'next big thing' and a 'one-man wrecking crew'. His impact was clear. Roy Masters said he made Lyon look 'pedestrian'.

Afterwards, everybody who had heard about him had one thing to say: it's true.

'I don't know what he's going to be. He's just going to get better and better and he will play for New Zealand, for sure,' halfback Brent Sherwin said.

'Sonny Bill Williams was great,' wrote Phil Gould.

Everybody who saw him play knew he was going to be better than the rest.

Chris Anderson, the former Canterbury coach, said he was as good as Brad Fittler was at the same age.

Everybody wanted to know his story.

SONNY BALL

Where did this kid with the unusual name come from?

John Ackland, a serious judge of football talent, had watched Sonny Bill Williams play for years, since he was ten or eleven, for Owairaka Primary School in Auckland.

Mark Hughes, Canterbury's recruitment and development manager, saw him play at fourteen in an under-16s competition. 'He was a skinny if not awkward kid, but you could see the potential.'

When he first started playing rugby league Williams was quick and strong and a standout because junior rugby league is nearly always about who had the most natural gifts. Then nature played a trick on him that would prove a wonderful godsend.

'I went through a stage when I was pretty young where I shot up and couldn't really run,' he said.

He was like a new foal, trying to grow into his legs. 'At thirteen I got really tall. I shot up to about six foot. When I was young I was pretty fast but when I shot up I went real slow.'

Without pace, Williams was forced to find other ways to dominate his rivals. The great benefit here is, despite the loss of pace, he suffered no loss of confidence. So he started playing football against them, developing his skills. Soon, there was not a tackle he would go into where he did not think he could offload the ball. He was often correct. By the time his muscles caught up to his bones again, Williams had added a serious arsenal to his game. By fourteen he was dominating, playing up a grade.

Canterbury had never signed a player so young but Ackland, also working for the Bulldogs, was convinced of Sonny's talent. So was Hughes. It quickly became a race.

About the same time Hughes saw Sonny play, former New Zealand captain Gary Freeman also saw him in an under-16 tournament. He looked around and saw the NRL talent scouts and was overtaken with a sick sense of dread.

'My concern was that the Kiwis would lose him because it's so tempting for kids that come over here so young to want to play State of Origin,' Freeman said. 'He was just this big, raw-boned thing, but he could play the ball at the line and I remember saying to John Ackland at the time that he was going to be an absolute superstar.'

There was no doubt Canterbury wanted him. He might have been only fifteen, which would have made him the youngest ever player signed to the club, but the Bulldogs also knew you don't wait for talent to come to you.

Sonny had concerns about heading to Sydney. Lee was concerned about him leaving home so young. It was Lee who got him playing rugby league, taking him to the local team, Marist-Richmond, when he was eight. Her father, Bill Woolsey, was already a bona fide legend at the club, one of the all-time great Kiwi players.

If Sonny was beginning to write his own narrative, his grandfather had long written his. They still spoke about the time Woolsey suffered a head cut so severe it required thirty stitches. Blood poured down his face. The coach on the sideline got suitably concerned, and sent a player to replace him. Woolsey reacted as you might expect: he grabbed the replacement by his jersey and marched him off again. It is after Woolsey that Williams got his middle name. Sonny is the name of his dad's brother, making his proper name Sonny William Williams.

'And Sonny William Williams sounds kind of funny, eh, so it was just Sonny Bill,' Sonny says.

Canterbury's offer was too good to pass up. Eventually he would have to go to Sydney where the Bulldogs had a gold-star reputation for looking after young players. So one afternoon, in the housing commission area of Avondale, Ackland put the contract on the bonnet of his 1984 Nissan Centra and Sonny signed for the Bulldogs. He was paid $5000 and given free accommodation that first year.

Williams arrived in Sydney with his father John and set about finding a manager. Everyone courted him. They took him to flash restaurants, polished their expensive cars to chauffeur him.

Gavin Orr picked him up and took him to a takeaway restaurant for a hamburger. He recognised Sonny was humble and took him where he felt comfortable, not where he thought he would be most impressed. It was a masterstroke. Williams signed up with Orr.

MARY and Peter Durose were Bulldogs fans. They were also houseparents to young Bulldogs players away from home for the first time. For more than twenty years some of the club's greatest players would come to know Mary's way. If anybody wants to know about these people be prepared to be covered in love. That is Mary's way.

One of those who landed on her doorstep was Sonny Bill.

It all started when Mary and Peter were at the Canterbury Leagues Club, where they often went for a meal. Over time Mary started noticing the younger players at the club, sitting nearby, watching her and Peter eat. Too shy to say anything, but their hunger betraying them.

'The young players would just sit there looking at our food,' she said. 'We'd ask them if they wanted anything to eat, but they'd refuse even though they were drooling. Back in those days they only got paid twice a year. They never had any money to buy dinner.'

Soon Mary and Peter were buying dinner for the players, and shortly after Mary was cooking great slabs of chicken schnitzel and legs of lamb and whatever else they could fit on a plate. She recognised a need and spoke to club patriarch Peter Moore, telling him she needed a house to fill with players.

The Bulldogs bought several houses around Belmore and those who did not live with 63-year-old Mary and her husband Peter were around there each day for breakfast and dinner, until they all moved into one big house in 1997. Inside the home she put up a sign: *Céad Míle Fáilte*, Celtic for '100,000 Welcomes'.

The house rules were simple: no women, no alcohol and no caps at the dinner table.

'Gentlemen don't wear caps in the house,' Mary said. 'It's only a little thing, but it's a mark of respect.'

Mary loved Sonny Bill. For all his size and talent he had a kind manner. He was a gentle boy who often got homesick. The Bulldogs flew him home as often as they could to ease his home-sickness. Backroom staff often invited him around for dinner and a change of scenery, keeping him from getting bored. It is the golden rule of management: when you have star talent, do all you can to keep him happy.

Years later Sonny moved into his own home, and his problems with the Bulldogs were reaching flashpoint.

Mary and Peter were doing it tough by now. One day, there was a knock at the door and Mary opened it to find Sonny standing there. Mary had lost her upper teeth to mouth cancer five years earlier but Peter was doing it tougher. He had begun suffering mini-strokes and also suffered diabetes, and was in hospital.

Sonny had arrived to drive Mary to hospital.

One afternoon he grabbed her phone and put his number in it. 'I want you to have my number so that if anything goes wrong you can call me,' he said.

Mary found it hard to reconcile that Sonny with the one who walked out on the club just a few months later.

'I love Sonny, I still do,' she said. 'He probably did the wrong thing, but that's not the Sonny I know. The Sonny I know is respectful and quiet – a loving guy.'

Just months after Sonny left Australia Mary and Peter, by now seventy and sixty-seven, with Peter confined to a wheelchair, closed their home, unable to look after the players anymore.

ALMOST immediately after his first-grade debut a debate began about where Sonny Bill Williams would commit for representative football. This is exactly what Gary Freeman was worried about when he saw the boy Sonny, still playing in New Zealand. Freeman worried he would be lured by the appeal of State of Origin football, and it was no small concern.

Since the first State of Origin game in 1980, it had emerged as the most intense football in rugby league, and possibly any of the football codes. You could drink until closing time arguing over that one, but it gets the vote here. Nobody can properly explain why because it makes no sense.

State of Origin was not meant to work. It came about only through the single-mindedness of one man. For more than seventy years NSW and Queensland played an annual inter-state series and by 1980 the series was nearly dead. Queensland had not won a series since 1960 and, in truth, had really only dominated for a period during the 1920s. Throughout the 1970s Queenslanders had become sick of being beaten by Queens-landers wearing NSW jerseys, all of whom moved to Sydney to play in the richer NSW Rugby League competition.

It wasn't fair, and leaning back in his office one afternoon at the Queensland Rugby League president Ron McAuliffe finally saw enough. McAuliffe was built with a fire in him. He did not come to run the QRL and later be a Senator in the Federal Parliament by doing what he was told to do. So on this day in 1980 he called Kevin Humphreys at the NSW Rugby League and put an idea to him.

State of Origin, he said. I want the Queensland players to come home and play for their state when they play the interstate series. It was an idea that had been spoken about before but, this day, McAuliffe was resolute.

Queenslanders, he said again, are sick of being beaten by Queenslanders.

By then the series meant so little and the NSW Rugby League was so strong they were playing the interstate series midweek so not to interfere with the Sydney competition. The NSW clubs had been poaching Queensland's best players for years and built the competition into a considerable strength.

And the reason was simple, the same as it ever was.

Money.

Backed by the poker machines in their Leagues clubs the NSW clubs were able to pay bucketfuls of money, sometimes literally. More than one player spent Monday mornings at the bank counting out twenty-cent coins to deposit into his account. Still the all-time favourite, as far as rorts go, is the Australian player who got the door at the Leagues club's post-match disco every weekend. With poker machines illegal in Queensland, how do you compete against that?

Queensland Rugby League no longer meant a lot to the NSWRL but Humphreys listened. He was obligated. As well as being executive chairman of the NSWRL he was also chairman of the Australian Rugby League. Eventually he agreed to give it a go. Some Sydney clubs sniffed at having to release their players to play for Queensland and refused. At this, Humphreys threatened to make it an officially sanctioned ARL trial, thereby making it mandatory that the players be released. The clubs backed down.

It was feared State of Origin would fail when first proposed for the simple reason that teammates would not play hard against teammates.

So they agreed to make the third game of the 1980 series a State of Origin. McAuliffe called the Queensland selectors and gave one instruction: 'Pick whoever you want,' he said, 'but Beetson's captain.'

It was somewhat unusual, for only one reason. By now Arthur Beetson was thirty-five and playing for Parramatta in the Sydney competition and struggling to stay out of reserve grade. He was an old man in a young man's game, although he was young once. He left Queensland as a young man in 1966 to play for Balmain and Australia and become one of those players that upset Queenslanders so much. He played for NSW seventeen times. Beetson, who would be named rugby league's Seventh Immortal, had achieved everything in the game except for one: he had never played for Queensland.

McAuliffe knew what he was doing, demanding Beetson be captain. He knew the quality of other players in that team – young men like Wally Lewis and Mal Meninga and Chris Close, and knew they needed a leader at this stage of their development.

Years earlier Jack Gibson returned from one of his trips to America, wandering around the hallways of NFL clubs, with a dossier from San Francisco 49ers coach Dick Nolan. It was a psychological study dressed like a questionnaire. It wasn't exclusive to the 49ers. Most teams in the NFL had it or something like it. It was the end of 1973 and Gibson had just taken the job at Eastern Suburbs for the following season. Ron Coote was captain at the time.

Gibson always did things his way, though. He had this dossier from the 49ers and there was no point having it if you were not going to use it, so he took out the questionnaire to get to know his players and when they filled them out he sent them all to America. The experts went through the papers and sent them back. On top was Beetson.

'The one on Beetson came back saying this man has the best leadership qualities of any person we've ever tested,' said Ron Massey, Gibson's right-hand man. We were talking about it one afternoon in 2011, and it was the first story Massey remembered after Arthur collapsed and died of a heart attack while riding a bike to a schoolboy coaching clinic on the Gold Coast.

'They put a special note in,' Massey said. 'We didn't know what to do but Jack said, "Well, we've gone to the trouble to get this done, why not take notice of it?" It was the best thing we ever did. It changed everything.'

With Beetson upfront in every sense, the Roosters won the premiership both years Gibson coached.

That was the man McAuliffe wanted.

Underlying Beetson's return to Queensland, enough in itself to send three shudders through the NSW players, was that tremendous sense of injustice Queenslanders felt. Certainly the NSW players had no inkling. They drank until up to a day before the game, the perfect preparation when walking into an ambush.

From all this, which we see only with the benefit of hindsight after all that has happened, came the moment. The Queensland fans sensed it themselves and got to the game at Lang Park in Brisbane well oiled.

Beetson ran onto the field with chalk powder on his chest, his sleeves cut off. Few noticed, but his right hand was strapped like a prizefighter. Oh yes, Beetson was coming.

Unlike Origin legend, he did not punch his Parramatta teammate Mick Cronin in that opening game. Cronin stood in a tackle because he could and Beetson, who knew this as well as anybody, knew one thing you did not do was let Mick Cronin stand in a tackle. So Beetson came in over the top in the tackle and his arm might have been swinging slightly, which was not good manners, and Cronin ducked under. Given there had already been several brawls, both sides figured it would have been impolite not to start another one.

Over time Beetson's swinging arm became a punch in the telling and was often cited as the great example that team-mates had no problem getting violent against their clubmates in Origin. Few know, but Beetson and Cronin sat together on the plane home the following day.

From that, Origin grew. Mostly through the intensity Queensland brought to the game.

Eventually NSW realised they had to match it or forever continue being beaten. With that, the game found something different in the community and began to appeal beyond rugby league fans.

It looked different. Players began wearing their surnames on the backs of their jerseys, like they did in American sport. Even casual fans could see something more was at stake than usual. By the time Williams was playing rugby league the three State of Origin games were the most watched programs on Australian television.

Origin emerged at the same time that international rugby league faded somewhat. As the Australian game advanced significantly on the back of better training and increased fitness, driven by the Origin bloodlust, other top-tier nations Great Britain and New Zealand failed to keep pace.

Separated by substantial distance, it came in a hurry. The closely fought 1978 Kangaroo tour gave way to the 1982 Kangaroos who, for the first time in history, toured England and France undefeated, a feat they repeated four years later. And except for the occasional win by the Kiwis against Australia, international football was dead.

WHILE playing for your country remained the pinnacle in terms of prestige, players soon realised that the greatest test was no longer in the Test arena, as it always had been, but in Origin. So did the Kiwis, who were ineligible to play but were appearing in greater numbers in the Australian competition.

By playing Origin football a player had to be qualified to play for Australia. This naturally ruled him out of playing for New Zealand. Plenty of New Zealand-born players still made that decision over the years, taking advantage of loose qualification rules to declare themselves for Origin and later play against their homeland.

Brad Thorn had even played for Queensland and then, when he switched codes to rugby union, played for the All Blacks.

Williams was already qualified to play for Australia after playing for NSW in under-17s in 2002. It was his choice to make.

He was captivated by Origin. He had his surname tattooed on his back, just like the Origin players, and soon many were waiting to see where he would pledge his allegiance.

'His mum is Australian and his dad's Samoan,' Gavin Orr said. 'I expect he'd probably want to play for the Kiwis but no one has ever asked.'

Just a week earlier another Kiwi junior, Benji Marshall, had declared his allegiance to New Zealand despite finishing his schooling at Keebra Park High in Queensland. The schooling was part of his scholarship with the Wests Tigers. Marshall played for Australian Schoolboys the previous season, drawing the two-game series against New Zealand. Another talented Kiwi player, Karmichael Hunt, was part of the same Australian Schoolboy side as Marshall.

Where Williams and Marshall were brought to Australia by their clubs, Hunt moved to Australia with his family in search of better opportunities.

Hunt would reflect this when he pledged for Australia, saying he wanted to play Origin football.

In reality, it was a short conversation. Williams was always a Kiwi.

What was more interesting is he gave little thought, if any, to the commercial benefits of declaring himself for Australia. It would have opened him to the Australian market more than he already was. He would also have made himself available for Origin match payments, which were not insignificant at $30,000 a game.

In many ways Williams is still a young innocent here in our story.

He showed as much just weeks into his NRL career when Canterbury travelled to Wellington to play the New Zealand Warriors, just after his debut. It was a home game for the Bulldogs, taking the game to New Zealand as a marketing ploy.

'This is a dream come true for me, playing against my idols, these players I've always seen on TV growing up,' Williams said after training. 'I've been getting a bit of stick from the Aussie boys because all the time I've been in Australia I've been talking about how good the New Zealand food is. They reckon the food hasn't been that good since we've been here. I'll have to take them to McDonald's and KFC. They're much better in New Zealand than in Australia.'

That weekend, after helping Canterbury beat the New Zealand Warriors 24–18, Williams was picked to play Test football for the New Zealand Kiwis.

Not everybody thought he was ready.

'We always thought he'd be a Test player eventually but not this season,' said Steve Folkes. 'Hopefully he'll do well and play strongly.'

Still, Folkes thought his selection was 'a bit premature'.

Once again, though, prodigious talent emerged. Williams turned up to camp nervous, feeling out of place. Williams is, in many ways, a slow thinker. He likes to listen, to absorb the information available to him, and let it bounce around inside before speaking. And he is a worrier, forever hard on himself. So it was surprising when he later revealed he started the season with what most would agree were fairly modest goals. He wanted to make his NRL debut, he said, surprising himself when he achieved that by round one. That done, he wanted to turn one game into five games and, with that done, he wanted to stay in first grade all season long.

Test selection shocked him. Perhaps sensing this, New Zealand coach Daniel Anderson roomed him with veteran Nigel Vagana who immediately started treating him like a man.

'You're here for a reason,' Vagana said to him. 'You have to aim up against Australia.'

The message clear, Williams put his head down and did what he always did in such circumstances. He watched and learned and developed at a great pace. Vagana took away from him the option of excuses. Test football was Test football.

Perhaps he sensed that Williams still harboured doubts about himself as a first grader, let alone as a Test player.

'Before I kind of thought I didn't belong in first grade, that I was just filling boots. But after that week I felt a lot better and I felt I was part of the team. I belonged there,' Williams told Iain Payten at the *Daily Telegraph*.

It is hard to adequately describe Williams' performance. Australia won the Test 37–10 and against any loss like that it is hard to stand out or indeed have a great stamp on the game. Unless you know what you are looking for. For those trained to look at the game through more than the scoresheet, it was in nothing, but it was in everything. Little things, insignificant to most people, like how they handle contact. Whether there was hesitation or not.

All those self-doubts dissolved in his performance. Immediately after the game Williams and Bulldogs captain Steve Price, who played for Australia, were named for Canterbury's game two days later against Souths. They won 34–8 but during the game Williams injured his ankle and was sidelined for twelve weeks. This was very bad news. Williams disappeared to heal.

Williams would go through tremendous change during this season. A non-drinker, he took his first taste of alcohol. Midway through the year Keith Galloway, a friend he played junior reps with, introduced him to those at the Violent Foundation, a charity for children with the horrific disease meningococcal. He would go on to become an ambassador.

'He's quiet and unassuming and he's got a big smile. He makes you feel good,' said the Foundation president, Colin Greenway.

THE Bulldogs were also going through great change. Right here in our narrative, the club was trying to heal itself after a spate of incidents that led to players making the news for all the wrong reasons.

The day after beating Souths the NSW Department of Public Prosecutions announced no charges would be laid for rape allegations made against unnamed players at the club in Coffs Harbour in February. It came at the end of a troubling time for the club that began two years earlier when they were penalised thirty-seven competition points and fined $500,000 after admitting to deliberately cheating the salary cap by one million dollars the previous two seasons. The loss of their competition points effectively took them from first place in the competition to last and was a defining moment in David Gallop's leadership of the game.

Just six months into the job at the time, Gallop called Bulldogs officials to an urgent meeting after details of systemic cheating broke in the *Sydney Morning Herald*. The Bulldogs officials denied the paper's allegation. Gallop told them he was going to leave the room for five minutes and when he returned he wanted their answer on how they would plead.

The Bulldogs confessed all when he returned. Shock soon turned to hostility within Belmore, a silent bitterness at the fact that they were not the only club cheating the salary cap, they believed, but had become the only club to pay the price.

The following February the club travelled to Coffs Harbour for a trial and pre-season camp when a rape allegation was reported to police. Police found no evidence to support the rape charges but bitterness festered within the club, at the media in particular for what they perceived to be unfair reporting, but also at the disgusted eyes that almost always accompanied the players wherever they now went.

Then came another allegation twelve months later, in February 2004, again at Coffs Harbour. Police investigated these allegations far more vigorously. Within days of the allegation details, which police believed came straight from their computer system, were broadcast on radio. A twenty-year-old woman claimed six players had raped her in the swimming pool at the resort where the players were staying.

Police sought DNA tests from all players. The entire investigation took almost two months but was marred by police leaks to the media. An internal battle was being waged within the force and the fallout was tremendous information being leaked to the media to colour the investigation. The media was being used and the Bulldogs were paying the price. Much of what was leaked was eventually proven wrong, some deliberately wrong. A dangerous and damaging game was being played.

'We were getting good evidence of an incident of consensual sex but not of a pack rape,' said Detective Senior Sergeant Gary McEvoy, who at one point led the investigation. 'In fact, we were getting nothing to suggest any crime had occurred at all.'

More and more damaging details were anonymously set loose. The intention appeared to be a determination to damage those running the investigation but it caused tremendous pain to the club, which was growing tired of a suspicious public and what seemed a growing unwillingness to believe the players' innocence. One rape allegation was bad enough, two was hard to come back from.

Eventually, on 18 March, football manager Garry Hughes was sacked and, four days later, chief executive Steve Mortimer resigned. Hughes would sue and win an apology in a wrongful dismissal case.

Almost immediately some investigating detectives questioned the validity of the allegations as they contradicted several eyewitness reports. Late in the investigation an insider showed me private information contained in the brief. I read two independent witness statements, both of which identified a sex act occurring in the pool but with no suggestion of non-consent.

'Before you actually walked into the enclosed area, I could see into the pool and I saw two people in the pool over in the northeastern corner of the pool. They were actually in the act of sex,' one statement said. 'There was a girl in the water with her back towards me and there was a fellow sitting on the edge of the pool. When I walked in, I could see what they were doing so I deliberately let the gate shut loudly to warn them I was there.'

It married up with the version some at the club had, somewhat embarrassingly, admitted to.

Where the Bulldogs fell down was their treatment of the girl. When she finished in the pool she tapped on another player's door looking for her friend and perhaps a little more and the player, who had become acquainted with her some nights before, told her to 'fuck off'.

Her feelings were hurt, something the club later conceded. A simple offer of cab fare home and just a little kindness could have saved the club much, much heartache. But it was not in the club culture at the time.

'There were things which happened in Coffs Harbour we are very ashamed of,' incoming chief executive Malcolm Noad would concede.

Williams was never a suspect in the investigation but, in a dip to his naïvety, came under notice during the investigation, before he had even played an NRL game. The players were in the city to see their lawyers and left that meeting to walk into the Sydney Police Centre for interviews about the allegations.

Williams and teammate Reni Maitua wore University of Texas T-shirts, and the smaller of their two problems was that they were wearing T-shirts and casual wear instead of something more appropriate. The bigger problem was that the front of their T-shirts bore the motifs 'We Play Dirty'. Given they were walking into the Sydney Police Centre to be interviewed over pack rape allegations, it was a look that angered the NRL and brought widespread criticism.

Finally cleared by the DPP in April, Willie Mason said the club was owed an apology. 'We've been smashed over this by the media for months,' he said.

Williams, who had said very little throughout, agreed with Mason. He said the team had been treated 'like criminals'.

The allegations would have crippled another club.

Not the Bulldogs. They were the best at circling the wagons when trouble struck.

When the Super League war broke out in 1995, for instance, four players originally signed with Super League before being enticed to change sides and sign loyalty deals with the NRL. Behind captain Terry Lamb, a blue-chip legend, they were the four best players at the club: Dean Pay, Jason Smith, Jim Dymock and Jarrod McCracken.

One evening they called coach Chris Anderson into a room to tell him they were leaving. Anderson's nickname is 'Opey', an abbreviation of opium. As in, he is so mellow he must be on opium.

Not this night. He kicked a chair across the room and right there, with half the competition still to go, the club looked set to split and die in its own acid. 'I can't believe you blokes,' he told them. 'You can all get fucked.'

But this was the Bulldogs, even by then well practised at abandonment. The same had happened in 1979 when four players walked mid-season to join Newtown. Then they went on to make the grand final.

After many poor weeks and an embarrassing loss to the Auckland Warriors in 1995 a meeting was called where it was all left on the floor. Some years later I was talking to the retired captain that season, Terry Lamb, and he told me how they turned it around.

'We couldn't ignore what happened so we got it out in the open,' he said. 'And then for the last six weeks, after every swimming session on a Monday, we went to the Sefton Hotel and had a few beers together. We didn't even speak about football, we spoke about everything but football.'

Somehow, over a few beers, the Bulldogs turned it around and found a momentum that was unstoppable. And with that a tremendous calm fell over the club. They were relaxed and playing beautifully.

For the qualifying final, prop Darren Britt turned up for the game and, reminiscent of Williams about to make his big game debut, reached into his bag and found he had no socks. Worse, he pulled out two left boots.

Lamb got changed next to him when he noticed his own socks missing. Then he noticed Britt standing next to him in socks that came only halfway up his shins.

The Bulldogs won the premiership a few weeks later in 1995.

The 2004 Bulldogs were about to respond to their own problems the only way the club knew how.

14

SMOKE AND MIRRORS

WILLIAMS returned from his ankle injury in late July against Penrith with six games left in his first season. It was a 46–20 win and he came off the bench where he would remain for the rest of the season. The Bulldogs were travelling by now. Penrith were the reigning premiers. Halfback Brent Sherwin was putting together the kind of season that had many talking greatness, his control over the game evident when he chipped ahead for Williams to regather and turn the ball back to him, putting him over for a try.

'It's so exciting for me to see a young guy coming through like Sonny Bill is,' captain Steve Price said in the post-match press conference. 'He is just getting better and better and his confidence is growing all the time. To think he could play so well after being out for so long is scary. It's like he was never injured and he's been playing all along.'

The confidence the Bulldogs had for the rest of their season was clear. The trick for coach Steve Folkes was knowing where to look.

'He's got a bit of what Andrew Ryan's got,' Folkes said after the win. 'I suppose, normally, I would replace Andrew with Sonny Bill. The guys who come off the bench, they always make an impact. I think we're going okay because we've got seventeen guys who can contribute.'

Praising Williams, Folkes gave an insight into the strength of their campaign. Any team that can field seventeen fit and contributing players this late in the season is in supreme shape. And when one of them was Williams, well, Folkes could hardly contain himself. For Folkes, that is.

'He's obviously a talented kid – sometimes his youthful exuberance gets the better of him,' he said. 'But he's obviously a player of the future and he created a bit of unease in the defence, I think, because he's got footwork and he's a big fellow. He can offload as well.'

And Williams was about to cut loose.

Williams turned nineteen during the week and came out and dominated North Queensland the following Sunday. He played like a man a dozen years older. The instant he set foot on the field he began to make a difference. He scored a try thirty seconds after going on, then set up two more. And that was after he came on nineteen minutes into the game, with the Bulldogs trailing. The win took the Bulldogs to the top of the premiership table.

Cowboys coach Graham Murray had one concern for the teenager. 'Someone will have to teach him how to play the ball because he has never done it,' Murray said. 'Gee, he got some offloads away, he's a pretty good player, let's not beat around it.'

Two games back, and with brilliant performances each time, Folkes began to backtrack on his praise after the Penrith game. Aware Murray was going heavy on the praise Folkes moved to ensure Williams did not get ahead of himself. He had, after all, just turned nineteen.

'There were thirty-three other players out there, weren't there?' he said after the game, the bark back in his voice. Price sat next to him.

When Folkes was sounded out about Williams replacing the injured Jamahl Lolesi for the following game, the logical choice, Folkes was curt. 'I think I'd be going with Ben Harris. Sonny gives us some good impact off the bench.'

If Folkes had concerns about Williams getting carried away with his success they were unfounded. More than anything, his far more experienced teammates were impressed with the way he went about his work. He fitted the Bulldogs' culture.

'Sonny Bill is very coachable,' Price said. 'He listens and learns and tries to improve all the time. The medical staff will tell you how hard he worked on getting himself right again after the injury. He's one of the fastest players in the squad as well, which is fantastic for such a big guy. I can't fault his work ethic in any way.'

In some ways, Williams is a worrier. He wants his teammates to know he is working hard, doing all he can to earn his place among them. He might be born with tremendous gifts, something he would never admit to them, but already he wants to be known as a teammate who works harder than the rest of them.

That was what they were finding with Williams with every new training session. He never relied on his talent, never assumed it would be there. He worked for it. They could not help but be impressed.

With all this going on the Bulldogs put a gag on him. From a newspaper point of view it was the great frustration of the business of the NRL. The game needs heroes and sells itself on those heroes. Along comes one and the moment everyone wants to hear from him they shut him down. It was a constant battle to stop good young players getting ahead of themselves and, from a club point of view, this was the safest route available.

Williams was fast reaching cult status at the club. When the Bulldogs' seventieth-year commemorative jerseys, worn against Penrith, were auctioned, the top bid went for captain Price's jumper at $2800. Williams' jersey was next highest at $2100.

Still. 'He's just too young,' said teammate Tony Grimaldi. 'You've got to let him earn respect, really, instead of people just blowing smoke up his arse too early. And he is earning our respect and he is a good player.'

Mason, never one to stick to the script, could not help himself. 'He runs like Gorden Tallis and offloads like Stephen Kearney.'

Former chief executive Steve Mortimer urged the club to sign him for life. Mortimer believed Williams had to be the cornerstone the club built its future on.

George Peponis agreed. He revealed they were soon opening negotiations to extend his contract. In the meantime, the Bulldogs made Sonny a goodwill gesture. His contract was $110,000 for the season but, fearing they would lose him if they failed to act, upgraded his contract to $350,000 for the season.

It was a telling moment for the club: by upgrading Williams' contract so significantly they had set a starting point for negotiations on his next deal. It also took a tremendous bite into their salary cap. The Bulldogs admitted privately they spent about $75,000 more than he was worth, but believed they needed to do so to keep him at the club.

Only later would club officials admit it contributed to squeezing out captain Steve Price, who took a deal to join the New Zealand Warriors the following season and, more significantly, Johnathan Thurston, who accepted a deal to join North Queensland. Thurston would go on to win three Dally M Player of the Year Awards, play in every game of Queensland's eight-year winning streak in the State of Origin series, win two Golden Boot awards as the world's best player and score more points than anyone in Origin history. The Bulldogs lost this little poker game.

For the moment, though, it was all sunshine and roses. With each fresh quote Williams was finding himself in uncomfortable territory. Praise made him tug at his collar.

'I said at the start of the year,' said Laurie Daley, 'that potentially Sonny Bill could be the best player to ever come out of New Zealand and from what I've seen in the past couple of weeks I see no reason to change that view. I can understand the Bulldogs wanting to protect him but when you're that good people want to know about you and talk about you. He's got great footwork. Fans love new heroes and this bloke is one.'

What Williams brought was second-phase football. In a game becoming increasingly sterile, weighed down by an over-reliance on structure, his offload and ability to bust a tackle made him trouble for any opposition defence.

'A great player,' said former Australian hooker Ben Elias. 'I think his vision makes him so special. It just seems like he's two or three steps ahead of the rest.'

Elias' former teammate Steve Roach, now working on radio, loved nothing more than a big man dominating the game and quickly developed a crush on Williams.

'He's got everything. But what about his power? He has aspects of his game that takes other players five or six years to develop. And what about the way he breaks tackles,' Roach said.

Trying to navigate through, Williams revealed to Dean Ritchie in the *Telegraph* that he had spoken to teammate Braith Anasta, the new sensation from four years ago.

'He's going great now but he was put up on a pedestal a few years back and when things weren't going great he was bagged,' Williams said. 'I've been listening to the boys. They're great to me. I'm just trying to stay out of the limelight.'

The NRL was feeling proud of itself around this time. Just weeks earlier Andrew Johns, the greatest player in the game, had knocked back an offer to switch codes after months of negotiations.

Some at the ARU had no interest in Johns in 2004. Initially, anyway. Eddie Jones was Wallabies coach and was unsure about his ability to switch but ARU boss John O'Neill knew what it would do in the code wars to poach rugby league's current great. Steered by that, Jones agreed to meet Johns.

It was the coming together of opposing philosophies. Rugby was over-complicated, highly technical. If the rugby backline looked up and saw a four-on-four match-up in the backline the rugby philosophy was to go one more ruck and try to drag a defender in, creating a four-on-three. If Johns looked up and saw four-on-four he had only one reaction.

Beautiful.

He backed himself to beat them and it was not even a fair fight. Johns told Jones that rather than avoid a situation it was something, in the tighter defence played in rugby league, he looked for. Then he explained to Jones how he would use the men around him to beat those four players. Jones walked away from the meeting convinced of two things: Andrew Johns was serious about switching to rugby and, when he did, he would change the way the game was played. The ARU went hard from there on.

The NRL initially dismissed the ARU's interest. Anybody but Johns. They believed it was a managerial ploy to drive up his market value by introducing a competitor. For a time, nobody knew what he was thinking. The NRL finally bought in and got third-party deals from Channel Nine and News Limited to cash up their offer to stay. Then it was announced Johns would reveal his decision on the *Footy Show*. As part of a cross-promotion between Nine and the *Telegraph* I went to the show's taping to get Johns' decision unofficially before he announced it on air. We wanted it in the early edition.

He was a wreck.

Before the show we walked into Ray Martin's dressing room, the host of *A Current Affair*, to talk. Johns slumped in a chair and ran his hands through his hair. The stress of a thousand waking hours told in his eyes. He looked at the floor a lot and kept shaking his head, repeatedly drawn back to the debate in his head.

This was the anomaly of the guy. On the field he was unbreakable. There was a game once, for all the marbles, and as time ticked down the pressure began to show in errors from everyone. Late in the game Johns walked to a scrum and looked at his opponent and smiled, 'How good is this.' Amid the chaos, he had such clarity of thought.

Off the field it was different. As he weighed up which way to go Johns had eaten little and slept less.

'Honestly, it's doing my head in,' he told me. He hadn't made a decision, he said. He didn't know what to do. Twice already he had privately made his mind to switch to rugby, only to wonder if he could walk away. He just wasn't sure he could.

This created quite a situation. Hundreds of thousands were expecting him to walk on set in just a few minutes and tell them what he had decided. The network had promoted it.

In the hallway outside Martin's dressing room host Paul Vautin left no doubt which way he'd go.

'Why wouldn't you go?' he said to someone. 'Eight hundred thousand and never have to make a tackle.'

When Johns went on set I was convinced he had decided to switch to rugby but did not know how to say it. With the same heavy eyes he had in the dressing room Johns said he couldn't make a decision. The air went out of the crowd.

The following day he announced he was staying in rugby league. In the end, he said, he stayed in league only because rugby would take him away from his son. Other than that, he was gone.

Soon after the Johns affair, Anasta revealed he was being courted by the NSW Waratahs. Unlike Johns, Anasta had a background in rugby. The Bulldogs were preparing to play Brisbane weeks before the finals and Anasta could see it all coming together.

'There's been a lot of interest from rugby union and the Waratahs and I have an interest in wanting to play union,' he told Peter Kogoy at the *Australian*. 'Switching football codes is certainly an option I'm looking at but for the moment my immediate priority is to help the Dogs win tomorrow to prove to the rest in the NRL that we are serious contenders for the premiership. When I look back on 2002 and think what may have been, this is our best chance since then to win it. His gives us as a team even more motivation to try that little bit harder.'

Anasta would stay in rugby league, but leave Canterbury after being offered a considerably reduced contract for 2006. The club was shuffling its salary cap to make room for the likes of Williams.

BY August the Bulldogs were premiership favourites, going on a run of ten straight wins before Melbourne ended their run two weeks before the playoffs. A week earlier, for the Brisbane match, they had made a pact to make a statement to the rest of the NRL. They did that wonderfully, levelling 12–12 at half-time, and pouring on six second–half tries to beat Brisbane on their home turf 46–18.

They walloped Newcastle after the Melbourne loss by 52–6 and went into the finals as the side everybody was talking about. Only the Sydney Roosters, premiers in 2002 when Canterbury were ineligible to win after being stripped of their competition points, were seen as a legitimate threat.

In some ways, their success was hurting them. A fortnight before the grand final Bulldog officials acknowledged they were hoping some players would take pay cuts to relieve pressure on the salary cap. Four players were asked to defer payments of around $100,000 so the club could keep the players together another season.

Immediately Gavin Orr, who represented Reni Maitua as well as Williams, pointed out the difficulty the Bulldogs were going to have, although he did say neither Sonny nor Maitua had been approached.

'Why should players have to take pay cuts when they are performing the way they are? Let's say they win the grand final. Why would they stick their hands up and offer not to get paid until next year? I think it is going to be difficult.'

It should not have been just difficult. It should have been impossible.

When Canterbury was caught cheating the salary cap in 2002 NRL boss David Gallop ordered them immediately back under. This was not as difficult as it sounds. The club was cheating the $3.25 million cap by about $500,000 a year over the two seasons they were busted. After a meeting of players, there was agreement they would take pay cuts to get the club under the cap again. The NRL allowed this to happen. It failed to consider two important facts.

First, the willingness of the players to take, in some cases, large pay cuts to remain together. These were highly emotional times, and the players were tremendously aggrieved, making them more willing to take pay cuts they normally would not because they believed they had been unfairly penalised in 2002. They had a point to prove.

Secondly, and of vital importance, the NRL did not consider that the Bulldogs had been able to illegally recruit their roster by cheating. In simple terms, when players were on the market the Bulldogs were able to secure them ahead of rivals by paying above market price through illegal accounting. The players might not have gone there if the club was forced to pay market value.

So while the immediate advantage of being over the salary cap was extinguished, the roster was the same as if it was illegally built, which it was. The Bulldogs had a tremendous advantage.

And now the NRL was considering allowing players to defer payments so they could not only have a solid crack at the 2004 season, but 2005 as well.

Thankfully, the NRL rectified this by the time Melbourne was caught cheating in 2010. This time, pay cuts were banned and Melbourne was forced to offload whatever players were priced to fit until they were below the salary cap again. It was the only fair way.

Not that it stopped the Bulldogs in 2004.

After an upset loss to North Queensland in the opening week of the finals they steamed through Melbourne 43–18. Their purpose, the one that began two years earlier, was clear.

Willie Mason called the players into a circle while still on the field. 'Enjoy the moment,' he told them, 'but we still have two games to go.'

The following week they went through Penrith, the defending premiers, 30–14. It qualified them for the grand final against the Roosters.

The game three years in the making was finally on.

Williams was brilliant against Penrith. Captain Steve Price went down injured and Williams went on for him. With Price unable to return, Williams took over the game. Even today, the game is known for Williams' shoulder charge on Penrith prop Joel Clinton. Less than a minute before half time Clinton took the ball forty metres out and headed for Williams. Williams set his feet as Clinton lowered his centre of gravity and, each man's intent clear, drove with his left shoulder and Clinton bounced back, a halo of spray glowing from his head.

'Ohh, Clinton is hit head-on by Sonny Bill,' Nine commentator Andrew Voss said. 'This is colossal.'

Paul Whatuira got some of the same treatment towards the end of the game.

'Mate,' Willie Mason said after the game, 'he's just a freak. You look around and see him in your team and can't help but be happy.'

Two days before the Penrith game Channel Nine reported Williams had been approached by the New Zealand Rugby Union about switching codes. He had a year to run on his contract and Orr had already knocked back an offer for an extension.

Coincidentally, or maybe not, Orr was in New Zealand when the story broke. Bulldogs chief executive Malcolm Noad said he knew nothing about it. For all anybody knew, Orr was there negotiating this very moment.

A game of smoke and mirrors was being played. With a new flurry of excitement New Zealand Rugby Union deputy chief executive Steve Tew put out a statement: 'It's the second or third time this has happened, and it's a funny coincidence that it always happens when players are negotiating a new contract. I don't know whether this is calculated to increase players' bargaining power but we are not talking to Sonny Bill Williams.'

Understandably, the NRL and its clubs were a little gun-shy. Wendell Sailor, Lote Tuqiri and Mat Rogers were all part of the Wallabies World Cup campaign just a year earlier and the game's biggest name, Johns, had since revealed just how close he was to switching.

And now Sonny?

The following day Orr denied the speculation, although it did not contain a fullstop: 'There was a report over here on the news last night that they were chasing him for $NZ850,000 ($793,533). That is not true. There have been no formal talks with that organisation at this stage.'

At the time, Williams had only one thought of New Zealand. Now the Bulldogs had qualified for the grand final, he wanted to fly his mum Lee to the game.

'It was my mum that got me into footy,' he said.

He had no thoughts of the All Blacks. 'I'm just happy playing with the Bulldogs and there's no way I'm going to rugby,' he told Brad Walter at the *Sydney Morning Herald*. 'I've loved rugby league since I was young, I've always dreamed about playing this kind of footy. To be in the grand final is unbelievable, I just can't explain it . . . But at the moment I don't want to talk to the club at all, I don't even want to talk to my manager about it until after the grand final.'

That's what had always made Williams different. It's something Canterbury officials spoke occasionally about whenever the threat of a code switch came up. He was always one of the few Kiwis to confess to having no ambition to play for the All Blacks. All the way back to his grandfather, Bill Woolsey, there was rugby league pedigree.

'He was really well known in league over there,' Sonny said of his grandfather.

GRAND final week was madness, and you wouldn't have expected anything less. The Bulldogs and Roosters had been circling each other for three seasons by now. Now the finals system had delivered the teams that finished first and second, the two top-ranked teams. An extra layer of tension was added after they played in round one and police and security guards at Aussie Stadium, the Roosters' home ground, were injured after brawls between the two sets of supporters. Referee Tim Mander stopped play midway through the second half when sections of the crowd hurled water bottles onto the field. This was a sign of the changing tastes in football crowds. Years earlier it would have been beer.

The Bulldogs also harboured a secret resentment for the Roosters. There had been tension since the Roosters won the premiership two years earlier and Braith Anasta received a phone call from Justin Hodges as the Roosters celebrated.

'Sucked in for getting kicked out, we won the comp,' Hodges said.

The Bulldogs sat on it for two years and spoke briefly about it as they prepared to play the Roosters, and Hodges, in the decider.

To kickstart the week both clubs held open days for the fans. The heavily supported Bulldogs open day that was later described as 'like being at a rock concert'.

While the Sydney Roosters held their open day at Aussie Stadium the Bulldogs were at rundown Belmore Oval, where Sonny no longer cleaned the bird shit off the seats and where fans waited more than two hours to catch a glimpse of the players.

Willie Mason posed for photographs, got a couple of I-love-yous from teenage girls and was even asked to sign a baby's forehead. He looked at the madness surrounding the players, and Williams in particular, and felt proud. Mason revealed that he deliberately gave himself the job of mentoring Sonny throughout the season. It was as odd as it sounds, given Mason was booed earlier this season by his own fans when he ran onto the field for NSW in the State of Origin match.

'I think it's been good for him and I know it's been good for me,' said Mason, who was still only twenty-four. He was talking to Alex Brown at the *Herald*. 'I remember when I was coming up, I was the same age as him. I've been through a hell of a lot the last couple of years, so I thought if I can teach him everything – like with the media and how people can take you for a ride and eat off you – it might be good. I didn't really have anyone. I came up [to first grade] and I was probably the only one that was my age for a couple of years. It was hard like that. I wish I had someone like that, a mentor.'

A lot of talk centred around the strength of the Bulldogs' bench. They would become a nod to the way the game was played. Until now, most teams picked their strong-est thirteen players to start the game and the next four, in whatever formation the coach preferred, made up his bench. So it was only natural that when the starting players were replaced by the bench players they suffered a dip in perfor-mance. The Bulldogs' four changed that. When they came on, Canterbury surged.

Melbourne coach Craig Bellamy believed the Roosters had the stronger side but said the Bulldogs bench – Williams,

Reni Maitua, Corey Hughes and Roy Asotasi – were enough to tip the game Canterbury's way.

'It is not often a coach has the luxury of having players come off the bench who are as good or possibly even better than the players they replace,' Bellamy said. 'That is what the Bulldogs have. You look at their bench against the Panthers, when Sonny Bill Williams and Corey Hughes came on, it just lifted the whole team another notch. They take Mason off for a rest and Sonny Bill comes on and there is just no respite.'

Bellamy had found the perfect phrase: no respite.

Gorden Tallis, who retired after the Broncos were eliminated in the finals, saw it too, saying, 'The thing I think of when I look at the Bulldogs bench is just the amount of strike power they have got there. When you are able to bring a player like Sonny Bill on to try and change a game you're in a pretty good position.'

The Bulldogs knew the value of their bench better than anybody.

'When they come on we are a whole different side,' Brent Sherwin said. 'They come on and they are enthusiastic and they go hard. They lift the rest of the team. It's a great boost having them come off the bench.'

This was typical of Sonny.

Afraid to let his teammates down he over-compensated, giving more than they had when he came on from the bench. Only the very special are capable of this.

His motivation, he said, was to not let his teammates down. 'If one of the boys pull off a good hit then Mark O'Meley is in your ear saying how good it was,' he said. 'That is what all the training is about. Players that I watched last year or the year before on TV, the stars, telling me "great stuff", that's awesome. I just don't want to let the boys down. I want to make all my tackles.'

In the *Daily Telegraph* Dean Ritchie was talking to Graham Murray, who was still coming to terms with what Williams had done to his Cowboys side just weeks earlier.

'I want to see how he handles an Adrian Morley bone rattler on Sunday,' Murray said.

Morley was the Roosters' enforcer. A few seconds elapsed as Murray thought about it. Then he gave up to logic. 'He probably will,' he said. 'Why wouldn't he? He can do everything else.'

After injuring himself against Penrith captain Steve Price was ruled out. It was a blow for Canterbury, but one that got squared up when Luke Ricketson failed to beat a high tackle charge and was suspended from the game.

It is hard to believe Williams had still played just fourteen games.

The 2004 grand final was about moments. When star teams collide, the moments always decide it. The crowd was waiting for theirs. When the players' faces were splashed on the big screens before the game the two biggest roars went up for the Roosters' retiring captain Brad Fittler and for Williams. Midway through the first half a shot of Williams sitting on the bench was flashed up on the big screen and a guttural roar went around the crowd. If anybody ever needed proof what this kid meant to the game, that was it.

Williams came on twenty-two minutes into the first half and almost immediately began creating his own moments, going straight after the Roosters' enforcer Morley. Williams knew where the battle was. Every time, his class was obvious. Next came a one-handed offload. As Sonny searched for victims Chris Flannery came on for the Roosters, sporting an injury that made most men wince. Five days earlier, Flannery was operated on for a ruptured testicle. Whatever pain he was suffering must have increased two-fold with his first hit-up when Williams, whom he should have been looking for, hit him high and legally and spun him like the hands on a cartoon clock.

'Ohhh,' said referee Tim Mander.

'It was a great shot,' Flannery said after. 'He hit me around the chest. If he'd hit me a bit lower I might have been in trouble.'

Every minute Williams was on he created moments. Midway through the second half the Roosters led by a point and were pressing hard when Williams reeled off three tackles, one after the other, and then played a part in a turnover to get the ball back for the Bulldogs. In a game of possession, it was vital. As the minutes wore on the Bulldogs bench was winning the game.

Folkes took Williams off for a spell in the second half and then sent him back on with ten minutes left with the Bulldogs leading 16–13. They held it right through, the premiership not decided until the final thirteen seconds when Michael Crocker dropped the ball as the Roosters threatened.

Willie Mason began clapping his hands on the sideline. After three of the toughest years in sport the Bulldogs were premiers. And they didn't care what anybody thought. Injured captain Steve Price left his position on the bench, where he sat while wearing his jersey over his dress shirt, and joined his teammates in celebration. Stand-in skipper Andrew Ryan called Price up to the podium to accept the premiership trophy with him.

'This will be the sweetest lap of honour I've ever had the opportunity to do,' Price said. He would leave the club in 2005 for the New Zealand Warriors.

15

THE WINNING STREAK

THERE was never any doubt Sonny's wonderful season would continue. Days after the grand final he was named Canterbury's rookie of the year, as if that was in any doubt, and then picked to tour England as part of New Zealand's Tri-Nations Test team.

'It's a bit overwhelming,' he said of his season so far.

The tournament once again created argument about State of Origin eligibility. Officials from the New Zealand Rugby League were using the Tri-Nations as a launchpad to argue they were disadvantaged by the 'exclusivity' of Origin football.

The Kiwis were arguing players such as Williams should be eligible to play State of Origin because too many, like Karmichael Hunt earlier in the season, were intoxicated with Origin football and turning their backs on New Zealand rugby league, to the detriment of their game. New Zealand chairman Selwyn Pearson led the argument. Once again the Kiwis argued the lure of Origin was convincing Kiwi players to switch allegiances.

'I can see New Zealand's point,' Australian Rugby League chairman Colin Love said. 'And we're looking at it, but I can see the other side of the argument. Selecting a Kiwi Test player would mean an Australian player missing out and I'm not sure that is such a good idea.'

Pearson planned to lobby the Rugby League International Federation, knowing it had no authority to change Australia's Origin eligibility but hoping it would encourage the ARL to consider his request.

The whole thing was a dog's breakfast. If anybody wants any idea how ridiculous the eligibility laws were, New Zealand picked Cairns-born Brent Webb to play fullback during their campaign. It got worse. Australia picked Tonie Carroll who, four years earlier, was playing for New Zealand in the World Cup when eligibility exemptions applied. It will never be resolved with any true satisfaction.

For now, though, the Kiwis had Williams rolling from one success to another. Kiwi coach Daniel Anderson put the polish on all the plaudits that followed Williams into the team.

'He is a supremely talented player. I can't think of a kid who has made such an impact for a long time. He is dynamic. He is top ten now – with a bullet. Hopefully he will be top five after the next six weeks. He's a bit like Andrew Johns. People go to games to watch him,' he said.

Anderson named Williams in the starting side and he immediately made clear his intent.

'When you put the black jumper on,' Sonny said, 'anything goes.'

By now Tonie Carroll was probably rethinking his decision to switch from New Zealand to Australia. 'I've no idea what he means,' he said, 'but it doesn't sound good.'

The Australian game plan was built on shutting down Williams, which was extraordinary to hear. Williams was starting his first Test against Australia's best players, just his second overall. His career was only fifteen games old, and yet he was the focus of Australia's game plan.

'I thought he probably wasn't that far away from being the best player in the semifinal series, to be quite honest,' Australia's assistant coach Craig Bellamy said. 'And to do that coming off the bench, he certainly has a presence about him. We've certainly had a look at him on video and I think we're aware of what his strengths are. We've spoken about a couple of ways where we might be able to blunt his effectiveness. I guess it's easy preparing for that, but actually going out and doing it is a different matter because he's such a wonderful player and everyone's aware of what he can do in a game.'

As Australia broke down his game, just how tremendously talented Williams was becoming clear. Everybody who ever plays the game has habits. Opposition teams learn them, and find ways to shut the player down, which is why so many players suffer much more in their second season than they do in their first.

Bellamy, who was coaching Melbourne and assisting Bennett with the Australian side, was known as the most thorough coach in the NRL. Premierships would follow. When he watched footage of opposition players he broke down their *strengths*. There was no point planning to exploit their weaknesses since they might fix them before you got a chance. Their strengths were always there, though, and you could count on that. Better players often went to their strengths under pressure.

Watching Williams, Bellamy saw the greatness in him. He could do what only the best could do. He was developing his game with frightening speed. Under the pressures of the NRL, few had the ability to change the way they played to counter their opponents.

'A guy who can hit with a shoulder charge and a guy who offloads as much as he can with the least amount of errors that come from those sort of things, I don't think I've ever seen that,' he said. 'I haven't seen anyone roll out of one of his shoulder charges. Usually they're fifty-fifty, sometimes you whack them and you get them in the right spot and they go down, sometimes they just roll out and go to the next defender. And with the footy, making that decision when to offload and when not to offload – he seems to have that down pretty well pat. I haven't seen him make too many errors. He did earlier in the year, but he's learned from that and that just shows what a mature player he is for his age.'

Williams was already a star.

The *New Zealand Herald* ran a cover photo of him in their sports section, casually sitting down in the gym wearing a pair of Jandals, the Kiwi version of thongs. 'Can Aussie Handle the Jandal?' went the headline.

Playing in front of a home crowd New Zealand battled Australia to a 16–16 draw. Williams was named man of the match and once again it was all there: a shoulder charge on Jason Ryles, the offloads, and a sixty-metre run late in the game that almost won the game for New Zealand. Both sides flew to England to complete the tournament with Great Britain, the third nation involved. Unfortunately that was about as good as it got for the Kiwis. After arriving in England they lost all three games. Australia went on to beat Great Britain easily in the final. The Kangaroos led 38–0 at half time and then punched their time clocks, winning 44–4.

The trip to England was a mixed bag for Williams.

He missed New Zealand's final game through a shoulder injury. At the International Rugby League Awards he was named International Newcomer of the Year and was the only Kiwi named in the World XIII. It was a given he was named New Zealand Rugby League Player of the Year as well. When he got home to Australia he was named Rookie of the Year at the NRL's Rugby League Players' Association Awards.

Before the night was over Brad Fittler pulled him aside. Fittler came into first grade at seventeen and only occasionally stubbed his toe on fame. He wanted to help Williams with what advice he could.

Fittler started telling his own story. He was still in high school when he was brought into first grade.

'You've got to enjoy it,' he said. 'But don't take anything for granted, nothing is going to come to you easily. I can understand what you're going through but you've got to keep your head down and work harder because it can all disappear if you don't.'

Williams was stunned. Part of him was star-struck.

'I couldn't believe it,' he said. 'He just came up to me and started having a chat. There's no way I would have gone up to him. He was really friendly.'

Fittler had no reason for concern. Despite his great success Williams still had that unusual insecurity streak that compelled him to work hard for approval. He still found himself looking at the Bulldogs' team photo and marvelled that he was standing next to Willie Mason.

16

SONNY IN THE MONEY

STEVE Folkes gave Williams time off after the Tri-Nations. It had been a long season and he was nursing a shoulder injury and fighting the need to get it operated on and the coach knew the rest would do him good. Shortly after Christmas Folkes got a tip-off: Williams returned to train with the under-20s three weeks earlier.

Williams explained himself by saying he did not want to appear to be a 'big-head' by staying away, as if he was getting preferential treatment.

Eyes followed him everywhere. As the new season rolled around discussion began on whether he could repeat in his second season what he did in his first.

'It wasn't as if he was a smokey last season. He had plenty of publicity. He won't find it too much different really,' Folkes said.

Canterbury have a great knack for taking the pretension and stress out of things. Folkes described it as being able to put drama to one side. 'That's what separates the professionals from the nearly professionals,' he said.

Williams was unconcerned about second-year syndrome. He knew what was coming.

'Of course it will be tougher this year,' he said. 'We won the premiership and everyone's going to pick it up against the Bulldogs, not just against me.'

With just ten players from their grand final team the Bulldogs travelled back to England and went down to Leeds 39–32 in the World Club Challenge. Leeds led 38–12 before Williams cut loose. Two shoulder charges started it, the first on Marcus Bai.

'I wasn't far from that,' Folkes said, 'it sounded like concrete hitting bone.'

'Everyone just stopped on the field,' said Luke Patten. 'I can't believe he got up.'

Then England fans got the whole treatment. The runs, the offloads . . .

'He's just a special talent and it was an honour to play against him tonight and to watch him out on the field,' said Leeds' Willie Poching. 'His footwork and his patience . . . he backs himself. He put Willie Tonga through with a couple of short balls and they were beautiful balls. He made a break towards the end there and put some massive shots on.'

BY the time Canterbury returned from England the officials were under all sorts of heat. Williams was coming into the last year of his contract, as were Willie Mason, Braith Anasta, Willie Tonga and Jamahl Lolesi. Chief executive Malcolm Noad knew the battle ahead to keep all of them.

The Bulldogs had them to themselves until 30 June. Under NRL rules, clubs were forbidden from negotiating with players at rival clubs until 1 July in the final year of their contract. This never worked in reality, but provided a wonderful ignorance for fans who got frustrated at revelations their favourite players were negotiating with rival clubs when, according to fan loyalty, they should have been concentrating on giving their all for the club. All it meant was a flood of signings in the first few days of July, of deals you think would normally take months to negotiate.

Any manager that had not begun negotiations well before 1 July was not doing his job. By February it was heavy on the rumour mill that the Sydney Roosters had tabled an offer. Roosters chairman Nick Politis was said to be a big fan. Brisbane was another club said to be keenly interested with money freed up from Gorden Tallis' retirement. As many as six clubs were said to be circling, while English club Wigan was another.

At a testimonial dinner for retiring NSW cricketer Richard Chee Quee on 9 February, Wallabies coach Eddie Jones was interviewed by compere Graeme Hughes, one of Canterbury's Hughes brothers. He asked Jones whether Williams would ever make it in rugby.

'He's too small to play number eight or blindside flanker and too slow for openside flanker,' Jones said. 'He doesn't have the body type.'

Well, didn't that upset a few.

'I tell you what,' said New Zealand Rugby League chairman Selwyn Pearson, 'he mightn't be the biggest bloke but by Christ Eddie Jones wants to get a doctor to have a look at the size of his ticker.'

Laurie Daley, Ben Elias, George Peponis, they all defended Williams. They might as well have shone spotlights on him, telling every rugby scout in the game to come look at him.

Eventually Jones claimed he was joking. 'Graeme Hughes asked me a question and I just had a bit of fun with the answer. Everything I said was all in jest. But why do we get thrown up every time a rugby league guy comes off contract? We have no interest in Sonny Bill at this stage.'

At this stage. We all know how that changed.

The Bulldogs knew how tough it was going to be. Then they got a reminder from Phil Gould in his *Sun-Herald* column.

Saying how he was recently asked what he would pay for Sonny, Gould said he was worth a million dollars. As Bulldogs officials picked themselves up from the floor, Gould acknowledged it was impossible to pay any player that much, but said he believed he was worth it to the club and the game.

Already Sonny was getting a taste of the financial problems troubling the League.

Gavin Orr signed Williams to a Gatorade sponsorship, a $50,000 deal that the NRL was investigating to see whether it was a legal third-party agreement. From Orr's point of view it was a way to earn Williams more money given the limitations of the salary cap.

For the NRL, it looked like a salary-cap breach, since Gatorade was a Canterbury club sponsor. The NRL had no problem with the drink company sponsoring him, but under NRL rules it had to be included in the salary cap which, in this case, it was not.

'We had no involvement with the deal. The first we knew about it was when someone saw the ad on TV,' Bulldogs chief executive Malcolm Noad said.

Orr was on a salesman's pitch, talking to Peter Badel at the *Sunday Telegraph*. He was starting to see the dollars come in as experts tipped Williams could earn as much as ten million dollars over the next ten years. Orr was steering him towards an international sponsorship with Nike alongside the two stars in their 2005 stable, Tiger Woods and Lance Armstrong.

'His name is truly unique,' Orr said. 'There are hundreds of Darrens, and Andrews, and Johns, but there's only one Sonny Bill. Every week I get stacks of letters from kids who say: "I want to be like Sonny Bill." In the past month, I've had twenty-five sponsorship proposals. That shows you the attraction of the guy. We'd like to see him get to where Jonah Lomu was – he transcended rugby union – and Nike wants Sonny to be recognised as an international athlete. In time, I think he can be on the same level, in terms of profile, in this country as Ian Thorpe. Ian has that international appeal because he swims in an Olympic sport but Sonny can have just as big a profile here and the fact he's a Kiwi would give him greater recognition in New Zealand than Thorpey.'

Orr knew exactly what he had. Before anyone else.

Eventually the Bulldogs were cleared of a salary-cap breach by the happy coincidence that Gatorade was also a game sponsor under the game's sponsor leveraging agreement. It was much the same way game sponsors Channel Nine and News Limited had weighed in with financial top-ups to keep Andrew Johns in the game seven months earlier. It was a nod to Williams' star quality. There might not have been another in the game given such consideration.

It was an unhappy season for Williams. After just thirty-two minutes of the first game against St George Illawarra he limped off with an ankle injury. He made it back the following weekend but then tore the ankle ligaments against Cronulla on 3 April, which might have been an aggravation of the St George Illawarra injury. He would miss seven games. A week later he announced he had re-signed with Canterbury, a great relief for the Bulldogs. They paid him $350,000 for 2006 and $400,000 for 2007.

The Bulldogs held a press conference at the Olympic Stadium, Sonny sitting next to Steve Folkes and Malcolm Noad.

'It was my personal decision to sign a two-year deal,' he said. 'I don't want to get relaxed. I want to stay on my toes. Hopefully it keeps me hungry and determined to be a better player. I had a good talk to my old man and we came to the decision it was best for my footy.'

He never seriously thought of leaving, he said, 'I have always insisted I wanted to stay at Canterbury and it was only a matter of time. It's over and done with now and I'm really looking forward to the future. I'm only nineteen and I have a lot more to learn about footy.'

The Bulldogs were investing in their future.

Here, as Williams spoke of his future at the club while nursing his injured ankle, a subtle subplot began to evolve. The Bulldogs were growing increasingly concerned at the rate of injuries. Club doctor Hugh Hazard, also the NRL's chief medical officer, oversaw a lot of the 53 weeks Sonny would total on the sidelines while at the club.

'I've spoken with Sonny about this before. Basically I've told him that he's got a long career in front of him and if he wants to survive in the game he has to learn to preserve himself,' Hazard said. 'He's just such an enthusiastic kid, but he'll get to the stage where he has to be conscious of his body.'

Right now, though, he had no hesitation about what he was doing with his new contract money.

'I want to bring my mum Lee over, my nanna Denise and my other sister Niall,' he told James Hooper in the *Telegraph*. 'I want to buy them a house in the Kogarah Bay area, just to say thanks and to look after them. They have been great to me and family is very important in my life. I already live with my other sister Denise, who is Niall's twin, and my old man John and brother John-Arthur live next door to me.'

His season was written off shortly after he returned. Just minutes into his return against South Sydney he took the ball up, his first hit-up of the game, and got up hobbling. He swore and called for the trainer. Fear went through Bulldogs staff that he had injured the ankle again. Hazard checked him on the sideline and a dejected Williams walked up the tunnel.

It was worse than he thought.

'He has a severe compression of two bones in the knee which has caused a trabecular fracture beneath the cartilage surface,' Hazard told Roy Masters. 'Over time the cartilage breaks down and exposes the fracture. It will heal but if we don't give him time, he'll end up with an arthritic knee. Old footballers have them but not ones like Sonny Bill, who turns 20 next week.'

It was a completely different injury. It was August 2005, and he was gone for the rest of the season.

17

BAD BOYS

THE charmed run came to an end in August 2005.

If there was one indulgence in Sonny Bill Williams' life, it was clothes. So when Italian design brand Diesel launched its summer range and an invitation landed in Sonny's inbox he was there like he had just stepped from the catalogue. Dressed in Diesel, all the way down. It was some party, girls dancing on podiums, a live DJ. Outside the store on Oxford Street was a flatbed truck and on the back of this truck was up-and-coming band Jones. And all the free alcohol you could drink.

Still, the police didn't need to turn up at 7 pm to calm things down. It wasn't quite that sort of party.

For Sonny, football was over for the season. Earlier in the day he was told he would not be playing again that year. Maybe something inside him relaxed. Maybe those around him got in his ear.

When the launch was over many inside left and went to the Paddington Inn Hotel and continued celebrating the fine clothes they had just seen. Why go home when you're having so much fun? Sonny spent much of the evening posing for photos.

Sometime about three in the morning he decided it was time to go home. He went and found his car, a sponsored black Land-Cruiser, and turned the key. He pulled into Kingsford McDonald's and an off-duty policeman saw his car bunny-hopping into the drive-through and thought it didn't look right. Nothing got past this guy, so he called the nearby police station.

Police arrived and watched Williams drive out of the carpark into Anzac Parade and pull up at a red light. The light turned green and the car remained motionless. Then it turned amber and Williams turned left. At that, the police sirens went on. Fifty metres down the road Williams told the officer he had two Smirnoff Vodka drinks. Then he blew into the bag and the breathalyser told the officer something else altogether. It read 0.075, and Williams admitted it might have been closer to between five and ten drinks.

Canterbury boss Malcolm Noad fined Williams $10,000, suspending five of it. NZRL boss Selwyn Pearson got his priorities straight. 'I've made that same mistake myself, too,' he said, 'but I'm sure a DIC wouldn't rule him out of the Tri-Nations, would it?'

As for Sonny, he was devastated that he had let himself down. And only he knew at the time how bad it was. It was later discovered he was on his P-plates, a provisional driver's licence, which has a zero alcohol limit. Then it was discovered his licence had actually been suspended months earlier after accumulating too many demerit points. A magistrate suspended him from driving for a further five months and fined him $700.

'I would never hop behind the wheel if I thought I was drunk,' he said the following day at training. 'Obviously I had one too many and I'm not using that as an excuse. What I did was irresponsible. I have let a lot of people down and I've let myself and my family down. This is definitely one of the lowest points in my life, especially after trying to get a good image out there and having a strong fan base especially with the young kids.'

He rang NRL boss David Gallop and apologised. He rang Canterbury's major sponsor and his own sponsors. Several private sponsors dropped him, he later revealed in court, including Toyota. The LandCruiser was gone. It was a young man's mistake.

There is a chance the drink-driving charge masked a deeper problem. Williams never touched alcohol before playing first grade at Canterbury but almost instantly fell into the booze culture that is part of the NRL. There is no doubt he was greatly frustrated at the time, unable to take the field. That, combined with his need to fit in with teammates, made him vulnerable.

To make things worse, the Bulldogs were in a small freefall. The reigning premiers, they would finish twelfth in 2005 and fail to make the playoffs after spending most of the season battling a crippling injury toll. Williams would play just five games while other significant players would also miss large parts of the season. Some of it was their own doing. Days before Williams went down for drink-driving Steve Folkes nominated that weekend's Parramatta game as a 'must win' if the team were to have any chance of making the finals. They lost 56–4, the club's worst loss in seventy years.

That weekend several players – Mark O'Meley, Willie Mason and Luke Patten – were kicked out of Club Troppo, a nightclub inside Gosford's Central Coast Leagues Club, for being too intoxicated. Anyone who has ever been to Club Troppo knows this is a feat not easily achieved. O'Meley and Mason continued drinking at another pub. Mason was then seen drinking the next night at Ravesi's in Bondi and then later at the Sapphire Suite in Kings Cross. In the scheme of things they were mistakes that many young people are capable of making. The trouble was, it was part of a growing pattern for the Bulldogs. The Bulldogs were paying too much attention to the third part of Bullfrog Moore's equation – party hard – without enough attention to the first two parts.

The Bulldogs failed to recognise it at the time, but they were struggling to handle their success. A drinking, partying culture had taken over at the club and, still hostile at the criticism of recent years, it was in no state to hear advice.

Earlier in the season Mason and Reni Maitua had missed the opening game against St George Illawarra, a heavy loss, after choosing to attend an Xzibit concert instead. In May Brad Morrin was arrested outside Melbourne's Crown Casino and detained in a holding cell after trying to force his way into a passing car. He was fined $5000.

The day after their season finally ended Bulldogs staff returned to work on Monday morning and thought they had been robbed. The office was trashed. After a small investigation Malcolm Noad had the embarrassing job of explaining a small group of players were responsible. While Noad refused to identify them Sonny, Reni Maitua and Roy Asotasi were identified as the three.

Williams later denied through his manager Gavin Orr being responsible.

'Essentially it was a practical joke which I've taken extreme offence to because I don't think it shows the appropriate respect for the office staff that support them twenty-four hours a day,' Noad said in the *Sunday Telegraph*. 'There was no urination, no atrocities, there were no breakages. Still, I am filthy about the incident because of the lack of respect they showed for the staff. We're talking two or three guys by the way. They would have thought in the early hours of the morning it was a practical joke.'

Publicly, Williams' reputation barely suffered a blip. Bulldogs fans defended him heavily against media criticism.

Just a month later he was named the Fave Rising Star at the Nickelodeon Awards, getting slimed as he accepted his award.

Clearly the culture was a problem for Williams. Not a big one, and without his profile he would not have been any different from any other twenty-year-old man in Sydney. But he also would not have been invited to celebrate celebrity hotelier Andrew Jolliffe's $26-million purchase of the Cremorne Hotel at Ravesi's, or turned up in the gossip pages partying at the

Sapphire Suite with other celebrities like AFL star Michael O'Loughlin and actress Ada Nicodemou. As he was learning, there was a price to fame.

THE good thing was there was always football. Nobody trained harder over the off-season. Williams pushed hard to make it back for the 2006 season and was forever working in the gym at Belmore. The same physical gifts he brought to his performance were also harming him. He was just beginning to learn the difference between playing through pain and playing through injury.

'When I hurt it against Souths I came back too early and I felt it when I was running,' he said to Brent Read of the *Australian* one afternoon in the Belmore gym. 'I was being a hardhead and saying "I'll be right, I'll be right." When I had scans it was buggered again. This time if it feels uncomfortable I tell the trainers or physio straightaway. But it's feeling good. I can't feel it at all.'

He wanted to be back for the trials but the club was more patient, just telling him to be right for the season opener.

'All of last year he was frustrated,' said Folkes. 'He wanted to get back on the paddock and play. He was always pushing the envelope as far as what he could do and what he couldn't do. There's no doubt he can be guilty at times of doing more than he should.'

He missed the trials. He also missed the opening game. And the next.

Williams pushed himself so hard he broke down with stress fractures in his feet and did not play until round six.

By then his teammates had long been calling him 'Chalky', meaning that he broke like a piece of chalk. He was less than pleased. He got through the game in round six and played the rest of the season, restoring the Bulldogs to genuine premiership threats.

Canterbury finished second on the premiership table and beat Canberra in the qualifying final to advance to a game away from the grand final. They went down to eventual premiers Brisbane 37–20.

WHILE the Bulldogs remained relieved Williams saw out the season staff already adapting his training. Conditioning staff took as much running out of his program as they could, replacing it with bike-riding. The problem with his injuries were they were all different, making it hard to pinpoint any reason why, beyond simple bad luck. Already, from the seventy-eight games the club had played in the three seasons since his debut in 2004, Williams was fit for just forty-one of them. He also missed the previous two end-of-year Tri-Nations series, and was unavailable for the 2006 series because he went in for knee surgery.

He knew how much football he was missing better than anybody. As 2006 closed out, the NRL held a charity launch at Luna Park a few weeks before Christmas and Williams was interviewed widely.

The games he had missed for the club were not far from his mind.

'I feel I owe the boys, my family and also myself,' he told Dean Ritchie at the *Daily Telegraph*. 'I'm grateful for their support. I want to make up for things. I'm working hard at training and training's been good, man. It is an exciting time. I just want to get some football under my belt. I just want to get the body right and get back out there.'

In many ways he was no different from every other good young kid coming through. In other ways he was the boy superstar. The previous season he had knocked back a $900,000-a-year offer from St Helens. That was some money in anybody's language.

Within an hour of talking to Ritchie he was talking to Glenn Jackson at the *Sydney Morning Herald* and, by now, his conviction was not nearly so strong.

'I don't want to rush anything,' he told Jackson. 'With the injuries that I've had, I guess they've opened my eyes a bit. I'd love to stay at the Bulldogs, but it's a business. You rarely see players playing for ten years these days. I do want to stay at the Dogs but I'm not going to be silly about it.'

In some ways it was typical Sonny. He was being led by the questioning, polite to a fault. It was also an indication of the pressure he was under. His contract was up for renewal after the following season and talks were about to begin. In times like those, players are often at the mercy of the last conversation they had, juggling managers, his family, his club and his emotions.

Steve Price leaving the club had forced him to reconsider his no-questions-asked commitment to the Bulldogs.

'Every player wants to be a one-club man,' he told Jackson. 'I never thought Steve Price would leave the Bulldogs. It just goes to show, five years after you stop playing, they're not going to be paying your bills. It's just you and your family. You've got to look after yourself.'

Contracts were on Jackson's mind because there was barely a conversation about Williams these days without speculation about where he would go. With his contract up at the end of 2007 some had declared he would be at the Sydney Roosters in 2008.

Williams wanted to begin negotiations with the Bulldogs as soon as possible, he told Jackson. 'I'm trying not to worry too much about it at the moment.'

He then added, 'I just want to really concentrate on training hard. If I'm playing shit footy, I'm not going to go anywhere.'

Who knew it was all about to end in tears?

Again it was the twin terrors, injury and alcohol.

Again his pre-season was filled with newspaper stories declaring how fit and ready Williams looked for the season ahead. Only sparingly were there references to his injuries and brief mentions that the gloss on all those predictions had worn off.

The Bulldogs announced him in their team to play St George Illawarra in a February 2007 trial.

'I'm feeling good man. I'm pumped up,' Williams said in the *Telegraph*. 'I've done my first full pre-season since 2004 and want to play every game this year and also hopefully play for the Kiwis. I'm really excited. I think 2004 was my best year. It was so good, like a dream.'

As Williams prepared to play the Bulldogs were in the process of withdrawing their three-year, $1.275-million offer for him. The deal would have paid him $400,000 his first two seasons before rising to $475,000 in his third season but had sat on the table for two weeks without any indication from Sonny or his manager Gavin Orr that he would sign.

Williams was under great stress as he decided his future. The deal was reasonably standard. A pay rise in his second season would have been more in keeping with standard NRL contracts, although it was not unusual. In his mind, though, Williams wanted the security of a longer deal. Given how many games he had missed since his debut, it was the smartest play.

Williams struggled with the decision.

'He's been grumpy and when he's grumpy and angry he's not nice to be around,' his father John said.

The games had begun. Every NRL club was contacted and asked if they would table an offer. Twelve said no, Cronulla said no comment, the Roosters said unlikely and the Warriors, who were constantly speculated to be interested, were unavailable for comment. In England, Wigan boss Maurice Lindsay said at $500,000 a year Williams had priced himself out of the English Super League, a quote that sheds new light on the $900,000 a year said to be offered by St Helens several years earlier. The Bulldogs gave him until 5 pm on Friday 9 March to make his decision. It was the day the season kicked off.

Just before the deadline the New Zealand Warriors came in with their offer. Williams spoke to his father, whose advice was clear.

'There were a couple of late offers but we just said, "close the book, work on staying. End of story,"' John said. With Sonny hard to be found, the *Australian* had found his father.

Williams walked into Malcolm Noad's office at 8.30 am that Friday saying he wanted a five-year deal. 'I couldn't imagine him playing with anyone else, to be honest,' John said. 'I am glad he stayed. It was never, ever about the money. I got sick of hearing it was about this and that. He didn't want anything. All he wanted to do was play football. He would play for a ten-dollar meal at McDonald's. He loves his football.'

Williams signed that afternoon. John Williams told the club Sonny sacrificed top-end money for a longer deal.

'I want to be a Bulldog for life,' Sonny said at the press conference announcing his retention. 'I don't want to go through this ever again. I've copped a bit of a beating from the papers the last couple of weeks. It's not just hard on me but also my family . . . my sister and my old man cop it too.'

The only person more happy than Sonny was his dad. 'It means I get my son back,' he said.

Two days later Williams went out and opened the season by hitting Andrew Johns high and hard, becoming the first NRL player sent off in the 2007 season. He got up quickly from the tackle, apologising. Johns got up a little more slowly.

Johns later had no memory of the incident but said, 'There are no hard feelings with Sonny. I sort of started to come around a bit about fifteen minutes after it happened apparently.'

The NRL suspended him for two weeks. On his return Williams destroyed South Sydney in a Friday-night game, the match of the round, with one of those games he was becoming famous for. Only two or three people in the world could have done what he did that night, creating chances with his one-arm offloads and running through holes in the defence when he went looking to do the heavy lifting himself.

The following night he made one of the great small mistakes of his life. The weekend off, the Bulldogs were out drinking when Williams walked into the men's toilets at the Clovelly Hotel. Shortly after, not by coincidence, ironwoman Candice Falzon also walked into the men's toilets. Supposedly a secret rendezvous between the star couple, what happened next was known throughout the sporting world the moment they locked the cubicle.

A day later the gossip columnists were onto a live one. All those around him could do was go into damage control. The Bulldogs refused to comment.

Orr said, 'Sonny had been there since 2 pm and I know he was really blind. I don't know anything about Candice Falzon – all I was told was that Sonny Bill was taken home in a taxi by Willie Mason's girlfriend just before midnight.'

It emerged security staff at the hotel reprimanded Williams and Falzon as they left the toilets.

Most troubling for Williams was he had a girlfriend, Genna Shaw. Falzon's manager Max Markson tried to claim Falzon was simply using the men's toilet 'because the lines are shorter', something he said she often did.

Any chance of killing the story ended when a photo emerged the following day. If anybody wanted to know the popularity of the game's new star, the blurry photo of Williams and Falzon in a cubicle, shot from underneath the stall, revealed just how big a star he was. It set a record number for hits on the *Daily Telegraph*'s website. Markson changed tack and tried to get the image removed.

The following day Andrew Johns abruptly retired, putting a brief pause in the news cycle. Johns had injured his neck in a collision with teammate Adam Woolnough at training a week earlier and scans revealed a bulging disc that might have been there for some time. Johns said it had nothing to do with the Williams tackle. While Johns dominated the sports pages Williams and Falzon continued to hold their own in the gossip pages.

The incident showed just where Williams was in the public mind. Nobody cared anything for it other than that it was terrific water-cooler conversation. 'Did you hear . . .' is the way it mostly started.

The Falzon incident had no bearing on Williams' popularity. Again, it was widely dismissed as a young man's mistake. Also, typical of him at the time, he took responsibility and set about repairing his mistake. Maybe that's why it had no bearing.

Williams was seen as a stand-up guy. As he spoke to Andrew Webster at the *Sun-Herald*, in an odd way this only reinforced that.

'I'm ashamed and embarrassed,' he said. 'I've really let down all my loved ones, especially Genna. I'm glad she's stuck by me because this house is lonely when she's not here.'

Everybody was keen to drop it in the mistakes basket and leave it there. We all make them from time to time.

'I know it sounds so stupid saying I can't remember but I can honestly say I don't remember anything. That's what cuts me the most. I think Genna knows if I had any sense about what I was doing, I wouldn't have done it.'

Williams sought Canterbury's club chaplain Ken Clendenning to ask if he believed he had a drinking problem.

'You don't have a drinking problem,' the chaplain said. 'You can make the same stupid decisions like any twenty-one year old. If you have a drink, make sure you're with people you can trust.'

Williams listened but started eyeing the waters. Perhaps too much. Two months later police caught him urinating in public after a night out in Cronulla and fined him $650.

Again, it was no hanging offence. More than anything, it embarrassed the game and embarrassed the player. In some ways, Williams was also paying the price for being a Bulldog, the bad boys of the NRL, and of a growing public intolerance of drunken misbehaviour.

Yet the Bulldogs did not help themselves and, by default, Williams.

By now the club's character was clear. They snarled too often when they should have smiled. It was an attitude driven still by a strong sense of injustice left after the salary-cap scandal in 2002, for which they were surely guilty of, and the twin rape investigations. They responded to each incident like it was 1964, circling the wagons and believing that by closing down it would simply go away. Internally it worked a treat. In the real world, though, it was a disaster.

So when they clocked up ten alcohol-related incidents over three seasons, while still at war with the media and almost every NRL fan not a Bulldogs supporter, they found a public short on sympathy. The incidents ranged from brawls at racetracks to trashing the club's own office to drink-driving charges — teammate Ben Roberts was charged with drink-driving just the week before Williams was fined – and, throughout it all, the club maintained the bad publicity was a massive over-reaction. Whose business was it but theirs, they believed.

What had changed was the times, and the Bulldogs were the last to realise. So it was no surprise they failed to help themselves, and responded typically.

As the fallout to his public urination fine continued chief executive Malcolm Noad said he would make a statement at 9 am and much of the Sydney media rolled through the gates of Belmore Oval.

'Ah, look at all the vultures,' Folkes said as cameramen started setting up their cameras, forgetting they were invited. A television journalist bumped into Williams as he headed onto the field and said g'day.

'Go fuck yourself,' Sonny said.

As the club figured out how it would respond to the police fine, clearly an incident at the lower end, another television journalist almost got into a fight with the Bulldogs media manager. Life at the Bulldogs was turning into a Monty Python skit.

WHILE many in the club did not believe the problem was worth addressing, and any admission was to show weakness to the media, chief executive Malcolm Noad knew he needed to appear firm, while delivering a small uppercut to the media given the chance.

So the Bulldogs response was to call the 9 am press conference and then have Sonny apologise by reading a prepared statement where he admitted he had a drinking problem at 1.55 pm. Roberts then delivered his statement more than two hours after that, at 4.30 pm.

Noad explained the delay by saying he was running late for an appointment.

'I have let a lot of people down over the last couple of months,' Williams read. 'I know that all the bad publicity I have had is alcohol–related and I know I have been in this position before. This time I have come to the conclusion that enough is enough. With the help of the club I will be taking drastic measures to make sure this doesn't happen again. I will be seeking professional help with regards to alcohol and until myself and the club feel this is under control I will be off the drink.'

The statement would later be used as one of the central wedges for why he felt justified leaving the club. Williams later claimed he was told to admit he had a problem when he never believed he did.

The Bulldogs are not so adamant it happened that way.

At the same time Noad, for the first time, conceded to the *Telegraph* the club might have a drinking problem. 'We are addressing significant issues, yes. We can't deny there have been a number of incidents that we are facing head-on. Everyone forgets Sonny Bill is twenty-one years old and admits he screwed up. He recognises he needs help and we recognise we have a problem.'

Noad also revealed Williams was warned that his career was in jeopardy. While it might have seemed like necessary advice, it was absurd, given Williams' talent. Someone would always pick him up. Noad's true motive was to get Williams right. Noad believed Williams, naturally humble, used alcohol to mask other problems while in public.

'Whenever he goes out, he's greeted with the same fame and adulation – like a pop star, and the truth is that does not sit well with him,' he told the *Telegraph*. 'He genuinely is a very humble young man, and he has trouble dealing with the attention.'

Always acutely aware of his career, it was Williams who approached the club for help, according to Noad. 'Sonny Bill came to us . . . he's the one who wants to do something about it. He's the one saying he wants to get off the drink. And we think we have a duty of care to help him. He's young, he needs our help.'

Among the help offered were more visits with the chaplain, Ken Clendinning.

'And whatever resources we need to get to help Sonny Bill, we will,' Noad said. 'You have to be mentally tough to do what he's done on the field, and he's mentally tough off it as well. I think that it took a fair bit of courage for him to face the media on Monday. Now, he just wants to be allowed some privacy – he's embarrassed.'

In May the following year, just months before he walked out, Williams denied the whole version. With big strong quotes, he told Andrew Webster at the *Herald*: 'It's no lie that I used to go out and party too much. I think I was very naïve to think that if every other twenty-two year old was doing that, why can't I? In the last six months I've woken up and matured as a person. To be where I want to be, to achieve the goals I want to achieve, I can't be doing that. In the last six months, I've grown up. Not just as a player but as a person. I respect the position I'm in a lot more. I've taken steps to make sure the things that have brought me down as a man do not happen again. I've taken steps to make sure I'm the role model I want to be, especially for a lot of the young Polynesian boys.'

A few months after that his stance had hardened, his anger now including the club: 'I feel like I was hung out to dry. I didn't want to go and speak to the media. I'm a friggin' twenty-year-old kid and the CEO says stand here and say that. What are you supposed to do? It's like you've been naughty and that's just the fastest way to make it right. I was very pissed off that I had to say I had a drinking problem because the only problem I had was being naïve.'

The pity of all that is everybody else thought Williams had handled himself superbly.

IN between there was always football. It was salvation of a kind. Williams destroyed the Sydney Roosters. Without State of Origin players Willie Mason, Andrew Ryan and Hazem El Masri, and with fellow Origin prop Mark O'Meley suspended, Williams came up with two tries and all-round havoc. Those tries he did not score he set up. Perhaps the best moment was trademark Sonny, when he took the ball to the line and reached behind the defender to pop a ball to centre Daryl Millard to score.

'I'm always expecting it when Sonny is running the ball,' Millard said. 'You know he's going to have an arm free.'

The 32–8 win over the Roosters was the first time throughout the 2007 season the Bulldogs, fighting to make the playoffs, won back-to-back games.

Folkes was pumped. 'He was the reason we were in front at half time,' he said. 'He really stood up for us and did a great job. I don't know whether he can play much better than he did tonight. If he can I would like to see it.'

And he just got better. Six weeks later he gave what just might be the most dominant performance of his career. He scored three tries and set up several more in a 52–4 win over Canberra. He averaged nearly fifteen metres with every run. At times he took the ball four times in a set of six, dominating possession as he dared the Raiders to stop him. When the Raiders' defenders came at him he offloaded to put players through gaps in the defence and when they held back waiting to see who he would pass to he ran through them. Such was his performance the league world lit up once again. Only the Bulldogs, masters of controlling their environment, were able to ignore it.

'He's just enjoying his footy, he'd probably like to be left alone to do that, and we support him with that,' Folkes said after the game.

Williams would not be talking.

That was as bright as it got for the Bulldogs. A month later they were eliminated from the finals with consecutive losses to North Queensland and Parramatta. Williams failed to play against North Queensland after being suspended for a high shot on the Cowboys' Johnathan Thurston the week before, in the final round of the home–and–away season.

The Bulldogs had gone close, but the ride was about to end. Willie Mason was about to leave the club after a dispute with Noad, released with two years still to run on his contract. Mark O'Meley was also moving on, squeezed out when the club redirected money to Williams.

The club was investing heavily in Williams, with no idea what was soon to come. For the moment he was the foundation they were building everything upon.

For the club and the fans, and as far as anybody was concerned, he was the Bulldogs.

Just three weeks earlier Canterbury Leagues Club honoured office worker June Burnes for thirty-five years of service. It was a Leagues Club function and the only thing June loved more than the Bulldogs was Sonny Bill.

As she stood onstage to accept her award the auditorium suddenly erupted, the crowd realising Sonny was walking through them towards the stage to present her award.

'Sonny,' she said, her eyes filling with tears, her voice breaking and barely picked up by the microphone, 'this means the world to me.'

PART III

18
SONNY'S NEW BEGINNING

IN a bright French shopping centre in August 2008 Sonny Bill is taking in the first sights of his new home with Anthony Mundine. He is overwhelmed by a tremendous sense of freedom. Little is made of it, but a new man is developing. Indeed, it would take almost a year before Williams is comfortable enough to talk about his new life, telling Brad Walter at the *Herald* the following July, 'When I hopped on that aeroplane it was like walking into the unknown, but walking into the unknown feeling that I was free, not that I was in prison or anything like that but that's just the way I felt.

'It didn't matter where I was going, it was just the fact I was getting out. I wasn't happy and I just thought, "I will take things into my own hands," but it wasn't until I started packing my bags that I realised this was it. I walked out the door and my girlfriend was crying but looking back now, I know I made the right decision for me and my family because I am just so much better off financially, mentally and physically as well. I've got no regrets. If I did do it all over again there would be certain things I would change but I wouldn't change leaving.'

Back home the Bulldogs were still confused. His former teammates were struggling through what would be the club's worst season in more than forty years. And as significant as the loss of his talent was, which the players felt considerably, the simple maths now meant the club was working under a $2.85-million salary cap when the rest of the NRL was at $3.25 million. Given one of the chief reasons of the salary cap was to level talent across the sixteen NRL teams by limiting payments, among the chief reasons Williams walked out, it left his former teammates at a significant disadvantage. So the Bulldogs players felt the let-down deeply. His walkout had affected their careers, too.

The Bulldogs finished with the wooden spoon, their worst finish since 1964 if you don't count their 2002 disqualification. Their final game, a 36–22 loss to Brisbane, ended Steve Folkes' thirty-year association at the club as a player and coach. The next day the players met for consolation drinks, a sombre Mad Monday celebration. They wore French berets.

FOR the moment, though, there was great relief in Sonny.

Walking through the shopping centre he started joking with Mundine, two bulls in the paddock. Mundine was openly cocky, everybody knew that. Williams could be but always with an undertone of humour. He wanted you to know he was joking.

A friendly push and shove broke out between the young men. Mundine put his hands up and started flicking jabs at Williams. Williams pushed his left foot forward and began leading with his left in the classic boxing stance, but had none of Mundine's balance and grace.

'He couldn't even hold up his hands, I was touching him every time I wanted,' Mundine said.

In some respects this should not be surprising. Mundine was the prize fighter. Williams was a footballer. But Williams' reputation was always as a bloke who could handle himself and Mundine's ease at landing embarrassed him.

'He had his long arms down and I just thought, "Son, you're in the wrong game,"' said Mundine.

Mundine thought nothing more of it. They were soon shopping.

So much had happened. Yet it was only six months earlier Williams sat next to Mundine and Ben Cousins in Tony Mundine's gym and nobody knew how close he was to being on the card himself. Williams had joked to Mundine about turning pro.

'He'd joked about fighting as a pro a few times,' Mundine said. 'Well, it must have been real in his mind but I thought he was joking.'

This is the way it starts with such men. A fire lit up in Williams that afternoon in the shopping centre. His whole life was about challenges, always had been. He was disappointed Mundine had handled him so easily.

The boxing bug started whizzing around his head. Could he?

For the moment though it was about rugby. With his legal problems now out of the way Williams began preparing for his rugby career. The big game early was English club Saracens.

Watching from the sideline was Saracens director of rugby Eddie Jones. The good news is Jones had lost none of the fire he had as Wallabies coach. With two players in the sin-bin for the final ten minutes and a 20–8 penalty count against them Jones made sure the referee knew his frustrations. Despite being without two of their best players Saracens beat the full-strength Toulon 32–27. It calmed Jones only somewhat.

The game gave Williams the chance to speak for the first time to the man who had spoken so warmly about him. Jones introduced him to the club's own league convert Andy Farrell and, from what he saw, Jones had no doubt Williams had made the right move.

'He is a really humble young bloke,' he said after the game. 'He is dynamite on the field and off it he is going to be just as big. They got double the crowd they'd normally get for a trial and I think all Toulon's games are now going to be sell-outs. What really impressed me was his willingness to learn. He had a chat to me and talked to Andy Farrell after the game to ask him about the code switch. It's that attitude combined with his obvious physical presence that is going to make him an All Black.'

Jones was proving himself an astute judge.

By now the growing threat of French rugby was obvious. Craig Gower was also in the south of France, playing for Bayonne, and developing into a true star. Mark Gasnier was just weeks away, waiting until the NRL season was over to settle in Paris to play for Stade Français under new coach Ewen McKenzie. He would be introduced wearing a hot-pink polo before going on to stun the French with his skills. Penrith's Luke Rooney was also not far from joining Williams at Toulon.

Back in the NRL the managers couldn't help themselves; many players coming off contract were linked to a move to France. The player managers had caught on, playing their own version of Sonny Ball. This was a tremendous new development for them – they now had the unspoken threat of fleeing to France as an option in their negotiations. They didn't even need a legitimate offer. Whether the players could play rugby or not didn't matter. Heck, it didn't even matter if they wanted to.

In the middle of negotiations to extend his deal at Wests Tigers, Benji Marshall's manager Martin Tauber mentioned casually that Japanese rugby might be an option. Bayonne was also rumoured to be interested in Marshall joining Gower. Marshall, who was learning the rules, then got up at the Wests Tigers' season launch and, his first word to the audience: 'Konnichiwa.'

Having watched many NRL players closely, Eddie Jones said Marshall would be a hit in Japan with the extra space around the breakdown but warned against him joining the local product, the Super Rugby competition between domestic teams from Australia, New Zealand and South Africa. It was a tip that proved sadly prophetic when, after the Tigers failed to honour a pay rise in 2013, Marshall signed with the Auckland Blues but lasted just six games in 2014 before being released. He returned to the NRL.

Right here, though, the switch to rugby was still considered a sure threat. And the NRL was getting nervous.

WILLIAMS was ideally placed to make his rugby debut at Toulon. Tana Umaga was coach and in many ways ideal for him. Like Sonny, Umaga also once played rugby league. He signed for the NRL's Newcastle Knights before returning to New Zealand after three weeks, homesick. Most of all Umaga was a centre with a deep knowledge of the subtleties of the position. For a player like Williams, who wanted to know not only what to do but why he was doing it, Umaga had the answers.

A week later Williams made his premiership debut, scoring a try in the 22–16 win over Clermont. It was a significant win. Toulon was back in the Top 14 after two years in relegation and Clermont were runners-up the previous season. Here we can see the Sonny Bill magic already beginning to take effect; a win against top-flight opposition. Like the great ones, his influence was not just in what he did when involved, but his influence over the players around him.

The following week Williams got injured. He played more than forty minutes with what he believed was a cork in his shin in a 3–3 draw with Brive. Nobody knew which was worse: that Williams was injured again or that two teams played for eighty minutes and could manage only three points apiece.

Perhaps embarrassed at being struck down by another injury, initial reports out of Toulon were that Williams was injured and would be out for three weeks. Bad, but not catastrophic.

Not far away, though, in Nice, the Queensland Reds were trialling. After the game Umaga was a surprise visitor in the Reds' dressing room and naturally the conversation turned to Williams. The Reds were spectators like everybody else. Perhaps believing he was talking among friends, Umaga revealed the news was worse than was being reported. Broken leg. Out six weeks. It travelled back to Australia at warp speed.

In the end, Williams' time out was almost double that. By pushing so hard to get back quicker than his injury could heal he suffered several setbacks. With so much emotion accompanying his arrival in France it was enough to make Toulon officials, and also Sonny, for that matter, blush. Criticism from back home that he was injury-prone, backed by the statistics of the many games he did not play, supported it.

Sonny knew he had to do something about himself.

Many years back an American coach, Mel Rogers, highlighted the problem of young athletes. If a boy devotes his life to becoming President of the United States, he said, even if he fails, he will pick up enough experience and information along the way to make a successful and fulfilling career at something. But a boy who devotes his life to becoming centre for the Los Angeles Lakers or the Chicago Bears, or a centre-fielder for the New York Mets, had better get there if he expects to get anywhere at all.

All Sonny had was his body and the body he had was letting him down. Nobody can continue signing short-term contracts for maximum money if that time is spent on the sideline. Frustrated, he began redesigning his life.

He couldn't find ice-packs to treat his soft-tissue injuries, so he searched the internet and found that by freezing vodka it made an ice gel-pack. The moment he got out of bed he started stretching and doing core work, sending himself to bed the same way.

He started eating cleaner to help his recovery and relieve inflammation. Nothing fancy, just smart and disciplined.

Seafood became a big part of his diet. Salmon, full of protein and good fat. While supermarkets and diet books advocate the advantages of 'fat free' diets, Williams saw the folly of that and introduced good fats like salmon, avocado and nuts, and cooking in coconut oil.

After promising much in the trials Toulon started the season poorly and after just three games Umaga was called to a meeting by owner Mourad Boudjellal to explain the poor start.

'I am angry,' Boudjellal said after a round-three loss to Mont-de-Marsan. 'That was the most shameful defensive bonus point in the history of rugby. Out of six halves we have played since the start of the season we've had only one good one.'

Boudjellal then found a different perspective on assessing performance while putting Umaga on notice. 'We have a team to finish between eighth and tenth. Above that will be thanks to the coaches, below it will be their fault,' he said.

Boudjellal was spot-on as far as the talent he had acquired. Toulon eventually finished ninth. How they would have fared if Williams had not missed ten games will never be known but the owner did not wait to find out. When the season was over he released sixteen players, by which time Umaga had resigned as coach while briefly returning to play in a bid to stave off relegation.

Sonny did not return until December and by then Toulon was struggling. And he was far from his best when he did return. He came back too early. Pressure from Boudjellal might have had something to do with it. There were complications in healing and while he managed to return and play on a leg still injured, the stress on the still-healing bone caused more problems. Eventually the bone would over-compensate and grow too large, putting pressure on the muscle. It would feel cramped all the time.

While injured, though, he used the time for growth.

On the one hand the broken leg knocked him around, with reports going back to Australia that he was homesick and wanted to come home. The Canterbury board even met to discuss the possibility of taking him back.

'He would have to try and repair the irreparable,' a club source told Dean Ritchie.

While the Bulldogs reluctantly considered it, Williams flat out denied any intent to return. He had already been through too much. The damage was too great on both sides, with Bulldogs captain Andrew Ryan unsure if he could even forgive.

'It would take a lot,' he said. 'He's hurt a lot of us.'

Williams was down, though. The injury rocked him. Nasser flew over again in late September to ensure he was okay. Mundine and Nasser continued to fill him with positive reinforcement.

Sonny being Sonny, he used the time wisely. He took time for reflection.

'I think I'm evolving,' he would say later. It was his life's philosophy. 'I'm always in search of bettering myself, how I can improve as a sportsman and as a person. I am my own man now, I can think for myself, whereas when I was twenty, twenty-one, I always wanted to please others. I do speak my mind a lot more than when I was younger. I guess that's just my Polynesian background. That's how we are, just sit back and try and fit in, try and make everyone else happy.'

He met a family from Tunisia, a Muslim family, and got friendly with them. Seeing the peace in their lives he also converted to Islam while in France. In the end it was an easy decision to make.

While he had already read plenty about Muhammad Ali and his struggles, many of them driven by his conversion to Islam, once again he picked up Alex Haley's *Autobiography of Malcolm X*. He saw wisdom and struggle within its pages, which he identified with.

His girlfriend Genna had yet to join him. Mundine and Nasser were still the most influential people in his life at this point, where they would remain for years.

'Just hanging around with "Choc" and Khoder has lifted my self-esteem and my confidence levels to the point where I can speak my mind even if it does come back to bite me on the arse,' Williams says. 'That's what I believe and what I stand for. I am my own man, and I'm proud of that. A lot of people just say things that other people want to hear, kiss arse, but at the end of the day they're not their own man.

'That's what I try and stand for. I stand up for myself or if I think someone is getting treated indifferently.'

The rest of the time, he trained. His whole life was in transformation. Eventually he gave up alcohol completely.

'The first thing I cut down was no drinking, then from no drinking you cut down being out late, you're up early in the morning,' he said. 'You get those looks from the boys like, "What are you doing?" but they're the first ones to come up and say, "You had a great game."'

Not that he was without struggle. For perhaps the first time in his life the insecurities he carried deep down nearly bubbled to the surface. Time on the sideline can do that.

'It's a lot tougher than what I thought it would be and there were stages there where I thought I wasn't going to make it, to be honest. But I kind of always had good people around me, who believed in me, and said give it time. I had to work on the fundamentals of the game because in league, the position I played it was just bash and crash.'

He played just sixteen games that first season and as he questioned his body he promised himself one more year.

'I have to give myself time,' he said to himself. 'Give it twenty games under my belt and then I will see where I am at after twenty games.'

It was a period of growth. His need to fit in helped him through. England World Cup hero Jonny Wilkinson arrived at Toulon for his second season and Williams went to him often for advice. The new coach, Philippe Saint-André, spoke only

French, forcing Williams to hasten his French lessons. In the end it only helped.

'I've been listening to the people I play against and the people playing with me, to just trying to pick up little things,' he said. 'You have got to pick up those fundamentals. It's been a hard road . . .'

It was no different from what we had come to expect. A year earlier it was Andrew Johns. Now it was Jonny Wilkinson.

19

FRENCH CONNECTION

BECAUSE the French Top 14 is played in the northern winter its season runs alternately to the NRL season in the southern hemisphere.

So, even before the French rugby season was over, Stade Français forwards coach Fabrice Landreau turned up to the Sydney Roosters' pre-season training in February 2009 to watch. Landreau admitted he had never heard of Mark Gasnier before he joined his club, but Gasnier had opened French rugby's eyes to an entirely new nursery.

Again, the supreme talents of elite rugby league were being identified. For years rugby league folk had claimed league produced the better athletes. It was tougher and more intense. Its only handicap was its smaller international profile. Union folk simply pointed to their international game as a rebuttal. Now the international game was coming to rugby league.

'I think a lot of players can play union in Europe with no trouble and I think now every professional rugby union club is looking for the best players in rugby league because if they can win a duel one-on-one like Mark Gasnier or break the line like Sonny Bill Williams, they can make a difference in a game,' Landreau said. 'For us, Mark Gasnier is fantastic. He is a brilliant player, he is very skilful and one-on-one he is the best. He can pass on the left and the right and he is very clever. After six months he has made big progress and if he continues like that he can play for the Wallabies.'

Another French agent, Frédéric Bonhomme, also flew into Sydney that February to look at Marshall, as well as Braith Anasta and Willie Mason. Mason would eventually sign with Toulon for the 2011 season. He played one game, tweeted 'I'm so fucking over rugby' then quit and headed home to Australia hoping to pick up another NRL deal.

For a while the only offer came from the Guyra Superspuds in Group 19 in northern NSW. Superspuds official Terry Vidler believed he could find a place for Mason. Nothing is known about Vidler except he has a wonderfully dry sense of humour. 'I'd have to put it to a meeting but, yes, we'd take him,' he said. 'We've got a tomato farm out here, it's a big deal. He could work there.'

The Superspuds did not pay its players, Vidler admitted, but he believed Mason was a special case where they could probably raise $250 a game for him.

Unfortunately for the Superspuds, Mason finally received an offer from Newcastle and signed, playing three seasons before shifting to Manly in 2015.

But not before he was voted by Toulon fans as the club's worst-ever signing. Mason was thirty-one when he landed in France and later admitted he switched too late but, given his time again, would have switched earlier. He understood the lure. Comparatively, rugby union was easier on the body than the much harder rugby league.

'It's physical, it's hard every week, it's twenty-six rounds, you don't get paid as much as when you can just fuck around in France or Japan, bash all the Japanese guys around and get a few million dollars for fourteen games,' Mason said.

For rugby league, it was the same eternal war with rugby union, just the battlefield had changed.

The alternate seasons meant Sonny was creating headlines on both sides of the world. Even as New Year rolled around Williams was still a big part of the Australian news cycle. As the French talent scouts landed in Australia news emerged that the Wallabies would play the Barbarians in Sydney in June. Given the timing, fears arose that the strength of the Barbarians would be severely hampered because the best New Zealand and South African players would still be involved in their own Test series. South Africa would have the British and Irish Lions in the country ready to play a three-Test series while the All Blacks were in France for a two-Test series. A Lions-depleted England side was playing Argentina also, ruling out more players. The fear was the Wallabies would take on a Barbarians side filled with Pacific Island, Japanese and second-tier Irish, Welsh and Scottish players. In other words, Drummoyne third grade.

ARU boss John O'Neill knew he had to save the game. He tried to put the fears to bed, revealing that the best of Australia and New Zealand's overseas players, such as Rocky Elsom and Dan Vickerman, were also being invited to play, and not only them.

O'Neill is a former bank executive but has a certain flair never found in the banking industry. After dire forecasts that were enough for New Zealand to pull out of co-hosting the 2003 Rugby World Cup he declared the ARU would take it on by itself and turned it into such a financial success that it became the model for every World Cup since. If O'Neill turns up at the Eskimo village with a boatload of ice, have no doubt — they're buying.

He revealed Williams and Craig Gower were on the invitation list. 'We'd have loved to have seen Mark Gasnier but his team almost certainly will be involved in the French championship finals,' O'Neill added.

He knew exactly the effect his words would have. Immediately the conspiracy theorists were off and O'Neill received publicity way beyond what the game would have usually received. Everybody had an opinion on Williams' return to Australia. Six years after poaching Wendell Sailor, Lote Tuqiri and Mat Rogers to help sell their World Cup the ARU was going back to the well to use rugby league to sell their game.

At least that's what the rugby league community believed and responded to. The ARU, whose growing financial troubles were still a kept secret at this time, denied it was an attempt to cash in on the celebrity of former NRL players. What did it matter where the truth was, what was important was that everybody was now talking about a game that five minutes earlier ARU officials were wondering how they were ever going to sell.

It was almost too easy. Another small front opened in the war and, sure enough, the league world came out behind the strong fists of former hardmen Tommy Raudonikis and Steve Roach in the *Telegraph*.

'It's an absolute disgrace,' Raudonikis said. 'He shouldn't even be allowed back in the country. They should send him straight back to New Zealand. I can't forget what he did to the Bulldogs. It was dreadful and unsporting. No one should go to the game. All Sydney sports fans should boycott the event. I reckon it's just a publicity stunt because the match is only three days after Origin I. I just don't rate Williams as a person. I would hate to be alongside this bloke in the trenches.'

Roach, who only years before joined the long line of Sonny admirers, still believed his walkout was unforgivable, saying, 'Only his family will go to the match. He has dudded everyone else. People won't forget how he left the Bulldogs.'

O'Neill said it was far from a marketing ploy. Williams, he said, was now a rugby union player. His league past was behind him.

Former Wallabies captain Simon Poidevin contributed to the conversation but appealed to higher ground. 'The more they call for a boycott, the more people will turn up,' he said. 'That is dumb in capital letters.'

Poidevin was one hundred per cent correct, even if he, too, had no idea that he was just lured into playing a subtler version of Sonny Ball. If there was one thing Williams was reconfirming it was not just the growing fascination we were having as a society with celebrity, but with its power.

Where it started is anybody's guess; the contest barely mattered anymore. When exactly this change occurred, nobody is certain. Before Mike Tyson came along promoters put a lot of work into matching opponents and making sure fans saw two evenly matched fighters, whether they were four-round novices or contenders on the rise. Then Tyson emerged, knocking everybody over and it didn't matter who he fought. He was the biggest name in world sport. These new fans did not care. They just wanted a victim. Soon, Tyson's opponent wasn't even featured on the fight posters. If he was lucky his name was featured large enough on the poster not to cause you to squint.

At the same time the major fight networks in America fell in love with the zero at the end of a fighter's record and realised it was not a contest the fans wanted, but the name. The zero bluffed the naïve into believing the fighter was as real as his record. Protect the zero, build the name and eventually the network put him in against another whatever-and-zero fighter and called it a superfight on the widening pay-per-view audience. People paid through the nose.

Soon, organisations realised if it worked for individuals in sport, why not promote the individuals in their sport? As marketing and sponsorship dollars became more important throughout world sporting codes also began to realise the value of individuals within their code, and the value of promoting the individual instead of the organisation. Who cared what kind of contest the Barbarians were going to give the Wallabies if Sonny Bill was part of the line-up?

Mundine had long followed a similar model. Williams could see all this happening around him. It only made sense then, that, come March 2009, IBO middleweight champion Daniel Geale announced he would defend his title against Mundine in May. On the undercard was Sonny Bill Williams in his professional debut. The fight was another 'KO to Drugs' promotion and Mundine approached Sonny to ask if he wanted to spar an exhibition.

Forget that, Williams said, he wanted to fight for real.

The idea of being a professional athlete in three different sports appealed to him. The promoters scoured the country long and wide to find a suitable opponent. He had to be big and look the part and not necessarily be able to fight. They found a live one, though barely, who came with the appropriate dossier.

New Zealander Gary Gurr was nicknamed 'The Baboon' and it took only a short search on the internet to discover Sonny was in tremendous trouble if you believed the advance press.

Said one boxing forum, 'He's mad as a bag of snakes with the speed, guts and determination of a Group One racehorse. I have personally watched him take down many high-profile sports stars in arm wrestles whilst chatting up the ladies and sipping away on a whiskey.'

Naturally this looked to be serious trouble for Sonny, a high-profile sports star. If anybody dared introduce some ladies and a bottle of whiskey at any stage during the fight, it was destined to get worse.

Outside of that he was expected to do okay.

WILLIAMS flew into Australia six days before the fight, on 21 May, and admitted he was a little nervous about returning for the first time since he fled the previous July. Nasser organised security guards to pick him up and drive him to Mundine's Boxa café in Hurstville.

By now, Sonny Ball meant Williams spoke only to the *Herald*, telling Brad Walter, 'I guess just hearing all the stories and the media reports, you tend to be a bit on edge, but it has been really good, a few people have come up to me and given me their best wishes and said I had done the right thing.'

It was not just certain media reports, as those in the Nasser–Mundine–Williams camp believed.

As Williams landed in Australia, market research company Sweeney Research released its findings on Australia's most marketable athletes. The big news was the fall of Australian cricketer Andrew Symonds from number ten in Australia down to thirty-five. Symonds' fall came from several incidents where his commitment to the baggy green was questioned, most notably missing a team meeting because he had gone fishing.

Williams also dropped, going from forty-four to seventy-eight in the wake of his flight to France, showing that the public unhappiness was with more than just the Bulldogs and several of us in the media, as some around him liked to pretend.

'There's no doubt misbehaving athletes are falling faster and further than they have in previous years,' analyst Todd Deacon told the *Daily Telegraph*. 'The whole notion of role models in sport is really on the rise, and when athletes don't live up to that, well, they are being discarded – quickly.'

Deacon said Symonds' fall was for similar reasons to Williams'. 'It had people questioning his commitment to the baggy green. I mean, playing for our national cricket team, it's seen as a great honour and not something to be taken flippantly. It's the same with Sonny Bill Williams and the way he treated the Bulldogs players, fans and the game of rugby league generally. It just didn't sit well with people.'

Another, less scientific, list ran in *Zoo Magazine*. The 'Fifty People We Love To Hate' voted Williams number one, beating Bali bomber Amrozi, who had to be secure with the number two spot. While this might seem a small catastrophe in the world of Sonny Bill it was superseded by a greater truth, that in the world of Sonny Ball, like the culture of celebrity, it was better to be spoken about harshly than not spoken about at all. You can't sell second best.

That night Bulldogs fans got what they had waited for. Williams went on the *Footy Show* to publicise his fight and got a warm response from the crowd, who can never be accused of overthinking things, and after a couple of soft lobs gave the apology fans felt was long overdue.

'It's definitely not the way I should have come out and done things,' Williams said. 'I was a little bit upset with myself that I didn't apologise to the boys. If I had my time over again I would have rung every single player in the team. I didn't apologise to the fans and I guess that's what I want to do, especially to the Bulldogs fans. To the young kids that really looked up to me, I just want to say I'm sorry for all the heartache and the problems I've caused.'

Some questioned whether his remorse was genuine or if he was looking to win back fans to sell his fight. So much misinformation had been spread it was hard to know anymore. At least half the population remained sceptical.

Asked whether he would ever return to the NRL Williams smiled. 'You never say never. You never know. Who would have said two years ago that I would be playing rugby union? Anything is possible.'

He was in a conciliatory mood. In almost a carbon copy of his *Footy Show* appearance, Williams told Walter at the *Herald*, 'One thing I want to do is to apologise to the Bulldogs fans, and especially the young kids that looked up to me. I just want to say that I'm sorry for the heartache and problems that I've caused. Even though I had to pay $750,000 to get out of my contract, I've got no animosity towards the Dogs. They will always be my team. I've got the Bulldogs tattooed on my arm and I still cherish the memories that I have of playing for the club. I had some really good times there, so I wish them all the best and I still go for them. I was unhappy with the way the club was run and the way I was treated but I played for them for so long that if you were to ask me who I was to go for, it would be the Dogs.'

Todd Greenberg remained cautious. 'It is worthwhile reminding him that under the deeds of his release he signed with us Sonny was not allowed to play with any other club in the NRL until 2013,' he said the following morning in the *Telegraph*. 'All Bulldogs fans have very long memories and remember the way he departed in the dark of the night.'

What Greenberg remembered that Williams appeared to conveniently forget was that, in all those meetings held before he walked out on the club, his concerns were never about the club supposedly forcing him to admit to an alcohol problem, or a lack of respect towards him. The club had done its best to please him and placate any ill-feelings. Just a week before he left, the Bulldogs even agreed to let Polynesian fans in for free in a bid to support Williams' ambition to be a leader in his community, unaware that Williams had already signed a letter of intent to join Toulon.

What Greenberg remembered in all of those meetings was it was always about money. *That* was how the Bulldogs were supposed to show him their love.

Now though, with the new Sonny, it seemed to be about more intangible matters, like respect and blame, which made it harder for the Bulldogs to defend themselves. Who knows what constituted the proper level of respect?

The hard-sell continued four days later, a Monday, when Williams sat down next to Mundine at the press conference for the fight in Brisbane.

Midway through a man in a black hoodie ambushed the presser with a loud angry voice. Among other sins soon to be committed, he interrupted Mundine mid-sentence.

'Did you start the party without me?' he yelled. 'Where the fuck is my seat?'

Mundine was stunned. 'Who is this cat?'

Williams, somewhat embarrassed, said, 'He's the guy I'm fighting.'

Gurr meant so little to the promotion he was not even invited.

'I don't even know how he got here,' Williams said after the press conference. 'He must have been camped outside our hotel.'

It was the biggest fight Williams got in the whole trip. Whispers had been going around for days that Gurr was a street-fighter of some note back in New Zealand and was promising all that and more when he finally got Williams into the ring. How he missed a spot at the table for the press conference was blamed on a tremendous oversight on someone's part. Unless, as some believed, it all went exactly to script.

That was as good as it got for The Baboon. Gurr knew little more than to walk forward and lead with his chin until Williams, cautious early, caught him with an uppercut midway through the first round. From there it was all one-way. Referee Cyril Cairns stopped the fight in the second round.

The night was marked by an ugly incident in the main event much like what had taken place a year earlier when Mundine fought Crazy Kim in Newcastle. Almost from the moment the fight started people – who knows if they were friends, associates or just blow-ins from the cheap seats – but they bypassed security and got themselves ringside. Almost immediately one stood over English judge Marcus McDonnell and, the moment he scored a round for Geale, began accusing him of racism. His scores were relayed to Mundine's corner.

'You are full of shit, c. . ., you are playing the game,' he said.

'Fuck off,' said McDonnell, more than once.

When McDonnell scored the tenth round to Geale the supporter again called him a racist.

The fact that Geale was also Aboriginal seemed to have been lost on him. Unless his intention was to be there solely to intimidate.

What was troubling about the incident was that the fight was promoted by Mundine, through his company Boxa Promotions. In other words, as well as being responsible for employing the referee and judges he was also responsible for the security, or lack thereof, for the ringside judges. He was certainly responsible for their welfare and for ensuring working conditions where they could not be harassed or influenced by maniacal fans. While there is no suggestion Mundine had any idea what was about to unfold it was a poor look.

Certainly Geale's team was concerned enough to protest to the IBO, after Mundine won in a split decision – with McDonnell scoring the fight 114–113 to Mundine.

'For the future, judges of IBO contests when involved in a Mundine fight, they do need to be protected. We can't have people behind us calling us names. Lucky I'm a thick-skinned Pom,' McDonnell would say later.

'But that's boxing, it happens. Yes, he did call me a racist, but to his credit he came and said sorry after the contest. Interesting to see how he would have been if Mundine had lost.'

The IBO eventually ordered a rematch after independent judges, watching a replay with the sound down, ruled for Geale. It never went ahead, Mundine preferring to drop the belt instead of taking the rematch.

As far as Mundine was concerned, there were bigger names to chase. Who knew Geale would get to them first, winning the IBF middleweight title four fights later?

Here we see Williams' wonderful versatility, though.

He went straight from the fight to a couple of days relaxing on the Gold Coast before heading into camp for the Barbarians ahead of their game on 6 June, just ten days after the fight.

Wherever he looked Wallabies were lining him up. Ryan Cross, James O'Connor . . . Wallabies captain Stirling Mortlock would mark Williams at outside centre and admitted before the game a few people had come up to him and asked him to 'put a good shot on him'.

'But it's all a bit tongue in cheek,' Mortlock said.

Williams, allowing that self-doubt to briefly pop and bubble, thought the game would give him the best indication yet of where he was in his rugby career. He was still gauging how good he could be in the new game and the international game would answer that.

Mortlock got his chance nice and early, after just three minutes when Williams moved from outside centre to inside centre and took a crash and bang hit-up. Mortlock, a strong defender, was pencilled in as the man most likely to deliver the welcome to rugby shot many wanted to witness. And with Williams moving to inside centre Mortlock was now tackling outside-in, which meant he was coming from Sonny's blindside, which was perfect.

Williams ran over him.

Just ten metres out he looked set to score before being chopped down by halfback Luke Burgess. Mortlock did get the chance to square up two minutes later, dropping him with a big shot which was followed by the Wallabies forwards piling on with a little extra vigour, a tactic they were able to repeat for much of the game.

'That's the way the big boys do it,' Mortlock said.

The Wallabies gave the Barbarians a hiding in the end, scoring eight tries to one to win 55–7. To be fair to Williams, it is hard to make any impact on a result like that, playing outside centre, when the forwards are being so spectacularly beaten. Beyond the score though it opened his eyes to the way rugby was played in the southern hemisphere, away from the ten-man rugby style so dominant in the northern hemisphere. Here, it was closer to rugby league.

'He was amazed by the speed and how quick that ball gets recycled and how much the ball is in play compared to playing at Toulon,' Barbarians coach Dai Young said after the game.

'Let's be fair to the kid. He is learning the game and he stood up and performed admirably, I felt. But he has a bit to learn.'

Channel Seven commentator Tim Horan, who played eighty games in the Wallabies jersey, said Williams was 'out of his depth'.

Williams sat in the dressing room icing ribs from the Mortlock hit.

He responded the only way he knew how. 'He seems like a good bloke and a very funny character,' he said. 'But I'd love to come back here in a few years' time and show him how I do it.'

While Williams was talking in the dressing room Nasser was being refused entry at the door. The security guard posted at the door was following the simple code of the industry: No Pass, No Entry. Nasser unbottled an explosive tirade while the security guard remained resolute: 'You can't come in.'

Eventually Williams emerged and left the ground with Nasser and a *Herald* journalist, leaving behind his Barbarian teammates.

In June he returned to France for his second season but things were starting to move. Almost immediately conversations began about his next contract. He was being mentioned for both New Zealand and Samoa, courtesy of his dad's heritage, for the 2011 Rugby World Cup while some interest was shown, apparently, from France, where he would qualify if he played a third season in the Top 14.

Williams knew he needed to get himself right, though. As everybody speculated he was still preparing to give himself twenty games to see if he could meet his own standards as a rugby player. Then a phone call changed everything. It was from All Blacks coach Graham Henry.

'What do you think of coming back?'

Suddenly, the All Blacks dream was a reality. Soon All Blacks assistant coach Wayne Smith caught up with Williams in Toulon to talk about him returning to New Zealand in time for the 2011 Rugby World Cup. Like much of what happens in Williams' life the All Blacks interest was denied at the time. He claimed Smith was in France to see Dan Carter and while passing through Toulon caught up for a friendly coffee.

Things started moving quickly. With Wilkinson now playing for Toulon the side improved dramatically, finishing second on the Top 14 table before being eliminated in the first semifinal. They also finished runners-up in the European Challenge Cup, a significant result given where they had come from.

Williams was not the only player about to move. The overwhelming publicity surrounding first his departure from Australia and then his return for the Barbarians match switched on a couple of very bright bulbs across the Australian sporting landscape. Who's to say a rugby league player had to switch to rugby union? Or that Sonny Ball applied only to rugby league?

Weeks after Williams returned to France, Karmichael Hunt stunned Australian sport when he announced he was quitting the NRL, where he was an Australian and Queensland State of Origin star, to join the Gold Coast Suns in their inaugural AFL season in 2011.

It made no sense, but it made every sense. Hunt showed he no longer needed rugby league, one of the golden rules of Sonny Ball. For the truly elite, of which there are but a few, the athlete is bigger than the club, even bigger than the sport. You can be sure of that because of who wields the power.

Hunt was not signed because he was identified as a player with the necessary skill-set to be a hit in AFL. He was signed to bully space in the media for the Gold Coast Suns as the expansion club tried to establish itself in a new market, southeast Queensland. He knew that, but was determined to be successful anyway. His success as a player was supplementary. Clearly the AFL had watched closely the publicity surrounding Williams' switch, which included both his successes and failures.

The same month that Hunt signed with the Suns, Craig Wing quit the NRL for a career in Japanese rugby.

'Sonny's move opened my eyes to a world outside of NRL,' he said.

Predictably, Hunt's signing sparked a move by the NRL's Rugby League Players' Association to have the salary cap lifted. The game needed to start matching salaries paid in other codes, otherwise the game's best players would continue to be poached.

The RLPA was getting noisy at exactly the right time. Emotions were high and emotive arguments always stand the best chance of beating a logical argument.

When Parramatta star Jarryd Hayne complained he was among the NRL's best players but that his salary was below what AFL players were being paid NRL boss David Gallop said, 'It's what the game can afford. There are many demands on the game's revenue and rugby league pays a greater share of revenue to its players than the other codes.'

Gallop had already proven as much. Three years earlier Willie Mason had suggested the NRL was keeping money away from the players, a hidden pot of treasure, and that the players were entitled to see more of it.

Gallop responded by hiring the big room at the Crowne Plaza in Coogee and inviting every NRL player to come and watch as he opened the books. He would explain where the television money went, and why the players were being paid as much as the game could afford. From four hundred players a little more than thirty bothered to turn up.

Gallop showed them that NRL players received 26.2 per cent of the game's revenue while AFL players received 22 per cent. In other words, NRL players were better paid than AFL players according to the game's worth.

Gallop's job that day was to make the upcoming television deal worth enough so that he could make the club grant equal to the salary cap and ease the financial stress on every club. It was achieved when the new deal was announced in 2012. Politely, as all these complaints were being heard, not once did he mention to the players the millions of dollars that disappeared from the game when sponsors, tired of drunken incidents, walked away and took their money with them.

This argument about fairness and equal pay between codes is almost unique to rugby league. Some years later *Forbes* magazine released its annual top earners' list, with *Forbes*' Indian edition revealing cricket captain MS Dhoni earned $27.43 million in 2014. The US version claimed it was closer to $35 million. Against this, Australia's top earner, captain Michael Clarke, earned about $6 million. Yet not a peep came from the cricketing fraternity complaining their earnings weren't comparative to the Indian players when, essentially, they were playing the same game. Fact was, cricket was far more profitable in India. Indeed, about eighty cents in every dollar cricket generates worldwide comes out of India.

The game was paying what it could afford.

With Hunt leaving, other ideas were also considered to artificially raise the cap. Hunt was paid a fortune to sign with the AFL, part of his contract not included in the salary cap because it was exempt as a marketing payment. It was brilliant thinking, and never better shown than when, the following year, the AFL raided the NRL again and came away with Israel Folau for the code's second expansion club in the 2011 season, the Greater Western Sydney Giants.

While Hunt would have some success in his new code, Folau was a bust. Yet at the end of that second season, in 2012, GWS chief executive Dave Matthews revealed that 72 per cent of GWS jerseys sold in Western Sydney had Folau's number four on the back.

The AFL was playing the long game. Any suggestion that either Hunt (four seasons) or Folau (two seasons) were failures were strongly refuted by the AFL.

'I think it's been worthwhile,' Matthews told Malcolm Conn at the *Daily Telegraph*. 'Some of the ways to measure it are still to come. That is, the conversations Hunt and Folau have put us in across NSW and Queensland. We find a lot of players coming to our [GWS] academy and I'm sure Gold Coast are finding the same, young players from other sports who are trying our game. I've got no doubt Hunt has put us into conversations the game wouldn't have happened before. Only ten per cent of AFL players come from NSW and Queensland and it's not enough. In time Hunt and Folau will have stimulated a bit of interest.'

They more than paid for themselves.

'Their payments, and player payments in particular, were quite modest in comparison to the way they were used from a promotional point of view,' Matthews said. 'There is a lot of heavy lifting to build two new clubs.'

It was a line of thinking that, if the New Zealand Rugby Union did not directly pinch, they certainly mirrored.

In comparison to Folau and Hunt, Williams was a far safer bet to make the jump. In terms of publicity and marketing it was a no-brainer. It's a thought that would have horrified Sonny and Nasser under the terms of Sonny Ball, where they were fitting neatly into the 'system'.

For his part Williams' mind was on the World Cup after Henry's phone call. By now he was watching the Super Rugby competition back in the southern hemisphere and saw a brand of rugby far more familiar, and suitable, to what he knew.

Williams wanted a legitimate shot at the World Cup. He didn't want to be the stick to motivate players already in the side, brought back to sit on the sideline. The only assurance he sought was that if his form warranted it, he would be picked.

He was given that. Either way, the New Zealand Rugby Union knew he was going to be a marketing goldmine.

So Williams knocked back a reported $2 million a year to sign with the Crusaders. The NZRU deal was said to be worth $500,000 a season, a significant drop in what he could have earned in a third season at Toulon. What was crucial was under New Zealand Rugby Union rules, players needed to be playing domestically to be considered for the Rugby World Cup. What was crucial as far as Sonny Ball was concerned, Williams had it written into his contract that he was allowed to pursue several boxing fights each season. It was a take it or leave it ultimatum to the NZRU. The boxing pay-per-view would subsidise the shortfall in contract money.

He confirmed the deal, oddly, in another appearance on the *Footy Show* in June. Yes, that was Sonny in Australia for another fight on another 'KO to Drugs' campaign on a Mundine under-card. The announcement irked many people.

Here was Sonny, whose big news is to announce he is fighting on a boxing promotion, confirming he is leaving one rugby union team to take up a deal with another rugby union team and doing it all on a rugby league program on the game's official broadcaster. For a guy so happy to walk away from the game he was sure having a hard time staying away, and happy to use the game when it suited his purpose.

20

TRANSFORMATIONS

SONNY Bill Williams, the code breaker, became just the fourth player to be picked for the All Blacks before playing a Super Rugby game when the All Blacks chose him for the 2010 spring tour. We should never have had any doubt.

Williams returned to New Zealand after his second season at Toulon but not before first punctuating the change of seasons with a fight, this time against someone named Ryan Hogan, whom he beat by TKO in one in Brisbane. While he was having a little trouble putting them down he was having no trouble, it seemed, stopping them. Hogan was stopped without hitting the canvas.

Williams signed with the Crusaders shortly after. First they made him play for Belfast in the Christchurch local competition, a third-tier game, in what he knew was the start of his bid to prove his worth for the All Blacks. He did not need to look far. All Blacks assistant coach Wayne Smith drove to the game to watch him play, a high-ranking observer at a match that normally drew about a hundred spectators. Smith claimed he was going anyway, given it was his own club.

'Sonny's presence will add a bit of spice to the occasion,' Smith said, 'they're picking pretty big bar takings afterwards.'

About 4000 turned up.

A hamstring injury ruled him out for a month. He returned to play for Canterbury against Bay of Plenty on 3 September and, the following night, was on the third floor of his team hotel when the earth moved.

'I thought the roof was going to fall in. I just stayed in my bed buzzing out in shock. It's Mother Nature. You can't mess with that.'

Christchurch had suffered an earthquake, 7.1 on the Richter scale.

Shortly after arriving in New Zealand, Williams signed a sponsorship deal with Rebel sports stores. Days after the earthquake he was supposed to be at a photo shoot but could not get there. Transport lines were cut. So Rebel sent a helicopter.

Williams called his mum and told her he was flying and then came up with an idea. He asked his mum to walk outside and had the helicopter give her a flyover so he could wave out the side.

Six weeks later Williams was in the air again when New Zealand Rugby Union chairman Mike Eagle announced the thirty names to tour Hong Kong and Europe. Williams might have heard the announcement if the plane had departed on schedule but it was delayed and when he got off his phone lit up.

'As soon as I turned my phone on about twenty messages popped up,' he said. 'The first one was from the old lady and she was pretty happy. I think when I first went to rugby I had a lot of self doubts, thinking I don't know if I can make it or not, and it's all turned out really good. I'm just trying to soak it up at the moment.'

Once again Williams was going through a transformation. He is brilliant at adapting to the environment around him, or at least appearing to. His great joy living in France was the anonymity it provided him. He seemed to mention it in every interview he did with media back in Australia.

Now he was back in New Zealand and the opposite was making him happy.

'The big thing for me coming back here was the amount of support I've got from the public,' he said. 'Not just in Canterbury, but going to places like Whangarei and Southland and little kids coming up to me knowing my name. That's really helped my self-confidence and as a person to grow. I'm happy with picking Canterbury to go to . . . and I think it has paid dividends to get into that system straight away. I've really taken to the boys and hopefully they've taken to myself, too.'

His on-field game was changing, too. He played just seven games with Canterbury in the National Provincial Championship, the level below Super Rugby, and worked hard with coach Rob Penney to develop his game. Particularly his great weapon, the offload.

'I made it a point when I came back here that I really wanted to work on the distribution part of my game because when you watch players like Ma'a Nonu, who's the best midfielder in New Zealand . . . you see that he can break a tackle, he can put players into gaps and that's what I wanted to add to my game.'

Williams was not the only one going through a transformation. The All Blacks were in the midst of making themselves the greatest team in world sport. Their transformation began seven years earlier after Australia eliminated them in the World Cup and Wallabies skipper George Gregan, his tongue dipped in acid, taunted them.

'Four more years.' For all their dominance between World Cups the All Blacks had become chokers on the big stage. Besides winning the inaugural Rugby World Cup in 1987 and despite going into almost every World Cup since as favourites they had yet to win again. Australia, meanwhile, won in 1991 and 1999 while South Africa trounced the All Blacks in the 1995 final, despite the All Blacks being overwhelming favourites.

After the 2003 disappointment the All Blacks management went away and realised they needed to change their approach to football. They were not the first organisation to experience this, despite their success. It was realised early that the All Blacks, who over one hundred years of Test match rugby had won an extraordinary 75 per cent of all games played, were focusing on results ahead of the process, which inevitably was costing them. They were getting ahead of themselves without even realising.

Rather than being driven by results, the All Blacks dug down to what they believed they ultimately stood for and realised it was values. What did the jersey mean to them? How did they want to leave the jersey when they retired? It became all about that black jersey.

Their job, they realised, was to leave the jumper in a better place than when they arrived.

It was a commitment some felt more strongly than others.

It was why incidents such as this happened one particular afternoon, when the All Blacks were gathered for a team meeting. There was nothing unusual about this one. The coaches spoke and the players sat, as they do, and the big lock Brad Thorn taking note after note like he always did. Thorn loved to take notes. It was understandable. Like Williams, he crossed from rugby league to rugby union, his whole life about finding something new. It is fair to say Thorn is the most successful cross-code player ever. In rugby league he won three premierships with Brisbane and played eight State of Origin games for Queensland and three Tests for Australia. He switched to rugby and in 2001 won a National Provincial Championship with Canterbury before he withdrew from the All Blacks European tour because he did not believe he merited selection, that his selection was more about public relations. Thorn wanted to earn everything he got in life. He was wary his profile as a league crossover received as much consideration as his performance. Two years later he finally gained selection and, believing he was playing well enough to merit selection, played in the 2003 World Cup, playing twelve Tests that year and also winning the Tri-Nations Series.

He went back to rugby league and the Brisbane Broncos in 2005, winning another premiership in 2006 and playing Origin again that first season. He then went back to rugby and won the Super Rugby title with the Crusaders in 2008.

Wherever Brad Thorn played, he won.

So as Thorn sat taking notes and the coaches were talking the room fell strangely silent. They were shocked at the sight of the strong thick wrist Thorn was thrusting in the air.

'Coach? Can I say something?'

Thorn had never said a word in a team meeting. The respect he carried among the group was clear. Whatever he wanted to say now it sure must be important.

'Sure,' came the reply.

At that, Thorn stood and turned and grabbed the throat of a young half and picked him up out of his chair, the strength through his shoulders such that the player was up on the balls of his feet struggling for balance.

'I am fucking sick of you embarrassing me,' he said. 'Do it again . . .'

He then put his teammate down and sat back in his chair.

'Sorry, coach.'

The room sat in shocked silence, but Thorn's message was clear: embarrass yourself and you embarrass the All Blacks jersey. Embarrass the All Blacks jersey and you embarrass me. The player had been playing up on the drink.

In some ways, this culture was perfect for Williams. Since their 2003 World Cup loss the All Blacks had found a way to turn the intangibles into something measurable. Williams' way was thorough preparation: he got to training earlier, stretched longer, worked on extra skill drills after training.

Sonny's first tour with the All Blacks began with a Bledisloe Cup Test against the Wallabies in Hong Kong, the fourth of the year and a money-spinner for the Australian and New Zealand Rugby Union. The large expat community guaranteed both nations would be counting the dollars for some time.

The All Blacks failed to make the same mistake others had: Khoder Nasser was invited to attend the announcement and travelled to Hong Kong for the game where he was openly welcome.

Williams failed to play, though. Whether he would have been picked only coach Graham Henry knows, but Williams was quietly ruled out several days before the Test when he got off the flight to Hong Kong with great pain in his legs. The leg soon swelled and when Williams pressed on the swelling it reacted like playdough.

That's not good, he thought to himself. A team official took him to a Hong Kong hospital. Doctors feared it was a blood clot and told him that if tests confirmed it he would be unable to fly for six weeks, ending his European tour before it properly began. It was the same leg he broke in France. Tests eventually cleared him of a clot, however concerned doctors told him he was susceptible to deep vein thrombosis. Playing the Wallabies would be a bad idea. The good news was, he was able to fly with the team to England.

Williams said nothing of the injury publicly.

Days before the Test coach Graham Henry announced the team and subtly indicated Williams would have to earn his way into the Test side. Conrad Smith remained the preferred outside centre. Henry said the Test was 'a thank you for what the players have done this year'.

For reasons nobody can explain and no doubt everybody would like to review, the only positive many could find in New Zealand's performance was the potential of Williams to improve them. With the 2011 Rugby World Cup now less than a year away many commentators saw great wear and tear in the All Blacks and were already predicting they were wobbling ahead of the big tournament.

Perhaps the experts were looking for it.

He was impressing his teammates, learning as much as possible from them. He struck up a particularly strong friendship with the dynamic Ma'a Nonu, a monster inside centre who held the position Williams ultimately coveted.

'Ma'a's really taken me under his wing on the finer points of what we're trying to achieve as All Blacks,' he said. 'From the outside coming in I was probably a bit anxious to see what the boys were like. Everyone's been great, you ask a question you get ten answers.'

Williams flourished under the fresh attitude of his teammates.

'I've never experienced anything like this before,' he said while training ahead of the Test against England at Twickenham. He had no idea at the time, but Henry was about to name him in the starting side.

'The biggest difference to when I played at the top level in league is here you notice how different the games are. League's a pretty simple game. In rugby there a whole lot of set-piece, scrums, back moves and such to cover. It's been a big learning curve. I just try and be like a sponge. Hopefully, I get my shot soon. It's just like school. I go home, get that notepad out and jot things down. Last week was pretty tough, it was like a teething process. At the moment I'm feeling pretty confident with all the moves and what we're trying to achieve on the field.'

Williams was one of four changes made to the side beaten by Australia in Hong Kong when they called his name out to play England. Smith, nursing a tight hamstring, was rested.

It had begun. Sonny was coming. He had earned his first Test jersey.

The Test was played before 81,000 people at one of the great football grounds in the world. New Zealand won 26–16 after repelling a strong England fightback but, after the game, Williams was disappointed. Personally he had not played well. A couple of errors saw his head drop before Nonu, in his 54th Test, quickly told him to get his head back in the game.

'I was disappointed in my own performance and there are a lot of things I can improve on,' he said. 'But it is just like when I came back and started in New Zealand; hopefully it will be like a snowball effect where I get a bit more game time and express myself a lot more.'

Henry was unsure whether to retain him for the next Test against Scotland or bring back Smith. He eventually stayed with Williams.

Williams excelled against the lesser opposition of Scotland, just one rung below the top-tier nations. They won 49–3 and were continually opened up by Williams falling in a tackle and flipping the ball on. Few watching believed he could turn in such a man-of-the-match performance in just his second Test. You got the feeling his performance even surprised Henry and his staff. Certainly, you got the feeling they finally realised what kind of footballer they had.

'He has got an amazing ability to offload the ball in the tackle,' Henry said after the game. 'I don't think I've ever seen any rugby player with that sort of skill before. I think he'll get more confident and even go to a higher standard in future.'

Williams knew he had played to his strength.

'I guess it comes from my league days, it's natural to me,' he said. 'But I wouldn't be able to do that unless players were running the right lines off me. The great players I'm surrounded by makes it easier.'

He was not only doing all the right things, he was saying them as well. The All Blacks dominated the European tour as expected and, with the World Cup looming, were putting themselves in position to finally deliver.

21

IN THE RING

THE new year of 2011 began the normal way, by now, with a comfortable win in the boxing ring. Scott Lewis was a Campbelltown forklift driver whose most famous win was a TKO stoppage against NRL player Carl Webb a year earlier. Webb was a champion amateur boxer in his youth, and was regarded as the most educated boxer in the NRL, so the loss came as some shock. After witnessing the way Sonny Ball had added so magnificently to Williams' bank account Webb looked to do a little moonlighting himself.

It all came unstuck for Webb around the time he waited for the bell to ring to signal the end of the first two-minute round. He discovered then, much too late, it was a three-minute round. By the time the referee waved it away in the third he was punching on memory. You could have tied a thousand dollars to the top rope and he couldn't have raised his arms high enough to claim it.

It was a timely reminder that Sonny Ball is a two-part deal. There is the opportunity, and there is delivering on it. And there was the difference.

In many ways what Lewis showed against Webb proved he was perfect for Williams. When you cut away the hype of the win, what was left was a man willing and game, but hardly a boxer in some classical sense. In other words, for someone with such physical advantage like Williams, the only thing easier than winning the fight was selling it. Lewis was somehow built into some genuine threat following his win over Webb

At least the public thought so.

The one small concern in Sonny's game plan was Mundine's shock loss to Garth Wood seven weeks earlier. For months Mundine had resisted fighting Wood, privately concerned he was not up to it. He even offered Wood payment to not take the fight, wondering how he could ever sell it. But Wood was a fighter first, and held grimly to a contract that said that, as the winner of the television reality show *The Contender*, he had the right to fight Mundine. With Wood refusing to budge Mundine was finally forced into the ring. Wood knocked him out in the fifth.

Williams had returned from the All Blacks tour by then to be ringside. As he prepared for Lewis he kept the memory of Mundine's loss fresh to spur him on in training. His leg injury was still hampering him somewhat, and while he could move around a boxing ring he found there was pain in his leg whenever he tried to stretch out while running.

'The way he conducted himself [after the loss] pushed me,' Williams said of Mundine, telling AAP. 'I would have no one else but him in my corner because we feed off each other. Choc [Mundine] and I are the same. People are always saying we can't do this and can't do that, but we want to be the best and that's what drives us.'

Williams believed boxing made him play better football. It sharpened him. 'The last couple of years I have played my best rugby – that's due to the fact that I have done boxing,' he said.

Once again we see how Williams, when he commits, puts himself wholly into it. The moment he signed for the fight he started training twice a day in the gym, doing nothing but boxing training. He trained six days a week, sparring on alternate days against the likes of rising Australian prospect David Aloua and the New Zealand kick-boxing champion, Russian-born Alexey Ignashov. He even trained Christmas day. He did not go near a football or a barbell.

Days before the fight Queensland Reds number ten Quade Cooper told his management, IMG, that he was leaving the company when his contract expired in April. He linked with Khoder Nasser.

Cooper fit perfectly within the rules of Sonny Ball. He was a rare talent, currently the hottest name in Australian rugby, and he was agitating for more. It was clear the Australian Rugby Union was on notice. And so they should have been. Days after Cooper linked with Nasser in April the manager was talking about taking him to the NRL.

Williams went six rounds against Lewis and won every round. Lewis had a strong chin and not enough of anything else. This is not as ideal as it sounds in boxing. Too many fighters who go through too many fights this way invariably end up drawing ducks on the wall and feeding them, such is the damage. While no doubt game-chasing Williams throughout the fight, Lewis lacked the big weapon and the required fitness to put Sonny under any great stress.

After the fight Sonny spoke about becoming a professional fighter. 'A lot of people didn't want to give this fight credibility but I wanted to respect the sport,' he told AAP. 'I think I really showed that I respect the sport and it was a good fight. Hopefully I gave the crowd what they wanted.'

Certainly it earned plenty of money. While his previous two fights were on Mundine undercards, broadcast on pay-per-view around Australia, his return to New Zealand rugby opened the New Zealand pay-per-view market. While a much smaller market than the Australian pay-per-view audience it was a wonderful little bonus. Excited by their new toy, New Zealand fans delivered more dollars than the Australian market.

Certainly his trainer, Tony Mundine, wanted him to consider retiring from football to concentrate on boxing fulltime. 'I said to him in twelve months' time he could be the second [Muhammad] Ali. He could be anything,' Mundine told AAP after the fight. 'I saw him about twelve months ago. I really thought he moved like Ali. He needs more fights . . . If he keeps on boxing seriously, he will be the second Ali.'

Old Tony was identifying Williams' natural potential and it is possible to say, without being locked away forever, that few, if anybody, possessed more.

But the next Ali? Perhaps most impressive of all, Williams had no idea what he was doing and yet he was still delivering. His combinations were all wrong, for instance. He would throw a straight right hand followed by a left hook. It was backwards. The straight right is a long punch, thrown from distance. The hook is a short punch, delivered close. As anybody knows, if the right hand lands then his opponent can't possibly still be there for the left hook. Turn them around, though, and it is music.

While comparisons to Muhammad Ali looked a little ambitious, with a little imagination that was enough to see what had Tony Mundine excited.

TWO days after the fight Williams reported for training with the Crusaders and once again his commitment was whole. Straightaway the Crusaders ordered him to strip five kilograms from the 108-kilogram frame he carried into the ring. As everybody else was wondering whether he could make it as a professional fighter in the wake of Tony Mundine's comments, he declared he was not going to let boxing interfere with his World Cup dream.

'I can have another fight if I wish during the season – it is in my contract – but if I feel that it is going to jeopardise my playing ability in any way I won't do it because rugby is first right now,' he told the *Sydney Morning Herald*. 'But if it doesn't, if it feels like it would give me that kick which I feel right now – I feel mentally strong and I could play eighty minutes easy of footy after that – then I will do it for sure. It is back to rugby now. I'll have to train hard and change focus but that is all right. I don't like to be idle, I just like to work hard and I can't wait to get stuck into it.'

First he needed to get his leg right. It was still worrying him. X-rays revealed the injury was improving but it was line-ball whether he would be ready for the first game in three weeks.

Ultimately he missed the first two games, eventually making his Super Rugby debut in round three against the NSW Waratahs. By then, small things like leg injuries hardly seemed to matter.

Before the second game the Crusaders finished a training run at Rugby Park and headed to the showers. Sonny was in the pool, the weight off his leg. Then the ground began to shake. Players in the showers grabbed towels and ran to the field. Suddenly waves formed in the pool.

'The kids, the kids,' somebody started yelling. Williams looked. He could not see the kids behind the waves.

Williams jumped from the pool, saying, 'I ended up getting out of the pool pretty quickly.'

It was confusing and frightening, but eventually everybody made it safely out.

Upstairs in the office Crusaders media manager Patrick McKendry was on the phone when the force of the quake threw him to the floor.

'I looked up and saw [coach] Todd Blackadder with a shocked look on his face and I knew it was pretty serious,' McKendry said.

The earthquake was 6.3 on the Richter scale, smaller than the September quake, but its centre was closer to Christchurch and the fallout was far more devastating.

Williams had no idea how serious things were until later when he went into the city. 'It was like a scene out of a movie,' he told the *Herald*. 'I was with a mate and we went down to the cinema to find his wife and kids and there was just devastation everywhere. They're saying there is about sixty-five people dead, but from what I saw it is going to be a lot more than that.'

Williams immediately panicked for his sister, staying with him while she studied in Christchurch. Phone lines were down so he was unable to make contact. All the mobile-phone junctions were also knocked out. That night he slept at a friend's place, his apartment too damaged to enter.

Anxiety filled him. 'It was pretty scary because she was studying in town, and one of the first things I saw when I came out of the pools was the PPG building and it had just collapsed,' he said. 'It was just that feeling you get where you cannot get through because all of the phones are down, it's a yuck feeling, a feeling you don't ever want to feel. Some people had the same feeling, but it didn't come right for them. They never get to see their friends and family again.

'It really puts things into perspective and you really understand the thing that we do is just a game and there is more to life than that.'

The earthquake killed 185 people and changed the city forever. It would underscore the Crusaders' entire season. With their city in repair, and AMI Stadium damaged, the Crusaders moved their early home games to Nelson, some 130 kilometres away, as a stop-gap. The earthquake devastated Christchurch to the point that, with the Rugby World Cup just seven months away, the city was removed as a venue, given the damage.

Williams debuted for the Crusaders at their first home game after the earthquake. It was an emotional trip to Trafalgar Park, Nelson. And the funny thing about Sonny is that even when he was not trying he had a thing for moments. Against the Waratahs he was everything they believed he would be. Raw and dangerous. The Waratahs had no answer for his offload. He had plenty of whack in defence. He busted holes in the defence with his running. He scored a try.

He was also in the ideal team to fast-track his talent. The Crusaders were full of All Black talent, including some of the greats like skipper Richie McCaw, number ten Dan Carter and lock Brad Thorn, by now so big a part of the All Blacks mentality.

Week after week, Williams earned the plaudits coming his way. Another try in his second game but, more importantly, a performance where he manhandled the ACT Brumbies. It came with the trademark play: a one-handed offload to put Sean Maitland over for a try. He was proving the real deal.

The Crusaders were nomads in 2011. After beating the Highlanders in the round five game in Dunedin the Crusaders travelled to England for a special match against the Sharks. Money raised supported the Red Cross Earthquake Appeal. In the first 30 hours some 30,000 tickets were sold. The Crusaders were becoming everybody's second team, their sentimental favourites. With England fans getting a chance to witness their very own Super Rugby game – a game some sneered at as little more than 'candyfloss' footy because it did not follow the dour, ten-man rugby style popular in the northern hemisphere that is oh so boring – Williams took advantage of a directive from All Blacks coach Graham Henry to run the ball more and cut loose. The Crusaders won 44–28, and Williams starred. Stick that in your ten-man rugby.

In Australia the Queensland Reds were putting together their own great season. The Reds had never won the Super Rugby title. Under coach Ewen McKenzie, back from France, and behind the rare skill of Quade Cooper the Reds were putting together some season. In a part of the world where fairytales are lived every day, two were coming together at once.

Shortly before heading to England for the Sharks game Williams announced he would fight again in June. It was an extraordinary commitment. The Crusaders had the bye the week before the fight, giving him seven days to switch from rugby player to boxer, but would play the Blues just five days after. The Super Rugby finals would start just a fortnight later and last three weeks, with the All Blacks then set to start their final preparations for the World Cup, with a Bledisloe Cup series against the Wallabies to start a fortnight after that.

With each new move Sonny was winning back the public. Those he had yet to win back, anyway. Already a vast majority had chosen to forgive his walkout on the Bulldogs as they marvelled at each new accomplishment.

Williams was working hard on himself. He donated $100,000 from the fight to the earthquake victims while broadcaster Sky committed to donating all profits from the fights to the earthquake appeal.

When the Crusaders travelled to South Africa in May, Williams' first trip there, one website compared the hype to when Jonah Lomu landed in South Africa sixteen years earlier.

Crusaders' backs coach Daryl Gibson witnessed as much, saying, 'They are saying it's Sonny versus the Stormers – that's the impact he is having on this competition.'

The match sold out in Cape Town, a crowd 50,000 strong. The 20–14 win marked the Crusaders as the team to beat. A one-handed offload from Williams set up a try for prop Wyatt Crockett and the Crusaders went on with it from there. The thing about the win was not just that they were playing away, but that they were without All Blacks Richie McCaw, Dan Carter, Brad Thorn, Andy Ellis, Sam Whitelock and Ben Franks and then, during the game, lost Israel Dagg, Sean Maitland, Kahn Fotuali'i and Adam Whitelock.

When Williams finally announced his opponent for the 5 June fight all concerns about his welfare and how he would get through such a hectic time and remain in one piece were quickly allayed.

Alipate Liava'a was a 43-year-old gospel singer who stood twenty-one centimetres shorter than Williams but, in more positive news, enjoyed a significant weight advantage over him. Everybody who saw him immediately thought the same thing: he would make a wonderful Buddha.

'He's a tall guy and, what, I'm too short?' Liava'a said when queried about their height difference. He appeared offended. It was a terrible mismatch. Liava'a looked like you could pop him with a sharp elbow. All Sonny's talk about respecting the sport appeared little more than tokenism when anything more than a casual look was thrown over Liava'a. His record was 4–7 and Williams seemed to be catching him at the right time, on the end of a seven-fight losing streak. His last win was against a fighter having his one and only fight.

It got worse the week of the fight when it was revealed Liava'a was under investigation for claiming sickness benefits. He had tennis elbow and was unable to work. Some wondered how he could be well enough to fight if he was not well enough to work.

'It's very bad but it's good enough to hit somebody,' Liava'a explained to a New Zealand TV reporter, clearing that up. 'It's not a hundred per cent but don't tell Sonny Bill.'

The happiest man of all was All Blacks coach Graham Henry. There was minimal fear Williams would get hurt and without such fights Williams would not be also preparing to head into a World Cup with the All Blacks.

'He wouldn't be in New Zealand unless he could box,' Henry said. He was being queried about the fight, and why the New Zealand Rugby Union was so willing to let Williams get in the ring. 'He can play rugby for bugger all and boxing makes up for the contract.'

Now you see how it all begins to make sense. While Williams was donating $100,000 to the earthquake fund, and admirably so, he was earning about $200,000 each time he stepped into the ring, according to those in the industry. His contract allowed him up to three fights a year and the soft fights subsidised his rugby wage. Everyone came out a winner except, perhaps, the sport of boxing.

None of the giggling about Liava'a mattered anyway. Nobody was buying it to see a real fight. They were buying to gaze on Sonny. Of more concern when the fight was over, certainly more than Sonny winning in six without losing a round and Liava'a going home to ice his elbow, was how Sonny was unable to stop him earlier. It had some questioning whether the talent matched the hype. Nobody wondered out loud how Ali might do against Liava'a.

EVEN before he got to play in the finals with the Crusaders speculation began about where Williams would play the following season. Reports surfaced he was concerned at living in Christchurch after the earthquake. Some believed the Waikato Chiefs or Auckland Blues stood a good chance of securing him given they were in the North Island and it would put him closer to his mum. As some suggested both league and union clubs around the world were also interested; Nasser said the New Zealand Rugby Union was in the box seat to sign him. That only secured him to playing Super Rugby, though, and not who for, which gave both Auckland and Waikato a shot.

Then a day before the Crusaders beat the Stormers in Cape Town news broke that Williams had signed with Waikato Chiefs, the deal not to be announced until after the final the following week. Williams was joining All Blacks assistant coach Wayne Smith. Smith was quitting after the Rugby World Cup to become the Chiefs' assistant coach.

Little was said of it the week of the final. Most interest centred on Cinderella and her twin. Who was who depended entirely on where you came from. One was the Reds, finishing minor premiers and about to claim their first Super Rugby title after playing the most exciting brand of rugby all season. The other, more sentimental, pick was the Crusaders. They did nothing more than pick up a devastated city and, playing every game on the road, raised spirits as they overcame all to reach the final. When it was tallied up, the Crusaders had travelled more than 100,000 kilometres that season.

'You get a choice,' skipper Richie McCaw said. 'You can use it as an excuse or you can decide not to. I'm really proud of the way the guys all year haven't used travel as an excuse. We made a decision when all the carnage happened at home we wanted to stand up for the people at home and what the Crusaders meant.'

Williams had other things on his mind, though.

The Crusaders arrived in Brisbane early. It was a big week for the city. Bigger than the Super Rugby final on Saturday, Brisbane was hosting the third and deciding game in State of Origin which, if that wasn't big enough, also doubled as captain Darren Lockyer's final Origin game. Lockyer was as big as it got in rugby league. He was twice a Golden Boot winner as the world's best player, had played in three Brisbane premierships and captained them to another. He had played more games than any NRL player, more Origin games than any player and more Tests than anybody had played for Australia. They named a highway in Queensland after him.

So amid all this Channel Nine came up with a decision many thought was odd, and some were outright angry about, deciding to interview Williams, the code-breaker, at half time in the Origin game. As a little aside, Nine had the Rugby World Cup rights and was looking to capitalise on a little cross promotion. So there he stood, wearing a Queensland scarf of all things, talking up a rival code on what was rugby league's showpiece event.

Do not feel too sorry for rugby league here. The game continually allows itself to be treated like the ugly stepchild. Just a year earlier Israel Folau followed Karmichael Hunt into the AFL and despite the fact he signed midway through the NRL season, and would from that moment on be a pawn in the AFL's marketing strategies, Queensland still picked Folau in its Origin team. And the NRL allowed it to happen. So why should the game be upset about Sonny turning up at Origin?

Certainly Channel Nine boss David Gyngell was happy. 'I'm a big Sonny Bill fan,' he said, defending the network's decision even though there really was no need. Nine was broadcaster of both Origin and the coming World Cup so commercially it was sound. 'He is the most famous player in the world at the moment who has played both football codes. He is iconic in both sports and when we learned he was at the game we knew it was a good opportunity to use him. I don't know the details of why he left rugby league, but he's an ornament to the game he is playing now.'

Learned he was at the game? He watched the game from Channel Nine's private box, sitting next to Dan Carter. NRL boss David Gallop had no idea it was happening and it is fair to say that if Gallop had a machine gun with him he was better than even money to have used it that night. But why wouldn't Nine have thought it a good idea given the way the NRL so often allowed itself to be treated?

'We have raised our disappointment about it with senior Nine people as soon as it went to air last night,' Gallop said. 'It's not what we want to be talking about during a record-breaking night for the game, but trying to be on our stage is a form of flattery. I've raised it with Gyng today and he understands our view.'

Didn't mean Gyngell cared.

Nasser defended Sonny's choice to wear a Queensland scarf by saying he once played with Queensland halfback Johnathan Thurston while fellow Queenslanders Greg Inglis and Justin Hodges had watched his fights in Queensland. Forget the little matter of Sonny having actually played for NSW as a junior. Loyalty, remember, lost importance long ago.

'It's obviously designed to cross-promote the forthcoming rugby coverage, but I have no doubt genuine rugby fans would be filthy to see SBW using our game's biggest stage to promote himself,' said Todd Greenberg.

In the end, Queensland won the Origin game and the travel got the Crusaders. After leading 7–6 at half time Brad Thorn had a try disallowed before they pushed it out to 10–6 following a Carter penalty goal. The scores eventually got levelled at 13–13 before Will Genia took advantage of a tiring defence in broken play and scored the match winner on one of those long, wonderful runs he did so well.

BECAUSE of the looming Rugby World Cup the Bledisloe Cup was played over just two Tests in 2011. The All Blacks had two more Tests against South Africa. Effectively, they were warm-up games.

And they were nearly the end of Sonny Bill Williams as a rugby player.

Williams made his Test debut on home soil against South Africa on 30 July, coming off the bench late in a performance where he appeared oddly nervous. At one point he tried to do up his laces as a scrum was packing down. Then he lost the ball in a tackle, turning it over. In what was a comprehensive 40–7 All Blacks win, the turnover was one of the few chances the Springboks got.

Still, all this before he ended it in trademark way, a one-handed offload that led to a try.

For the first Bledisloe Cup Test against Australia coach Graham Henry picked as close to a full-strength line-up as he could. Henry, if you had given him the choice, would have been more than happy to send this fifteen on as his starting line-up in any World Cup final. Like he had against South Africa, Henry went with Ma'a Nonu and Conrad Smith as his centre combination.

Henry was banking on experience to get the All Blacks through the World Cup. It was his best chance against years of underperformance and the near overwhelming expectation they faced as they played this World Cup on home turf. Everybody expected them to win, simple as that. So Henry picked what was the oldest Test side in the history of the All Blacks. It was not the risk it might seem. When Clive Woodward won the 2003 World Cup with England his side was at times ridiculed for their advanced age. Grumpy Old Men, Dad's Army – they got all of that. Their combined age was 423 years but in such advanced years Woodward knew he had a squad that found a purpose. They were two things: they were battle-hardened and aware this was not only their best chance but, for many, their last. Such things motivate and then some.

Combined, this All Blacks side was ten years older than Woodward's England. More significantly, they had more Test caps than any side in history. This was a team ready to win. Over a hundred years of Test-match football the All Blacks have shown themselves to not only be the best rugby nation in the world but one of the best teams of any sport. You know this by looking in the win–loss column. Over those hundred years the All Blacks have won more than 75 per cent of all their Tests. If there is another international team anywhere that can better this they are well hidden.

Whether this formed any part of Williams' or Khoder Nasser's considerations is doubtful. Certainly Williams was unhappy at how he was being treated. After Henry again decided to give him just a few minutes towards the end of the Test against Australia, a 30–14 win in Auckland that retained the Bledisloe Cup, Williams was in no mood to celebrate with teammates.

He headed back to the hotel where Nasser was staying with Anthony Mundine and Quade Cooper. Williams turned up, still in his socks and shorts. That was as good an indication as any at how angry he was.

'Fuck him, bro,' Mundine said. He was talking about the coach, Henry. 'Let's get on a plane. Let's go shopping in LA.

You need some new clothes. He's got the world's best player in his team and he leaves him on the bench. Who the fuck does he think he is?'

Mundine pulled out his mobile phone. 'I'll book the tickets now, bro, we can be on a plane in the morning.'

Nobody, it seemed, was doing anything to calm Williams. Or Mundine, for that matter.

Williams felt used. His one stipulation when he returned to New Zealand was that he would be picked if his form warranted it. Most agreed he was the standout inside centre during the Super Rugby season and yet Henry decided to go with Ma'a Nonu against South Africa and Australia.

The easy thing to consider here is what would have become of him if he had got on that plane. Having walked out on the NRL team that developed him and then the rugby team considered the pinnacle of the sport, would there be anywhere left to go?

The answer is of course. Somebody was always willing to pay.

Williams would later admit he felt 'lied to'. His Super Rugby form warranted selection. That Henry preferred to remain loyal was, apparently, less important, or that he believed players like Nonu provided more flexibility, as he said, also did not seem to matter. Sonny always tried so hard to stay true to the core values of the team. This was one of the few times the mask slipped.

And it nearly fell apart.

With the Super Rugby season over and the World Cup looming Williams was on the verge of re-signing with the New Zealand Rugby Union for another season, where he had already agreed to join Waikato if the deal with the NZRU could be done. By now Sonny was no longer feeling the love, much like his crew had complained about in his last year at the Bulldogs. When the NZRU rejected a private sponsorship agreement the noise grew. Williams had done a deal with a

South Pacific Brands energy drink that was a direct competitor to All Blacks' sponsor Coca-Cola Amatil.

The Coca-Cola deal called for at least three All Blacks to be seen in imagery used in marketing. It seems no big deal. Yet reports in New Zealand raised fears the fallout between Nasser and the NZRU over the deal would see Williams leave the code. This marked some change from just twelve months earlier when Nasser all but dismissed commercial endorsements. Such deals, you might remember he told the *Good Weekend*, 'means that you are licking the arse of some corporation'. Williams was estimated to be earning $2 million a season in New Zealand after also signing personal sponsorship deals with the Rebel sports store chain and Adidas at the start of the year. Eventually a deal, facilitated by the NZRU, was reached where Coca-Cola Amatil agreed to use Williams alone, as the face of Powerade, which it also owned. Around this time I was in Melbourne for the Melbourne Storm–Newcastle Knights semifinal when I got a tip that the NRL's Sydney Roosters had signed Williams. This is always wonderful news to take delivery of when you are working against a deadline, even if this one sounded a little hard to believe.

'Not for next year,' I was told. 'For 2013. It's done.'

That made more sense. Under the terms of his deed of release with the Bulldogs Williams was not allowed back until then.

I called the sports editor Ben English from outside the press box and told him it was a big one if I could stand it up. The hard part was to come. I called Roosters chairman Nick Politis and got an international dial tone. Wherever he was in the world, I woke him.

He denied it. 'Haven't spoken to him,' he said.

I asked a dozen different ways if a deal might have been done – club officials like to say they haven't spoken to a player, for instance, because they know the truth is they have done a deal with the manager so technically they did not speak to that player – but Politis gave the same answer to all dozen.

'We haven't signed Sonny Bill Williams.'

And he hadn't agreed, either. Sometimes they will say the player hasn't signed a contract when they know they have got the player to sign a letter of intent or shaken hands on the terms but are yet to sign a document. It all means the same except in the literal sense, but allows them to bend the truth a little.

Politis' denial was so strong it left no story.

Thinking about it later that night I put it down to the games being played with the New Zealand Rugby Union. Privately, whispers emerged that Williams' non-selection for the All Blacks was 'agenda driven'. Just thirteen days before the World Cup Mundine had tweeted to Williams: 'Bra the more I think of this bullshit the more I think I gotta get yu out of that environment'.

The tone was set for the World Cup. For a man driven by achievement like he was, his limited role in New Zealand's World Cup did not sit well.

New Zealand would win the World Cup but Williams' input was minimal. He started the first game against Tonga and then played on the wing against Japan. In the final pool game against the only true threat in their group, France, he was named on the bench. It was where he remained as the All Blacks got serious about the job of winning a World Cup they could not lose. Against Australia in the semifinal Williams tried to involve himself in a fun way by spending much of the week texting Quade Cooper, the Wallabies number ten. Then he came on in the final moments and lasted just a little while before being sin-binned for an illegal shoulder charge. On Cooper.

He did not feel part of it. In some ways it was a little like his NRL grand final where he won himself a premiership ring but came off the bench to get it and believed that most of the heavy lifting had been done by others. Sonny liked to do his own lifting.

He was an unusual problem for the New Zealand Rugby Union. Every World Cup throws up a cult figure. At the previous World Cup it was France's Sébastien Chabal, nicknamed The Caveman, and you can bet he filled every square inch of that nickname. Even as Williams struggled to force his way into the team he remained the most popular player at this World Cup when it kicked off on 9 September.

At one point the NZRU emailed 120 of the worst affected families of the Christchurch earthquake to attend a private training session with the team.

'To begin with I thought, is this genuine? But it was so low key and beautifully written that eventually I thought it must be real,' said Crystal Monroe, whose brother and sister-in-law were travelling on a bus that was crushed by a falling building, orphaning their children. 'We've been so beautifully treated, with such respect. It's just been very nice.'

Many there had lost children in the tragedy. And all the All Blacks players were there, comforting the families and chatting to them and helping them laugh, but one remained a standout, signing autographs and continually handed babies to be photographed with or asked to stand next to children.

It was Sonny.

22

THE MACHINE ROLLS ON

HERE, now, Sonny Bill Williams becomes once and for all the hired gun.

His résumé is thick with achievement. Williams has helped the Crusaders to a Super Rugby final and the All Blacks to their first World Cup since 1987 and his reputation is that wherever he goes he improves them. Not just on the playing field, either. The marketing department think he is a wonderful addition to the organisation. Yet even as he prepares to play his first game at the Waikato Chiefs, and even with another fight coming up, he is seen having lunch at Circular Quay with Khoder Nasser and Sydney Roosters chairman Nick Politis and former Roosters board member David Gyngell.

Politis is the big guy. And, more importantly than being a former board member, Gyngell is the boss of Channel Nine, which makes him almost equally as big. As the game's free-to-air broadcaster Gyngell can make a deal with Sonny that is not part of the salary cap under the NRL's third-party agreement, just like Nine did with Andrew Johns seven years earlier. You don't need to ponder this long to understand what a terrific advantage that must be if a club can convince Gyngell to invest. He just needed to see a return, which Sonny brought by the barrow. The Roosters need to do a little less convincing than others.

So even before he plays a game for the Chiefs there is evidence Williams is already planning to return to the NRL in 2013 when his deed of release with Canterbury expires. Andrew Webster reported that Williams was unhappy with the way the All Blacks treated him his first season, playing him off the bench when he felt he deserved a starting position. A day earlier Matthew Johns said on his morning radio program, 'From what I hear, one hundred per cent he'll be at the Roosters; there is only the details about his boxing career to sort out.'

Williams denied any interest in returning to the NRL.

'I've signed nothing, for the record,' Williams told James Hooper at the *Sunday Telegraph*. 'I've been sponsored by the Channel Nine network for about five years now, so I go way back with them. I've known Nick since I was seventeen or eighteen and he's always wanted to get me to go to the Roosters. We always seem to have a good laugh about it. I had organised to go to breakfast with Dave Gyngell and he's good mates with Nick, and Nick wanted to come. He was saying to me, "come back to league", and I was telling him, "I'm happy where I am". Everyone can have their opinion about everything, but for me right now, I'm concentrating on this fight. If I start worrying about anything else or let anything affect me, this big fella's going to knock my head off.'

Again Williams was showing his tremendous experience with the media, throwing off interest, deflecting the conversation to his upcoming fight. He is a lesson for every professional athlete on how to handle the media.

He said he was in Sydney to continue training with Tony Mundine even as newspaper reports said he has told friends he wants to return to Sydney. So much of the truth of Sonny is revealed in gossip columns.

The Roosters also denied Williams was headed their way in 2013 and sent out a press release saying it. It meant nothing. There was no way any deal could have or would have been formally done at their lunch, legitimising the formal denial, but deals are never done this way. As we have seen, boxing now formed a part of any deal Williams made and under the terms of the NRL contract, income earned through a club releasing a player to fight would be included in the salary cap. For those who immediately argue a player should be allowed to go and earn what he likes and that it should have nothing to do with the NRL or its salary cap, this is, again, a necessary safeguard. If a club wanted to be devious, nothing could stop a rich benefactor organising a fight night and putting a dozen of his club's best players on the card and then underwriting the promotion. No matter whether the night is a financial success or a bust, the players all walk away with a fat cheque to top up their contract money. And best of all, you could put them in against any stiff you like to ensure their toughest battle of the night was to break a sweat.

Some might say it sounds ridiculous. Others, extremely plausible.

So NRL salary-cap auditor Ian Schubert watched very closely all this talk of Williams joining the Roosters and the boxing as well.

Williams dulled the noise by announcing another fight. This time for the New Zealand heavyweight title against somebody called Richard Tutaki. Regular fight fans struggled to recognise Tutaki but it mattered little – the title gave the opponent the appearance of legitimacy. Trouble emerged, though. As the thousands of Sonny fans got excited that their man was fighting for a title and confirmed their fierce support, news came that the fight was off because Tutaki was in jail. He got arrested in New Zealand for failing to turn up to court to face ten criminal charges, including possession of methamphetamine and drug paraphernalia. A guy on sickness benefits had now been replaced by someone who self-medicated, leading some to wonder about the true quality of his opponents.

The news barely slowed interest, and not even when more confusion soon surrounded the bout. It turned out there were several boxing organisations in New Zealand, much like the alphabet soup of boxing titles on the world scene, and the belt Williams was fighting for was not only vacant at the time but, according to reputable boxing source boxrec.com, had been fought over just four times in thirty years.

This belt had almost disappeared through lack of interest. Nobody cared much. Yet the pay-per-view was expected to be significant, with the numbers a closely kept secret.

Still, to show exactly how Williams was coming along at the right time, thirty years earlier Mark Broadhurst was a Manly frontrower, a Kiwi Test player and a former New Zealand amateur heavyweight champion. Yet Broadhurst could have turned pro and would not have made forty cents. In 1984 Canterbury hooker Billy Johnstone fought for the Australian middleweight title and would have been flat out earning cabfare home except the fight was promoted by the Bulldogs, the ring set up in the middle of the Bulldogs home ground, Belmore Oval. The money this fight was generating was just a dream to them. Such is how times change.

With Tutaki now otherwise distracted Williams came up with the New Zealand-based American Clarence Tillman as his new opponent. Tillman was fat and the moment you looked at him you knew it didn't matter how well he could box, he was never going to have the condition to pressure Sonny through ten rounds. Again. His only chance was to get him early. His lack of condition negated any boxing experience he had over Sonny, and then some. On first look Tillman had a credible record of 11–10 with six knockouts against Sonny's 4–0; if you did not bother to look too closely it might appear to be a fair fight. Yet only a small magnifying glass was needed to reveal the truth. Of Tillman's ten wins only two came against opponents with winning records – and one was 1–0 while the other was 2–0. In other words, he beat novices.

I wondered at the time in my newspaper column whether Sonny would ever actually fight someone who could punch back and what might happen if he did. It was not received well. Positive publicity was what they appreciated best, even if it barely resembled the packaging.

Not that I was wrong.

Refusing to pay $44.95 to watch the fight in all its small glory in Hamilton, where he was watched on by many of his new Waikato teammates, I waited until it should be over and turned on Fox Sports News to be met with the simple story: 'No need to show you just the highlights,' said the newsreader, 'we'll show you the whole fight.'

So Tillman went out in the first round. The fight was over so quickly it was carried in its entirety in the news package. What failed to make the package were the moments after the fight when a man got in the ring and challenged Williams next. It was Richard Tutaki, out on bail, bless him.

While it was easy to be dismissive and critical of Williams' boxing career – one where he kept promising to respect the sport even while he failed to realise it was bleeding to death – part of you could not help but feel sorry for him, too. There was a more serious problem here than a failure for the fight to provide value for money. It seemed to be completely missed in all the applause after the fight about Sonny being a national champion and on the road to greatness. While I have no sympathy for those who bought the fight and failed to see a proper contest – they get what they deserved – the biggest disservice of all was to Sonny. He was not learning how to fight with such easy victories. What did he truly learn from the Tillman fight that he could use in his next fight? Thicker wraps for his knuckles?

I was watching the Saturday-afternoon fights on ESPN one weekend when Teddy Atlas, Mike Tyson's early trainer, started talking about prospects and how you developed them. Immediately I grabbed my pen.

If a fighter has had more than 150 amateur fights, Atlas said, you move them along a little faster. Williams had none. For a fighter with more than 50 amateur fights, not below average – he liked them to start with two four-round fights, followed by four six-round fights and then four eight-round fights. After ten fights, he said, they could step up to ten-round fights.

At the same time, the opponent was important. 'I make sure that when he goes six rounds I put him in with guys that are maybe a little bit slicker,' Atlas said. 'Then he is going to think. Not just throw punches. He has got to think.

'And when you at the beginning, they're fighting ninety–ten fights. Ninety per cent chance of winning against ten per cent chance of losing. Then it goes to seventy–thirty. Then I step them up to sixty–forty in eight-round fights. It's much more competitive. Then he's getting ready for the ultimate ten-round distance where, historically, they're going to be fifty–fifty fights.'

That was how a professional did it.

Sonny's progression was all over the place.

The big job of managing any fighter is to make as much money as you can for him so he does not spend his retirement years rattling a cup full of pencils and looking for his next shower. In these terms, Nasser was the best in the business. For several reasons. Most of all he had fighters he could sell to the public and they happily bought in. Secondly, and not to be underestimated, he was honest. Fighters got paid everything they were promised. And for minimal risk.

Yet the more difficult trick of promoting is match-making, being able to keep your fighters safe while also finding opponents who will challenge them enough that they will learn and grow. The best example of this is the excellent job trainer Johnny Lewis and promoter Bill Mordey did with Jeff Fenech, who took it all the way to the International Boxing Hall of Fame.

Fenech turned pro with a wonderful backstory, robbed of Olympic gold in Los Angeles in 1984. Their job was to progress

Fenech first into the world rankings and then to a world title and keep him winning along the way. So in the early days of Fenech's career Lewis found a variety of fighters, all offering something different from the other.

It was standard match-making. For this fight they might find him a fighter with footwork, so Fenech would learn to cut off the ring and to corner his opponent. The next fight, the footwork might be missing but the opponent might have a granite chin, so can't be discouraged by Fenech's offensive intensity. The next, he might have quick hands. Or a heavy punch. The next might be tall with a longer reach. The next, short and stocky and coming on like a bull. With each new fight Fenech was problem-solving. Adding skills to what he already had. As Atlas said, he needed to think and not just punch.

Besides punching, it was hard to tell if Williams learned anything in any of his fights. It would come close to costing him a whole lot.

WILLIAMS missed the pre-season games with the Chiefs but it hardly mattered. His teammates were in the crowd when he fought Tillman and knew he had a fight to take care of. The Chiefs finished last in the New Zealand conference the previous season but they had recruited well and many expected improvement. As well as Williams, All Blacks Aaron Cruden and Richard Kahui and New Zealand under-20s players Ben Tameifuna and Brodie Retallick joined the team. They also had a good new coach in Dave Rennie, the former New Zealand under-20s coach, and Wayne Smith's influence.

If the forwards could match the threat of their backs they might be a chance to do something.

Almost immediately Williams' impact was felt. It started like it always does, with a professional at work. Arriving at training early, staying late, and working on all those little one-percenters he so firmly believed in. Teammates can't help but be influenced by it.

Nasser always told him: play well and the rest will take care of itself, and Williams was proving that every day. Who cared if they lost their opening game, going down to the Highlanders? The Chiefs went on a tear, winning their next nine games to take them to the competition lead. It was clear they were the real deal and Williams was emerging as a force within the team. While many privately speculated that he was upset with his lack of involvement in the World Cup Williams used it as a tool to spur him on rather than sulk. Driving everything he did with the Chiefs were performances built around high energy, high involvement.

'He's become a clear-thinking rugby player,' Wayne Smith said after the Chiefs beat the Bulls.

Eventually they would finish the season in second place, winning the New Zealand conference. Cruden would finish the season as Super Rugby's highest point scorer.

In round nine, though, the conversation around Williams and his superb form began to change. The *Herald*'s Brad Walter, with his close contacts to the Williams camp, revealed in his Friday column that Williams had attracted interest from Japanese rugby and could also feature in a fight in South Africa at the end of the year. The next day Walter upgraded the story from a paragraph in a gossip column to a fully substantiated story.

'Panasonic is interested in getting Sonny Bill Williams and has made an offer to him,' Hitoshi Iijima told Walter. Iijima was general manager of the Panasonic Wild Knights in the Japanese Top League. They finished runners-up the season before.

'We will offer two years and we will offer the best offer of the company because he is the best player. It will be the top offer by our company.'

The offer was enough to give Nick Politis indigestion. Panasonic was offering $1.2 million for twelve games. On a pro rata basis, it was almost three times what anybody could pay in the NRL. And Japanese rugby was a long way from the grind of NRL football. Most believed the average NRL player could play until he was forty with no large stress. Craig Wing, the former NRL player, now thirty-two, was happily showing that, playing for Shining Arcs.

Iijima had no concerns that Williams would provide value for money and worried little about what the Roosters might think. 'He is very famous in Japan and if he was to play in Japan we believe many non-rugby fans would know him,' he said. 'We don't know anything about him playing for the Sydney Roosters. We have offered a two-year contract and we hope the negotiations will be good.'

At first it was speculated that the deal would end any chance of Williams joining the Roosters because he would not be available until February. He would miss almost the entire off-season.

Nobody counted on how flexible Politis was prepared to be to get his man.

The bigger question would be the effect it would have on his relationship with the New Zealand Rugby Union. Certainly the Chiefs wanted him going nowhere. At a pinch, they admitted he would be welcome back if he did.

But the NZRU had a history of not allowing what they termed 'sabbaticals' to anybody except those who had given extreme service to the black jersey. It was a reward, a chance to top-up their earnings, while remaining committed to the All Blacks. Players who went anyway, without permission, were looked dimly upon and rarely welcomed back into the All Blacks jersey. Keven Mealamu and Tony Woodcock both played more than a hundred games for the All Blacks but were not granted sabbaticals. Neither was Andrew Hore, who played eighty-three Tests. The NZRU was finally forced to consider sabbaticals when fly-half Dan Carter was offered a reported £750,000 for a season with French side Stade Toulousain. Carter was still in his prime and with a home Rugby World Cup coming, New Zealand rugby feared it could lose him, so eventually allowed Carter to sign a deal with French club Perpignan, where he was reportedly paid £30,000 a game.

In May 2012 Ma'a Nonu returned to the Blues after a summer sabbatical with Ricoh Black Rams in Japan, just the second player after Carter to be granted a sabbatical. Now the NZRU was considering what to do with Williams, who had given the All Blacks none of the service Carter and Nonu had.

His case did differ slightly. Unlike Carter and Nonu, Williams was not contracted beyond that season, so he was free to leave if he liked. It could only raise problems if he ever returned. In good news for Williams, the NZRU's general manager of professional rugby, Neil Sorensen, opened the door in May when he said the game would treat sabbaticals on a case-by-case basis.

'We are still learning about this,' he told the *New Zealand Herald*. 'This is new territory for all of us and I think if we have a player say he really wants a playing sabbatical, we'd be able to talk to him about the experiences of both Daniel and Ma'a and that would be helpful. We remain open to the idea of players taking time out, getting away and enjoying different experiences during their careers and if some want to play rugby, or go tramping in Nepal, we will see if we can accommodate those requests.'

The Chiefs had no idea what to think.

'He knows how I feel,' said Wayne Smith. 'He knows how all the boys here feel. But he will make his own mind up. I just hope that if he decides to go that he comes back; he does what Dan and others did and comes back to New Zealand rugby. I'd love to see that. He hasn't made a decision and we don't know what that will be. But whatever he does, he wants to win a Super Rugby title.'

Again, Williams was polarising opinion. None of this is unexpected. Increasingly, those close to Williams – who, by some coincidence, could also benefit by his talent – were prepared to make concessions to later benefit from that talent. Those with less to lose, but nothing less personal at stake, resolutely defended their sport. As such, like his walkout on the Bulldogs four years earlier, speculation that Williams was putting himself above the game again angered the rusted-on fans, but this time in his new code. They believed no one had been afforded the privileges he had, and with players the calibre of Woodcock and Mealamu not given sabbaticals Williams, too, should be made to earn his opportunity.

On 9 July Williams looked past all that and announced at a press conference in Hamilton that he would play with Japan's Panasonic Wild Knights over the summer.

Then he said he would return to the NRL in 2013.

'This is due to a handshake agreement made a few years ago before I even came back to New Zealand with an NRL club,' he said. 'I haven't signed anything yet and I'm not in a position to elaborate on that.'

Nobody at the press conference picked up on the irony that he was returning to the NRL to honour a handshake deal when four years earlier he walked out on a written and signed contract.

Williams told the press conference he was enjoying his rugby but did not want to go back on his word.

There were still reservations within the NRL about his return. Memories are long in this game. But not too long.

'It's a massive gamble but I love the fact the Roosters look like they've been able to entice Sonny back into the NRL,' Brad Fittler told James Hooper at the *Sunday Telegraph*. 'The only question mark I would have is how long is Sonny Bill going to stay for? Recent history says Sonny only likes signing short-term deals. For me, that's a risk.'

Hooper spoke to another former Roosters skipper, Hugh McGahan. 'If he's coming to the Roosters, I'd be over the moon. My only reservation would be what's the term? If this is the start of the new wave of professional players, then I don't know what sort of culture they are looking to breed within the club. They've cleared the decks to allow him to come to the club, but are they talking about loyalty to the team and the players when they're only signing one player to a one-year deal? Without knowing the terms, it's hard to comment now, but he is a special talent. No one's been able to do in regards to what he's done in rugby league, rugby union and boxing.

Another former captain contacted was Royce Ayliffe. Ayliffe was an old prop with the soft hands of a Group One jockey and, from the bush, believed strongly in the strength of your word and how you honoured it said a lot about you. 'From the club's point of view I would rather see the money spent on up-and-coming talent,' he said. 'You're asking me if it's a good buy for the Roosters, no I don't think it is.'

It didn't matter. He was coming.

The one-year deal at the Roosters was worth a reported $850,000. With his $1.2 million pocketed in Japan Williams stood to earn more than $2 million, a significant upgrade on the $500,000 he would earn if he remained at the Chiefs. On top of that, Politis also agreed to let Williams fight and he would fight in February after returning from Japan. His fights brought him an estimated $150,000 to $200,000, depending on the night.

'The whole Japanese thing came about, I knew I was going overseas next year, they come and give me an offer and first I turned it down. But they come back with an offer that I pretty much couldn't refuse,' Williams told the *Daily Telegraph*.

Finally confirmed, the reaction across much of New Zealand mirrored the reaction in Australia four years earlier when he walked out on the Bulldogs.

New Zealand television presenter Peter Williams was savage, writing online, 'He's nothing but an immoral, money-grabbing, and dishonourable piece of work, being manipulated by an appallingly greedy management team that have been way, way too clever for the naïve coaches and administrators from

New Zealand rugby. I don't know which is more galling – to see the considerable investment that New Zealand rugby has put into this guy not reach its full potential, or the way the NZRU and Chiefs people have put on smiley faces as their investment goes off to that powerhouse of powder puff rugby, Panasonic, and wish him well with not even a mild complaint about his behaviour.'

If anybody doubts this is a business, be aware that almost immediately after his return to the NRL was confirmed the Canterbury Bulldogs started lobbying the NRL to kick off the 2013 season with a home game against the Roosters. Oh yes, they knew where the dollars came from.

Almost as quickly, Danny Weidler wrote that the Roosters were lobbying to have the same game played at their home ground so they could benefit through the gate. Weidler also wrote that Nasser was having none of it. Williams, Nasser told Weidler, was considering withdrawing from the game when they played the Bulldogs.

As the figures started to sprout and articles like Peter Williams' started to multiply, Nasser moved to ensure the perception was not about Williams chasing the dollar, pointing out to Brad Walter the money Williams had sacrificed around the world to pursue his dreams, including leaving behind a two-million-dollar deal at Toulon to chase his All Blacks dream.

'If anyone wants to imply that we try to get the best price and that we go from club to club, or if any CEO says that I have rung them or approached them, that is a blatant lie,' he told him. 'Sonny Bill Williams, Anthony Mundine and Quade Cooper – their reputations precede them. I have been lucky enough to represent three athletes who I have never had to pick up the phone to ring anybody for. I am just constantly taking calls on their behalf. I thank God that I have the easiest job in the world.'

Nasser was confirming the rules of Sonny Ball. Power is in the athlete. Their rare ability gave him the power to tell clubs, and now codes, to 'Go fuck yourself'.

Williams' decision to leave was made easier when the Chiefs won the Super Rugby title in August – another box in his growing list of achievements ticked. Williams starred a week earlier when the Chiefs eliminated his former team, the Crusaders, to qualify for the final. He set up both his team's first-half tries with offloads. Nobody else could have done it.

That was merely a preview of what was to come in the final. The first scoring chance of the game came when Williams got the ball and ran over one tackler, stepped another and then took on a third to put on a try for his cousin, winger Tim Nanai-Williams. He then iced the game five minutes from fulltime when he ran on to a pass from man-of-the-match Liam Messam to score his own try, finishing it by running and leaping into the crowd. The Chiefs beat the Sharks 37–6.

He was expected to leave New Zealand then. When he signed with Panasonic, All Blacks coach Steve Hansen said Williams would not be considered for The Rugby Championship against Australia, South Africa and Argentina. The Rugby Championship ran from 18 August to 7 October and the deal with Panasonic called for him to be in Japan for the team's first game on 31 August.

But once again, his talent was needed. The All Blacks' midfielders Conrad Smith and Richard Kahui suffered injuries. While Panasonic was less than pleased, they had to accept it. Williams played two Bledisloe Cup Tests against the Wallabies before ending his New Zealand commitments.

In two years he had won himself a World Cup, two Bledisloe Cups and a Super Rugby title. That is called success.

23

LAND OF THE RISING SONNY

ALMOST immediately when he landed in Japan in September 2012, Williams went into training – not for the Panasonic Wild Knights, since he was already in superb trim for football. He found a boxing gym and starting hitting the big heavy bag with the dull heavy thud of heavyweight arms. Then he began moving around the floor, flicking out jabs like he saw Mundine do so many times, like a lightweight, airy and light. They were unusual mechanics, like catching flies. Sonny was keeping to his life's pattern of total dedication. The deal with Panasonic included a November fight, and the big news was that it was against South Africa's former world title contender Frans Botha. This was some big deal.

Botha was once a serious heavyweight and almost pulled it off in 1995 when he beat Axel Schulz to win the IBF heavyweight belt, one of the four big belts. He held the title for as long as it took for the post-fight drug test to return. There it was discovered his sample contained anabolic steroids and the heavyweight title was no more. In the years since, Botha had fought and been defeated by the best fighters in the world. He led Mike Tyson on all three cards in 1999 before Tyson, as he is prone to, hit him with a short right hand high on top of the head in the fifth and the White Buffalo discovered his skull was not nearly as thick as it needed to be. Lennox Lewis took him out in two rounds in 2000, with the WBC and IBF belts at stake, and he was back again two years later trying to wrestle loose the WBO belt from Wladimir Klitschko's waist. Klitschko got him out of there in eight.

At his best, Botha was almost good enough. He was far more advanced than Williams.

This fight with Sonny rested on one question: how much did Botha have left?

He would be forty-four when he got in the ring against Williams and more than a dozen years past his best. But a Botha anywhere near his prime was going to be pure trouble for Sonny who, in all six fights, had not learned anything more than to punch.

It was not impossible. Others had taken big steps in quick time. Jeff Fenech won his first world title in his seventh fight, stopping Satoshi Shingaki for the IBF belt with his own particular brand of brutality, while Anthony Mundine challenged Germany's Sven Ottke for his WBA belt in just his eleventh professional fight. With no amateur career to speak of, Mundine put in a mighty performance before Ottke knocked him out in the tenth. 'Man Down' was the headline the following day, sitting over a photo of Mundine sleeping soundly on the canvas.

Sonny's problem was he had developed so little in his fights, the quality of his opponents so poor he took little from each win. In some ways Botha fit the mould of his previous opponents. He was past his best and not in the shape he would have preferred. But Botha also had something all the others did not. It is called ring craft.

Sonny was so raw he was vulnerable to anybody who might pressure him or refuse to stand in front of him and allow himself to get punched, as others seemed willing to do. It exposed itself only briefly in some of his previous fights when, met with a little resistance, his composure dropped and he went from being a boxer to a brawler and revealed his shortcomings. An experienced fighter like Botha had the ring savvy to exploit it.

And Tony Mundine was not going to be in his corner this time.

Anthony Mundine and Khoder Nasser were no longer speaking.

In July 2012, Mundine finally made good on his promise to fight in America. Mundine and Nasser had promoted almost all his fights together until then but, for this American fight, Mundine sought Jeff Fenech's help. Fenech, a mortal enemy of Nasser, had trained fighters and promoted fights since retiring and still had many contacts in America. A dozen rumours filled Sydney's boxing gyms about what went wrong between Mundine and Nasser. A big part was their disagreement over Mundine's future. Mundine wanted to go to America. 'I want to fight the best,' Mundine would say, and next fight he would announce he was fighting Rigoberto Álvarez and, at that, everybody would have to do the same thing. They would have to go google poor Rigoberto.

Nasser saw no sense in it. Why risk fighting in America when they got a good payday every time they turned out in Australia? Against what was minimal risk? From a promotional point of view Nasser had it one hundred per cent right. Mundine was making good money in Australia with little threat to his wellbeing.

But Mundine was, at heart, a competitor. And Nasser did not quite understand the internal flame that burned inside the athlete, the fire to dominate. It burns differently to the rest of us and sits inside these athletes like a conscience. The one person an athlete can't con is himself, and Mundine could go on talking forever about being the greatest fighter in the world and of all his many talents but, while most of America had no idea who he was and the Mayweathers, Cottos and Pacquiaos were off fighting other top-shelf opponents – and he remained in

Australia fighting nobody particularly special – he was fooling only himself.

Eventually Nasser and Mundine split, and Mundine got Fenech's help to establish roots in America. Mundine told the *Telegraph*'s Phil Rothfield the fallout with Nasser would not impact on his friendship with Williams, who remained close to Nasser. Yes, Mundine and Rothfield were talking after more than a dozen years without a word being spoken. Fenech had got them together.

'He's actually not a bad bloke,' Rothfield said.

'We're brothers, man,' Mundine told him of Williams. 'We'll always be there for each other. Sometimes it's hard in situations like this. My dad has done what any father would do for his son. As for Khoder, I don't want to go there. I lost my trust in him.'

Rothfield speculated the split was over money. It came as a surprise to many. If Nasser had done anything dishonest in the finance department it would be the first time for that, something Mundine later, when they resolved their dispute, admitted he got wrong.

There were more troubles for Sonny. Unfortunately, the Panasonic experiment did not work out quite like he'd hoped. After missing the first game to acclimatise after the trip from New Zealand he lost two of his first three games and got frustrated at his lack of effectiveness. Again it was typical Sonny, humble and with the promise of better. 'I just felt really disappointed and frustrated,' he said after a loss to Toshiba Brave Lupus. 'I just want to pay back my teammates and the Panasonic supporters. They have shown a lot of faith in me and a lot of love. And when we lose I feel the weight on my shoulders.'

His form slowly improved until round eight, when he injured his shoulder against the Kintetsu Liners. Moments after the game Williams tweeted: 'Going in for MRI hopefully just a small tear?!!'

Then: 'Hurt today . . .' he tweeted, 'results back nothing serious, small tear so hopefully still be able to [fight Botha].'

But the injury was worse than initially thought. Instead of a shoulder tear Williams had torn his pectoral. He had played his last game in Japan.

By now it was late October. Instead of fighting Botha in November as he was supposed to, the fight was cancelled and rescheduled for February.

Then Williams returned to Australia and confirmed for the first time, on the record, that he would join the Roosters the following season. The handshake deal, made three years earlier, was with Politis.

'If I'm honest with myself, I must admit it was pretty tough for me to honour what Nick and I had agreed about, but that's what I'm here today to announce,' he said, his arm in a sling after an operation to repair the torn pectoral. 'I guess when I first went to rugby, the first year or so I thought about rugby league a lot but I've really enjoyed my time here. It [the NRL] is going to be a massive challenge. I've met the boys. They're a great bunch of blokes, a bit like the Chiefs, real young, real enthusiastic and real welcoming, too. I'm looking forward to getting back out there in a game I grew up playing and hopefully put my best foot forward and play as best as I can.'

It was perfect Sonny, and it created fresh uproar.

'To be honest, I can't lie, not really,' Hazem El Masri said on Channel Nine when asked if he was happy to see Williams return. 'I think the way he left the game, I think the game should never let him back in. I am not here to cause headlines, that is just my opinion.'

El Masri was one of those Williams abandoned in 2008 and not your garden-variety footballer. A Lebanese Muslim, he was a leader in the playing community and emerged as a voice of strength when the streets of Cronulla erupted in racial riots in 2005.

'We need to put our differences aside for the sake of harmony,' El Masri said in the *Telegraph*, in a voice that spoke banners.

'This is a question which is hard to find an answer to but violence is not the answer.'

Such was the depth to his integrity that after he retired in 2009, El Masri was seen not only as someone smart enough to go into politics, and was approached by the Liberal Party for preselection in 2011, but was smart enough to reject it. El Masri's feelings on Williams' return hung heavily across an NRL that remained largely silent. This, despite his opinion being shared and supported by a vast majority. Nothing too important, just those who believed in the game and what it should stand for.

It did not necessarily equate to winning, though.

The backlash grew strong enough that eventually Nick Politis bought in. Politis joined the Roosters in 1976 as a sponsor and changed the game when he lobbied the NSW Rugby League, which ran the game, to allow him to put his car dealership, City Ford, across the chest of the Roosters' jersey. Politis, who turned 44 that year, made his debut on the big competition in town seven years later when he entered the *Business Review Weekly*'s Rich List in 1983, his worth estimated to be $30 million. On this day, when he came out to defend Williams, he was worth about $410 million with dealerships across much of Australia and America.

'You tell me what other athlete in the history of the NRL has had to pay a $750,000 release fee, serve a five-year suspension and then get treated like a criminal because they want to come back and play rugby league,' Politis told James Hooper. 'It's completely unfair. Look at all the other rugby league players that have gone to rugby union and then come back. They didn't cop the grief Sonny has had to put up with. Mark Gasnier, Wendell Sailor, Lote Tuqiri and Mat Rogers were all welcomed back with open arms. With Sonny Bill, it's like a case of tall poppy syndrome. We shouldn't be treating him like a criminal because he wants to return to our game, we should be celebrating having such an elite athlete back.'

Quite cleverly, Politis was changing the terms of the argument. While Gasnier, Sailor, Tuqiri and Rogers did indeed leave the NRL for rugby and return, and were welcomed back, their leaving was never the issue. It was the manner in which Williams left, happy to dud his teammates and refusing to show them the kind of loyalty that Politis, ironically, was now showing him, that upset nearly everybody.

This was no tall poppy syndrome. Williams was adored right up to the moment he reneged on a contract and, worse, abandoned his teammates. So much so he was even able to overcome several embarrassing personal scandals with little public bruising. What was also overlooked was that Williams had apologised for abandoning his teammates, an apology many had not seen or simply chose to ignore.

Williams' arrival at the Roosters also raised another question that marks a significant shift in Sonny Ball.

It began to be asked how the deal was done at all. Khoder Nasser was not an accredited NRL agent. Gallop had acknowledged as much four years earlier when sending his reminder email out to every NRL club, when all he needed to do was send it to Canterbury. Was he once again proving too smart for the NRL administration? Or was the NRL acknowledging an inconvenient truth?

Under NRL rules no contract could be registered unless the manager was accredited by the NRL. Managers paid more than a thousand dollars for accreditation under a scheme that would soon be revealed to be worth nothing. Nasser had never applied for accreditation, which was no surprise because it was unlikely he would ever be granted it after the way he manoeuvred Williams out of the game in 2008.

What did he care?

NRL salary-cap auditor Ian Schubert was slow to register the contract. You could tell Schubert was doing his job well by one simple criterion: all the clubs hated him equally.

Schubert worked on the basic principle that there was always another stone to kick over. He was reluctant to register the contract because of the handshake deal Williams spoke of. When was it made? Was it connected to the lunch eleven months earlier when Williams and Nasser sat with Politis and Gyngell at Circular Quay? Schubert investigated whether Williams' five-year $750,000 deal with Channel Nine was a down payment on him eventually playing at the Roosters. In the end there was no evidence to suggest it was. He wanted assurances the Botha purse was not an inducement to join the club. He also looked at Nasser's involvement and how that should be treated. The Roosters got around that by presenting evidence that Williams had been offered a 'vanilla' contract, a standard NRL contract with no added clauses, and simply had a pay-by-the-hour lawyer look over it before signing.

Underneath all this, and barely considered, was the moral stance of allowing a player back after the way he left the game.

But Schubert was part of an older generation by now. David Gallop had moved on months earlier. The ARL Commission now ran the game as it waited for Dave Smith to begin work as the new chief executive the following February. There was pressure from within the NRL to get Williams registered. He was regarded a tremendous coup for the game, the return of the prodigal son, a strike back against rugby union. Much later, many, many months later, the NRL announced the Roosters would be fined an undisclosed amount over the negotiation of Williams' contract for failing to provide documentation, but what did the Roosters care, they had their man.

With the fight delayed it meant there was time to repair the friendship between Mundine and Nasser who, in the meantime, announced a fight to take on fellow Australian Daniel Geale for his IBF middleweight belt. One of the first things Mundine did was introduce Nasser to Rothfield, a move that upset some at Fairfax. Mundine started hostilities for the rematch weeks earlier when he attacked Geale, who is Aboriginal, for marrying 'a white woman'. Then he joked that he thought all the Tasmanian Aboriginals were dead – Geale had moved to Sydney from Tasmania. The quietly spoken Geale said nothing throughout.

Finally Mundine was in a real fight and, having steered away from so many of his previous fights that did not seem to come against legitimate opponents, this time I headed along to Star Casino in Sydney for the press conference.

'Anthony,' I said at the press conference, 'can you tell us in your last five fights, the last couple of years, what we can look for that can convince us you will beat Daniel?'

Mundine stood from the table and walked to the lectern, gently shouldering MC Ben Damon aside. He was exactly where he wanted to be, centre-stage.

'Listen man, everyone respects me except for you, Paul. I know deep down in your heart you've got a little respect for me. But I know that you, and a lot of other people, doubt. I don't know, you just want to hate on somebody. You just want to hate because, I don't know, because I'm me, and I'm raw. I want the best fighters and the biggest tests. So what's going to get me up for this fight. That's what I need. That's all I need. I want the biggest stage, the biggest test. That's all I need. I don't need nothing else. That's what gets me off because it's going to satisfy me so much that people like you, I'm going to prove wrong. And you keep writing, dog. But tell me after this fight, when I win it, when I win it, I'm the best athlete ever, man. Ever. And if you give me the same accolades as Geale, you should.'

'You say you're the best athlete ever,' I said, 'but you're the only one that says it . . .'

Somebody in the crowd tried to shout me down.

'Well, can you name me one other person that has said it?' I asked.

'You name me someone that done what I did and conquered two sports like I did.'

'Bo Jackson.'

'That's team to team. We're going from a team to boxing.'

'Ambrose Palmer.'

'Never heard of him.'

'Aboriginal boxer, also played AFL.'

'Never heard of him. I'm talking world titles. I'm talking records, doing what I done. You know they gypped me in football, that's why I left the game. You had the [Australian] coach Chris Anderson coming out saying, "We don't pick him because of his off-field characteristics." I left it at its height, and I was the highest paid player in the league at the time. Money talks.'

'You left the game because you said it was racist,' I said, 'and there were Aboriginals in front of you. The five-eighth in front of you was Aboriginal.'

'How?'

'Laurie Daley.'

'How was he Aboriginal? He didn't claim to be Aboriginal, he was like this fella.' He pointed to Geale. 'He never claimed to be Koori.'

Daley, who surely is Aboriginal, had a stock answer whenever Mundine claimed to be a better player, which was often. A three-time premiership winner, a NSW and Australian captain, he said he was too busy polishing his trophies to hear Mundine's comments. Yet here on this day at Star Casino Mundine was exactly where he wanted to be. He needed to be aggressive like this to become the athlete he needed to be, which was why he always picked fights before stepping into the ring. And the deep truth here is that with someone challenging his over-the-top statements, as I was, rather than being annoyed, he was portraying himself exactly as he wanted to be. It was what he sought to create – a little Muhammad Ali–Howard Cosell-type moment.

'The chairman of selectors was Arthur Beetson,' I said. 'How do you claim he was racist against you?'

'Because they're all Uncle Toms, baby, just like him [Geale]. He's an Uncle Tom.'

'You're saying Arthur Beetson was an Uncle Tom?'

'No, I'm saying they're joined to the system.'

'Did you say Arthur Beetson was an Uncle Tom or not?'

'No, I'm saying there's Uncle Toms out there, there is Uncle Toms out there.'

'Arthur Beetson was chairman of selectors.'

'Yeah, but he don't make the decisions. He might be chairman of selectors but he don't make the decisions – it's set up to crumble, man.'

'You're rewriting history.'

'Listen, you just come Wednesday night and witness the best athlete you've ever seen. I'm a likeable guy, man. I'm easy-going, just down to earth. I give everybody time. But when you have people that want to see the downfall, want to wish bad, doubt you, criticise you – what I've done ain't ever been done.'

'We want to see you finally do what you're saying you're going to do.'

'You just be at the fight,' Mundine said, and walked off.

'Good questions, Paul,' yelled a man in the crowd.

'Nice Google-searching, dickhead,' yelled another.

I was disappointed with myself afterward. I had incorrectly identified Ambrose Palmer as Aboriginal. The rest was spot-on. And Mundine was not completely wrong, either. I did respect his talent as a fighter, and the best of what he had done – it was just the rest of the act I had a hard time learning to enjoy. And he had a right hand that could stop time when he threw it properly.

Geale took the decision on points. As soon as the final bell sounded Mundine leaned over the ropes towards me sitting at ringside. 'You owe me an apology, man.'

I looked at Geale's promoter, Billy Treacy, nearby. 'Does he think he won?'

Before the decision he walked to Geale's corner to apologise to his wife, Sheena. With the dignity of the mighty, she turned her back. All three judges scored it for Geale. One judge 116–112 and the other two had it 117–111 for Geale.

Mundine claimed he was robbed, that the system was against him winning. The moment the decision was announced he left the ring, bitterly.

In an odd way, Mundine's performance was such that it resurrected his career. As Mundine remained sour on the result afterward Williams posted a photo of himself, Mundine and Quade Cooper on Twitter, with the comment, 'Hanging out with @Anthony_Mundine celebrating a victory. We don't pay attention to corrupt judges!'

THE following day, Williams apologised as his Twitter comment about biased judges sent talkback radio into a small meltdown. NSW Combat Authority boss Denis Fitzgerald confirmed the judges were considering legal action and a pall fell over the fight. Once again, Mundine and his crew had overshadowed Geale's victory.

'It's disappointing,' Geale said, 'I wish I had a dollar for every time I said there was something disappointing when I'm speaking about Anthony Mundine.'

Williams was just little more than a week away from fighting Botha and Cooper, his ally this night, was making his professional debut on the undercard. It was a promotional masterstroke by Nasser. With Sonny going into New Zealand and NSW, Cooper's inclusion would shore up the Queensland market, a nice little Sonny Ball moment. Again the pre-publicity was staggering, with Cooper commended for not taking on a 'powder puff'. His opponent Barry Dunnett, it was said, once fought for a Queensland Muay Thai title. It came after two pro boxing fights several years earlier, split with a win and a first-round knockout loss. That the Muay Thai fight lasted about a minute, including the standing eight counts against the stricken Dunnett after he climbed back up after the first time he was knocked down, was left out of the publicity brief. Cooper was strong but had little idea how to box. He would keep Dunnett's record intact with a first-round knockout.

What happened in Williams' fight with Botha could be interpreted any way you like. He was magnificent early and surprised many. He got on top of Botha. Once again, the athleticism on display was staggering. You watched him move and punch with a fighter like Botha and thought, 'What a man.' He was doing it all with just a small clue of how to fight.

Botha was the one thing none of Williams' previous opponents were, though. He was resilient. With each round he turned up, hitting Williams late, leaning on him, applying all those tricks learned over twenty years in the fight game. By the ninth it was clear Williams, leading clearly on all three judges' cards, was wearing down rapidly.

Botha saw his opportunity. Two big shots thrown around the referee stunned Williams and an argument could be mounted that they were illegally to the back of the head. What did Botha care? He was making his run and when he was penalised a point for continually punching after the break he changed nothing. He knew the points did not matter by then, he was too far behind to win on points, but he also knew they were having a telling effect on Williams. He ended the ninth in a poor state. He seemed fragile.

Sonny came out for the tenth round, still distressed from the round before. Doctors would later say he was concussed throughout the round. He would tell others he had no memory of the tenth. The biggest surprise, though, was the announcement that it was the final round.

'Confusion ringside,' commentator Andy Raymond said at the start of the tenth after hearing referee Tony Kettlewell call it the last round. 'We had it marked down as twelve.'

Not just the MainEvent commentators believed it was a twelve-round fight. So did the judges, who had marked their cards for twelve rounds. So did Botha, who needed every minute.

A short right hand over the left ear stunned Williams early in the tenth and from that moment on Botha threatened to steal the fight. Williams hung on, and hung on, until Kettlewell eventually stripped him a point for holding. Williams finished the fight wobbling, leading to calls that the round was cut short to prevent Botha knocking him out. It wasn't cut short, although many believed the fight had been.

'When the ring announcer said over the loud speaker that it was the last round, that was the first we knew of any change,' said Alan Moore, vice-president of the Australian National Boxing Federation and a ringside judge.

Moore scored the fight 98–94 to Williams. The two other judges, Adam Height and Steve Marshall, both scored it 97–91 to Williams for a unanimous decision.

Moore was cornered immediately after the fight by the *Australian*'s Dan Koch, who knew the first rule was to get to them quick. 'Any international title fight is meant to be fought over twelve three-minute rounds. I have no idea what happened. Sonny was in more trouble than the early settlers there at the end of the tenth. Botha came back out of nowhere and Sonny was hurt and struggling to stay up. I don't think there is much doubt there is going to be a bit more said about what happened though.'

The fight was scheduled to be a twelve-round fight on boxrec. com, although it has since been altered. Everybody watching the fight believed it was a twelve-round fight because that was what the commentators had portrayed.

Botha was convinced there was a rort.

'He is a fine gentleman but this is bullshit,' Botha said.

While it appeared an investigation might be called, that was extinguished when Botha's promoter, Thinus Strydom, confirmed he was told moments before the first round that the fight was reduced to ten rounds and that he told his corner not to tell Botha. It explained Botha's confusion, though he did not want to settle. The following day he called Williams a coward, saying if he was any kind of man he should give him a rematch.

In the days that followed the whole scene got more ridiculous, causing Williams deep embarrassment. First came an allegation from Botha that, days before the fight, Nasser had taken him for a drive and offered him a bribe to take a dive. Then came an allegation leaked to the *Herald* that Botha had failed a drug test in pre-fight testing even though no official blood sample for drug testing had been taken. Fighters are routinely tested for HIV and hepatitis before fights but not by recognised drug laboratories like the Australian Sports Anti-Doping Authority.

The unfortunate part was it all overshadowed one of the more stunning performances you will ever see in a boxing ring. After just six fights and having never fought past six rounds Williams dominated for most of the fight against a fighter such as Botha, who showed he still had many of the smarts, if not all the skills. It was one of the more incredible athletic performances you are likely to ever see. It should have been remembered as some-thing noble but instead it is forever remembered as something that is not.

24

SBW: OMG

SONNY created a fair storm before he even turned up to Roosters training in February 2013, after which he would change *everything*. The Roosters had finished thirteenth the season before which, for a man driven by success like Politis, was somewhat less than satisfactory. Making it worse was they finished unlikely grand finalists two years earlier in 2010, teasing the club that success was coming, before plummeting to successive seasons out of the top eight.

When Politis and the Roosters board finally realised the 2010 grand final was the aberration and not the bottom eight finishes, they moved and sacked coach Brian Smith. The new coach was Smith's former assistant, Trent Robinson. This was greeted with much joy among Roosters players. After coaching the Roosters' defence in 2010 Robinson took a job in the English Super League, coaching French club Catalans Dragons and making everybody take notice. Few outside the NRL recognised his name but it mattered not at all, as the one group Robinson needed to convince were already convinced. The players knew they had a serious coach coming home.

Securing Robinson was design. After that the Roosters had what is necessary in any premiership campaign, and that is a great deal of luck. Before Williams committed in November the club already knew another top-flight player, future State of Origin player James Maloney, was joining them. Then came Williams. In January Penrith sacked State of Origin centre Michael Jennings to free up room in their salary cap and were forced to contribute part of his contract wherever he landed. He landed in Bondi, home to the Roosters.

Then came another former Origin star, Luke O'Donnell. O'Donnell left the NRL at the end of 2010 to play in England but, tired of grey skies, wanted to return to Sydney. O'Donnell joined the Roosters less than a month before kick-off, on Valentine's Day. He was past his best but beyond tough. And so ideal for a club with many good young players coming through who needed to be shown what it took to get the job done.

By accident and design, no club recruited better in the entire NRL for the coming season.

The big difference, though, was Sonny Bill Williams.

This might sound odd in the world of professional sport where it is the job of such professionals to know these things, but he taught them how to prepare to win. His self-discipline and dedication were relentless. Nobody had seen anybody so thorough. Few knew, but Williams had been turning up at the club since before Christmas, arm still in a sling as his pectoral muscle repaired, working on his rehabilitation. He began going through video sessions, getting himself used to the game and how it had changed. His new teammates were already aware of his talent and once they saw the preparation he was bringing to help them succeed, it was enough. He had them at hello.

They watched him eat and saw his devotion went every-where. Food was a source of fuel, not an indulgence. Driven by Williams' devotion, with the likes of skipper Anthony Minichiello chipping in, the entire club changed its diet.

Food was cooked in coconut oil, for example, instead of olive oil. Why? Because unlike other oils, and among other advantages, coconut oil metabolised medium-chain saturated fatty acids immediately in the liver and immediately converted it into fuel for the brain and muscle function rather than storing it in the liver. They were not walking around in lab coats, but the Roosters knew their stuff.

His impact was everywhere, and rugby league made the most of his return. Roosters' membership rose by 23 per cent. The club sold out its corporate boxes.

Even the networks started playing Sonny Ball. While Channel Nine televised the Roosters' first game, the season opener against South Sydney, Fox Sports had the rights to all trial games and announced it would televise the Foundation Cup, the trial between the Roosters and Wests Tigers, for the first time on 23 February. It was trumpeted as the first glimpse of Williams in his Roosters jersey.

Then he withdrew from the game, a move that industry experts believed cost Fox Sports as many as 100,000 viewers. Here, it is vital to remember Williams was sponsored by Channel Nine.

A week before the Roosters kicked off the season in the competition opener against South Sydney, Nine began advertising his arrival, simply and effectively, with just six letters: 'SBW: OMG'.

Nine knew what they had. Gyngell said he believed Williams was the 'most talked about footballer in the world'. Moments before Williams went on, midway through the first half, Nine took us into his private world, playing pre-recorded audio over the commentary of Sonny narrating his own return.

'I can either freeze,' he told viewers, 'or just walk through it.'

The game was almost a sell-out at Allianz Stadium, with 36,000 people turning up, almost double the crowd from the same game played on the same weekend the previous season. Among the crowd was a group of Canterbury supporters who took their seats at one end of the ground and unfurled their sign: 'We Haven't Forgotten'. Police made them put it away.

Williams was named on the bench in the number sixteen jersey and when he finally came on, as everybody knew, there waiting for him was South Sydney's own version of SBW, Sam Burgess. Burgess had arrived at South Sydney in 2010 and with Sonny off playing rugby, assumed the role as the game's most intimidating forward. Burgess began putting together numbers and a brand of hurt that were staggering. He became the reminder that, as often happens in the NRL, when a great one goes somebody soon fills his place.

Unfortunately for those waiting for the miracle that day, of which numbers were many, they would have to wait longer. South Sydney ran out winners 28–10 and Sonny was solid but not excellent. He had just six touches but tackled strongly. The game did find the moment, though, two minutes before half time after a Sydney Roosters dropout. The ball found Burgess, who for weeks had been reading about Williams' return and who was not used to sharing the column inches, and so with the ball in hand Burgess opened his gait and took big long strides and headed straight towards an advancing defensive line . . . before veering straight for Sonny.

Ray Warren, the greatest commentator in sport, nearly popped a valve at the collision.

'Burgess!' he said, going up an octave.

Williams went high and backwards and Burgess almost rolled over the top of him before Williams took a second grab and brought him down.

There, in that moment, was everything everybody had waited for: the appetiser to what would become a hell of a season.

Nine later revealed that ratings figures not only won the night but, driven by Williams' return, were the highest season opener since the new ratings system began twelve years earlier. It remained the highest-rating competition match all season.

The Roosters travelled to New Zealand the next week to play the Warriors and as everybody waited for the second game to better analyse his return, he did what he was so good at doing and talked football and effort and all those things teammates liked to hear.

Patience, he preached.

'It'll take me a few weeks yet to feel fully comfortable,' he said. 'It's been five years out of the game and coming back from injury as well. I'm just trying to do the basics well and concentrate on my preparation.'

He moved away from talk of immediate miracles. 'Everyone is looking for the magical play,' he said. 'But for me, it's just about doing my core skills as good as I can and making that "ad" line in attack and defence. When I keep it simple like that, the big plays usually come off.'

You could chisel that in stone right there, the mantra of Sonny Bill. While everybody was waiting for the big play Williams went out and played a full 80 minutes against the Warriors that spoke more of the strength of his return than any single play.

'He's probably further than I would expect him to be after two games,' Robinson said after the game. 'To leave him out there for 80 minutes, after a short preparation back in rugby league, I think he's done exceptionally well, so very happy. I had a lot of faith in what he was doing. That's why he played the 80 minutes, which is a great sign for a coach, to have someone like that out there for that time.'

He was gone five years and upon his return found a very different game from that he left. The game was tighter, less expansive. The big change was every team wrestled, making the game a whole lot tougher, not just week to week where competition was far more evenly spread than rugby, but even tackle to tackle.

'I like the challenge, week in, week out, of trying to play good, consistent footy,' he told Dean Ritchie at the *Daily Telegraph*. That marked another change in Williams. He seemed to be on a charm offensive, happy to talk to all media.

And the returning, more mature Sonny said all the right things.

SONNY BALL

'I want to be consistent rather than one week you are on
fire, the next week you're not. I see it as a massive challenge.
I don't worry about what is going on outside and what people
are saying and things like that. I just worry about doing my
job and doing the little things well. I am feeling good. It's about
doing the little things well, the one percenters, and making sure
I have been diligent in my preparation. If I do, then the big
picture always seems to fall into place.'

A month in his game went to a new level when Robinson
switched him to the opposite side of the field, the right edge where
he was more comfortable, and it led to a 50–0 rout over Parramatta.

Williams continued to charm the game a fortnight later when
the Roosters played the Bulldogs. Five years in the making, and
it was over almost as soon as it started. His first touch of the
ball he drifted down the right sideline and drew several defenders before throwing a cut-out pass to unmarked winger Roger
Tuivasa-Sheck. The winger did the rest, scoring in the corner. It
prompted the crowd to start cheering 'Sonny', almost in defiance
of the thousands of Bulldogs fans determined to boo him.

The Roosters ran out 38–0 winners, far too good for a
side that was a grand finalist the previous season. After laying
on the try for Tuivasa-Sheck Sonny scored two himself and left
the game with one of those wonderful small touches he is so
capable of providing. It came after his first try, a diagonal run
to the tryline through several Bulldogs defenders that saw him
slide over the line and skip to his feet and, without breaking
momentum, skip across to the fence where a couple of young
Roosters fans, just children, hung over with their arms stretched
out for a nice big high five from Sonny Bill Williams. Nothing
wins the people like looking after the little ones and Williams
was wonderful at it.

It was the third time in four games they held the opposition scoreless. Suddenly, the Roosters became part of the NRL
conversation. This was a team going somewhere.

By midway through the season the Roosters sat a win off the competition lead and Robinson knew he had a team not only capable of a strong top-eight finish but with the potential to take it all the way. Robinson and his coaching staff sat down and charted what they were doing. Aware they had a team capable of winning the premiership, they adjusted expectations and training.

The Roosters were going for it all.

Part of it was dealing with the distraction of Sonny. By mid-season media talk had begun again about his future, whether he would remain in the NRL or return to rugby union the following season, and what the game would do to try to keep him. Already the game had committed a massive blunder when Israel Folau contacted Parramatta at the end of 2012 looking to return to the NRL after a very average two years playing AFL. Attempts by the Eels to contract Folau turned into small comedy. Given his two years out of the game Folau had no true salary-cap value so instead would be assigned a notional value. Notional values were necessary to prevent clubs trying to register high-priced talent such as Folau below market value, because of anomalies such as this, where Folau had not played for two seasons and so had no current market value. The Eels contacted the NRL and asked what Folau's notional value would be so they could find room in the salary cap for him, even if it meant releasing other players already contracted. This was necessary to get Folau at the club. You don't gamble with the rent.

The NRL said no, you lodge a contract and we'll tell you if it is high enough. The Eels thought it was all backwards. The NRL was wary of being low-balled. So the Eels lodged as small an amount as possible to save as much room as they could in the salary cap while making the rest up in third-party agreements, only to be told it wasn't enough.

Parramatta lodged another contract, listing Folau on a higher base salary with less third-party money. No, said the NRL, he is worth more than that. And back and forth it went for several weeks before the NRL finally agreed on the most recent figure Parramatta submitted . . . by which time the NSW Waratahs had had enough time to negotiate and promptly announced Folau as its new signing for the 2013 season. He was not returning to the NRL, he was going to Super Rugby.

With that in the background the NRL was hard at work trying to find a way to keep the salary cap fair, or at least the appearance of it, while ensuring the likes of Sonny Bill Williams stayed in the game and Israel Folau could one day return.

The Roosters were certainly showing what Williams was able to provide. The wins continued until all the way through to the end of the home-and-away rounds when, almost as if planned, a little magic dust was sprinkled. South Sydney led the competition by two points over the Roosters. Normally that would afford them a good headstart on winning the minor premiership heading into the last round, but not this year.

To get a little idea of the venom about to be unleashed it is worth remembering the history of the clubs here. Both were foundation clubs, turning out that first year of rugby league in 1908. They were neighbours and yet appealed to vastly different social demographics. The high-flying Roosters were Bondi beach and A-list celebrity.

The Rabbitohs, with their inner-city bones and government housing, were working class bordering on the disadvantaged, but with the game's proudest tradition. Shortly after actor Russell Crowe took ownership of the Rabbitohs in 2005 he produced the *Book of Feuds*, a secret binding that highlighted all the wrongs the Roosters had perpetrated on the Rabbitohs over the years and, presumably, how Souths might have squared up.

So while Souths held a two-point lead in the standings heading into the final round, the Roosters had a better for and against, meaning if they won and picked up the two competition points available they would snatch the minor premiership from their rivals on percentages.

The game drew the biggest ever crowd to a non-finals game: 59,780 went to ANZ Stadium to see Souths start fast and lead 12–10 at half time. Those waiting for the sprinkle of magic dust would have to wait until the second half, and it came in the set after James Maloney sent the Roosters ahead 18–12. Working out of their own territory Williams took the ball on a standard run but punched through the two pretty handy defenders, Roy Asotasi and Chris McQueen, to go on a 50-metre run before putting Mitch Pearce away to score. The Roosters won 24–12 and took the minor premiership.

Early the next week the NRL launched its finals series, a disaster on board the HMAS *Leeuwin*. The captains of all eight finals clubs stood on the ship's deck under a baking sun without shade. You could have sold water for a thousand dollars a bottle and there wasn't a person there who wouldn't have lined up twice.

Dave Smith was among those working on their tans when he was cornered about Sonny Bill as speculation rose that Williams was on the verge of returning to rugby union. Smith confirmed the game was looking at ways to retain him. Williams still had not committed to a team next year, or even a code, and the NRL remained hopeful he was in league to stay.

'I think he is a fantastic talent,' Smith said to the assembled media. 'I thought he had a wonderful game on Friday night. I think we always said we wanted to keep players like Sonny in the game. He is an ambassador for the sport. Part of that is why we are looking at the salary-cap review and this whole marquee-player idea. I am going to work as hard as I can to keep Sonny in the game.'

Smith was asked if he had spoken to Williams about it. 'I spoke to Sonny on a number of occasions. I absolutely want to keep him in the game, Sonny has to figure out what Sonny wants to do and you have to support him all the way whatever that is. I hope he stays in the game. As I said, partly that's why we're looking at the salary cap so we do have the flexibility where we need it.'

THE Roosters went through the finals unbeaten, beating Manly 4–0 in the qualifying final and then Newcastle 40–14 in the preliminary final to qualify for the decider, where they would face Manly again.

By then Williams had it all worked out. With the Roosters now in the finals interest in his future was only going to intensify so, heading into the finals, Williams approached management and said he wanted to do no more media.

Despite arriving at the biggest games of the season, when the NRL seeks to cash in on the hype surrounding the game, Williams was dictating terms. He disappeared after that, spotted only at training and games. All interview requests fell dead. He was a no-show at the Roosters' grand final fan day despite attendance being an NRL requirement. The Roosters explained he was getting treatment for a calf strain, which was just a small lie. The NRL allowed it to pass unpunished.

'The last month,' he told the *Herald*, 'I just asked the club if I could not do any media and just concentrate on my thing, that's winning this competition, or doing my part. I went into my shell, changed my number, went off social media and just dedicated myself to the cause that we were trying to achieve.'

His comments were a small clue to the big change in him. He had left the game five years earlier, raw and ready to be shaped. By the time he returned he had a tremendous awareness of himself and what he could do, which only the great ones have. He was still not fully formed though.

Come the grand final, that awareness of what he could do was the difference.

The Roosters had an unhappy time of it early. For forty minutes the game was balanced, Williams coming up with uncommon errors as he tried to take advantage of the aggression in Manly's left-side defence. Both Kieran Foran and Steve Matai, defending in front of him, liked to get up quick and hard, and Williams tried getting around them.

At half time, leading 8–6, he apologised to teammates.

'I'm going to rub that first half and go out there and play through them,' he said.

Trent Robinson's mind briefly went back to the 2010 grand final when the Roosters were beaten by St George Illawarra. The Roosters led 8–6 at half time then, too.

Almost immediately Robinson's fears might have been valid. A penalty try just three minutes in gave Manly the lead 12–8 and soon after the Sea Eagles pushed further ahead, 18–8, following a try to Steve Matai.

Williams knew it was time.

The great ones sense the moment.

For the next ten minutes Williams worked his teammates, unseen before all our eyes. He started conversations, putting players in place around him.

Give me the ball early, he was saying, or run off me here. His first-half plans to finesse his way around the Manly defence were gone. Now he was getting physical, taking it to them. How many other players had the ability to change tack so substantially? Williams began putting his teammates in position, nominating defenders to target, trying to get them going.

When such effort is being exerted by such talent, a result is inevitable. A try to Aidan Guerra narrowed the score, making it 18–14, and then with the Sea Eagles suitably softened up by his previous ten minutes Williams cut loose.

Once again he took the ball to the line, knowing exactly where his support would be. It was James Maloney, who is quicker than most. Maloney went through the line and deviated to find Anthony Minichiello in support with a pass that might or might not have been forward, they are still arguing about it in some pubs, and Minichiello put Shaun Kenny-Dowall over and the Roosters had the lead, 20–18.

Then he finished them off.

With nine minutes left the Roosters were working out of their territory when Williams did nothing more than take the ball to them, full of running. It was perfect. He was too much man to handle and he went through them and deep into Manly's territory before running out of support. It was enough, though. Manly never recovered defensively and, before the set was out, Maloney dribbled the ball in-goals and Michael Jennings pounced to push them ahead 26–18, what would be the final score.

Afterwards, Williams sat in a sweaty dressing room, crowded with joy, and knew what he had achieved.

'This is up there,' he said. 'Because the NRL is such a tough competition . . . I've just been blessed.'

25

A STATESMAN SPEAKS

MOST expected Sonny Bill Williams to leave rugby league after the grand final. He had returned and played a significant role in the Roosters' premiership which, for the competitor in him, sat more comfortably than the first title with the Bulldogs. This time he carried much of the load.

'Winning the grand final was definitely a dream come true. This is just so much more sweeter than 2004 because after five years I had forgotten how tough this competition was. It's just so sweet looking down on this [premiership] ring,' he said in the dressing room.

He was talking a lot in the dressing room after the game. Later in the night the Roosters would leave the room and go to the middle of the field to toast their success and Williams would be the last out, still talking. Little had been said about the Bulldogs but now, with the air out of it, Williams thought back to his time at the club and gave his deepest insight into why he really left.

But first it is worth recalling a conversation Willie Tonga had earlier in the week with Dan Koch at the *Australian*. Tonga was one of two Bulldogs Williams told he was leaving the night before he left. Just weeks earlier he had signed a contract that would take him from the club at the end of 2008 to the North Queensland Cowboys, which was as far away from Canterbury as you could get in the NRL.

Normally people are so reluctant to talk about Sonny because they fear being cut off, from him or those around him, who knows. Tonga, a true friend, was past those barriers. In some ways, Tonga's explanation only confuses what we think we know of the Sonny Bill character, which you get the feeling is the way he wants it.

Who truly knows him?

How can anyone know a man on such an extreme journey of discovery he is constantly changing personality, picking up lessons he can learn and live by while discarding others? All we heard before he walked out on the Bulldogs was about money, and about how a lack of money somehow translated into a lack of respect, forget about the salary cap, and that if the Bulldogs did not compensate him he was going to walk.

Could it be possible that what he was most unhappy with was himself?

'We were like brothers, the three of us, so it wasn't a big surprise to Reni or me when Sonny told us he had made the decision to leave the Bulldogs,' Tonga told Koch. 'He hadn't been happy there for a long time – things had gotten out of control with the playing group and I was as much a part of it as anyone else. Sonny and I had arrived at the Bulldogs at the same time and I think we both got swept up by a pretty wild off-field culture and we were too young and naïve to handle that sort of life. By nature, we are both pretty quiet guys, so eventually that whole "train hard, play hard, party hard" approach became too much. We'd spent a couple of years struggling with injuries and it was obvious the balance between the working hard on the training track and the hours we were putting into enjoying life off the field had gotten way out of kilter.

'We had spoken early in the year about the fact we weren't happy with the direction our careers were heading and the fact things needed to change. It wasn't long after that conversation I made the decision to head to the Cowboys. When we talked about it a bit later, I said to him I needed to make the move because I needed a fresh start if I was going to get my football back on track. I remember him saying to me he felt the same way and that he wasn't happy with the life he had been living or the perception of him in the community. When he sat down with Reni [Maitua] and I on the Friday, he just said he needed to get out because he needed to get his life back together. He wasn't blaming anyone else – that's not Sonny's style, but he was really concerned about the reputation he was starting to get after a couple of off-field incidents.

'We all knew there would be fallout, but Sonny was adamant he needed to get away completely to start rebuilding not just his football, but his whole life. He knew he was going to cop some flak – though I think even he was surprised at how big a deal it became. But for probably the first time since he arrived at the Bulldogs, he was making a decision he knew was the right one for him in the long term. To see him today, I don't think anyone would dispute that and to be honest I think it also forced the club itself to address a number of things, which had led to the breaking-up of a group which should have, given the talent, built a dynasty after winning the 2004 title.'

A statesman could not have scripted it better. With an honesty missing from all the early narrative Tonga at once explained his friend and turned him into a sympathetic figure. Who could not understand that, a young man at the crossroads, struggling to find his way? Knowing he was blowing it?

Williams was not so much unhappy with the club as he was unhappy with himself. But the club, with its old-school, often hostile behaviour towards anybody that was not a Canterbury Bulldog, was turning him into a man he did not want to be. And he wasn't strong enough to say no at the time. He needed to get out, for his own sake.

Tonga told Koch about Sonny's first touch in first grade, at the trial in Coffs Harbour, and how, if not for what happened later that night when police came knocking, the trip would have gone down as the dawn of Williams' career. But, as we know, the police did come knocking and there went that.

'Looking back, it probably reflects that whole period at the Bulldogs — that some of the special things on the field were overshadowed by what was happening off it,' Tonga told Koch. 'We became a party crew and it got out of hand. All of us managed to end up in the headlines at some stage — some more than others. It's funny to look around the league now and, just about to a man, those same guys have gone on to become not just really good players, but leaders and positive role models. I mean JT [Johnathan Thurston, Cowboys], Nate Myles [Titans], Roy [Asotasi, South Sydney] and Braith [Anasta, Tigers] all became club captains and Reni [Eels] and Mase [Willie Mason, Knights] have come back after time away and become leaders at their new homes. But there is no doubt Sonny has undergone the biggest transformation. The bloke I drove to the airport that Saturday night when he took off to France . . . he never came back. The Sonny that came back is the one he set out to prove to everyone existed.

'He had a lot of critics and doubters, but he never wavered. I heard it in our conversations on the phone and saw it each time we caught up in person. He is the man — the best athlete in either rugby code. Players and coaches want him; young kids everywhere want to be like him; fans and sponsors just want to be near him.'

So in the dressing room this night Williams, requiring only a gentle nudge, touched briefly on it as reporters gathered around him.

'I never touched alcohol until I made first grade,' the *Herald* reported the next morning. 'I lost my way for a couple of years there but I'm proud to say I'm proud of the man I see in the mirror. I guess, looking back, I went through embarrassing times. I've got to take accountability for my actions. But I feel confident as a man, as a person that I represent my family as I was brought up to.'

It seemed a wonderful point to end the story right there. What sells better than redemption?

Yet if there is anything we have learned it is that Sonny Bill Williams is far too complex for that. Talk inevitably got around to his future. People wanted to know, where would he be playing next year?

'I'll try and get it out in the next couple of weeks,' he said. Williams knew the New Zealand Rugby League was about to announce its Rugby League World Cup squad on Tuesday and he also knew he had booked a holiday for when the World Cup was on, but he said nothing of it. He also knew a meeting had been planned for later in the week, the Thursday, with himself and Khoder Nasser and Chiefs coach Dave Rennie, technical director Wayne Smith and New Zealand Rugby Union general manager Neil Sorensen.

What was clear was Williams wanted to play in the 2015 Rugby Union World Cup and in the Sevens Rugby at the 2016 Olympics in Rio de Janeiro. It left 2014 as, described by some, a gap year.

Two days after the grand final New Zealand coach Steve Kearney announced in Auckland the Kiwi squad for the coming Rugby League World Cup.

Kearney said Williams was not part of the squad because he was unavailable due to 'other commitments'.

'What they are, at this stage we would all like to know,' he said. 'I'm sure we'll all hear about that after the next two to three weeks.'

Williams wished the Kiwis well, tweeting: 'Wishing the kiwis all the best in their title defence, having my first break since 2008. Looking forward to spending time with fam n friends'.

Several hours later it all changed. Williams contacted the New Zealand Rugby League and told them he'd changed his mind. He wanted to play. A series of discussions took place as the Kiwis tried to figure out what to do. Of course they wanted him. The problem was, they would now have to tell a player he was no longer going.

A day after being told he was going to the World Cup and celebrating by calling his family, Tohu Harris was told he now wasn't. He was dropped from the squad to make room for Williams.

New Zealand Rugby League chief executive Phil Holden was embarrassed. He spoke to local media, his comments reported in the *Herald* the following day. 'It has been a difficult time and for everyone involved it's been quite challenging. At the end of the day, whichever decision New Zealand Rugby League made, there were going to be some people saying it was a great decision and others saying it wasn't. We are pretty focused on winning the World Cup, we think he [Williams] is an undeniable talent – not only with what he brings on the field, but also what he brings off it is really important in terms of the [impact] he'll have on the team environment.'

Once again many believed Williams was afforded a privilege few receive. Once again, opinion was split between those supporting the decision to include him, under the principle of selecting the best players available, and others saying the Kiwis should have stood for something bigger, and remained with Harris, who wanted to be there all along.

And once again, Williams sought to appease.

'I'm really sorry about the Tohu situation. It was never my intention I just followed my heart, now I promise [I'll] play with all of it,' he tweeted.

Williams would explain it by later saying he wanted to live a life with 'no regrets'. I suppose it all depends on your interpretation of regret. Nobody could find him in the newsroom that day. His phone wasn't answered and anybody who would know wasn't answering either. And those who did answer, as the circle to call spread wider, knew enough to say they didn't know.

Somehow he turned up on BBC World Service, of all places. 'I'm really sorry about the Tohu situation and obviously he is hurting,' he said. 'I've not had a rest since 2008 and thought I could go on a vacation with my family, but I made a rash decision without thinking about it. Afterwards I thought what I would miss out on and remembered how bad I felt in 2008. I guess it took twenty-four hours and the team to be named for it to sink in. But a gut feeling . . . in ten years, would I have regrets about not making myself available? It can be played off as selfish, but I just left it in the coach's hands.'

At this my mind goes back to 2001 when I am sitting on my lounge and on my TV I see planes crash into New York's World Trade Center, and my mind flashes to Shane Webcke. The world plunged into great panic in the days after the September 11 terrorist attacks. Nobody knew when the next attacks would take place but suddenly any stadium that might be nearly full of people was considered a target. As the days wore on and our focus narrowed to our own piece of the world the Australian Rugby League responded to the fears and withdrew from the upcoming Kangaroo Tour to England. The unknown risk was simply too great. What few know is that before announcing it the ARL went to several senior players and asked for their support, talking them into a pre-emptive strike. They asked some senior players, including Webcke, to go public with safety concerns about touring, questioning if the tour should go ahead, at which point the ARL would sail in and take the decision away from them. The players agreed, some reluctantly.

The ARL did not count on the resilience of the world. Immediately there was a backlash in England and Australia. From there came an all-too-common phrase we hear these days: we are not afraid of terrorists.

The ARL changed its mind. The tour was back on.

At this, Webcke asked how he could now say he was going? He had come out publicly and said he was worried about going. In his mind he was left with no other choice. When the plane left for London Webcke remained home in Brisbane. For Webcke, some things were more important than a tour.

THE day after Williams wanted back in the New Zealand squad he met with the Chiefs about returning to rugby union at a restaurant at Brighton, on Botany Bay. It was believed he went into the meeting with a significant offer from Politis to remain at the Roosters. Like their rugby league counterparts, the Chiefs were generously accommodating to his requests. They were prepared to let him play in the Rugby League World Cup if he wanted to join them after it was over.

'We are really positive about that,' Wayne Smith told the *Herald*. 'We are Kiwis and I think it is great that he is playing in the Rugby League World Cup. That doesn't make any difference to us. It is no secret that we want him to come back to us . . . We hope he goes well over there, we are Kiwis fans, so we hope they can win again. But nothing has changed for us, we are sticking to our timetable, so that is what it is.'

For all intents it looked like he was returning to rugby.

The day after the meeting Williams announced he was staying at the Sydney Roosters one more season. Then he would return to the Chiefs in 2015 and bid to make the World Cup squad later in the season.

In all the good news, it emerged that NRL boss Dave Smith had met with Nick Politis for several months beforehand to help facilitate the deal. Smith had been texting Williams for some months, offering help should any problems arise.

'It's great news,' Smith told Brent Read at the *Australian* once the deal was confirmed. 'It's great for everybody. It's great for the NRL, it's great for the fans, it's great for the Roosters. It's great for the game in general. I am absolutely thrilled. He's a great player and a great chap off the field as well in terms of some of the stuff he does. The impact he has had on the Roosters team, the game in general, the season he has had, is phenomenal. It's a great show of confidence in us. I think it's the way the game is headed and how much he has enjoyed being part of it. The feeling is mutual.'

For twelve more months, anyway.

The deal was done even though Khoder Nasser still remained an unaccredited NRL agent and again had nothing to do with the deal. It was a vanilla-type contract again.

26

FADING SONNY

SONNY'S last season in the NRL belonged to Sam Burgess. Everything Sonny did, Burgess did it a little better.

He nearly saved it for himself, though.

While in England with New Zealand's Rugby League World Cup team at the end of 2013 he was named International Player of the Year and, at the flash banquet dinner where strong young men dressed in dark suits and pulled at their necks all evening, entirely uncomfortable in their suits and surrounds, there came one of those wonderful moments that nobody can ever properly explain, but leaves all those who witness it a little better for it.

Shortly after being announced the International Player of the Year his Kiwi teammates stood and, in honour of Sonny, performed an impromptu haka.

'I wasn't really teary until I saw the boys do the haka,' he told the *Daily Telegraph*'s Paul Crawley. 'That means the world to me. All I want is respect. I felt like after the way I left the game I lost a lot of respect but, this year, just the way I try to carry myself, just get across the real me, I felt I earned a lot of respect.'

It was a rare moment of vulnerability from Sonny. A peak inside a man people were trying hard to fall in love with again.

And then as quick as that it was gone.

Rugby league's new reality started two months later, 3 February 2014, when Burgess, the big Englishman signed by Russell Crowe five years earlier, flew back into Australia after an extended holiday in England following the World Cup.

Days before he arrived James Hooper broke in the *Sunday Telegraph* that Burgess received serious attention in England and was being scouted for a possible switch. More, he was seriously considering going. The Rabbitohs were quick to deny, as is their way. 'He's contracted for another three seasons,' chief executive Shane Richardson said. Some mocked the story entirely, saying the only way for him to leave was if Crowe released him. And do you think Crowe, the man responsible for recruiting him, was going to do that? To say nothing that his three brothers also played at the club or his mother Julie had also emigrated to Australia to be near her boys.

The story could not have been more right.

While some wondered whether Burgess would walk out on the club as Bath's interest slowly gained more legitimacy, at least publicly, Burgess did not consider going anywhere unless he had the club's approval. He spoke with Crowe and confirmed his interest.

On 17 February, just a fortnight later, Burgess confirmed Crowe had released him and he was returning to England to play rugby for Bath. The following day, Crowe claimed if Burgess was eligible to play State of Origin it might have been enough to convince him to stay. It was a totally emotional swipe, one without any real logic – State of Origin football is a step towards eventual Australian representation, and Burgess plays for England so he was completely ineligible – but it again stirred the bruised hearts of NRL fans. Once again that old argument started about different ways they might keep players in the game.

The NRL administration again came under attack as most realised two of the biggest names in the game were leaving. At least the other two players that sent a crackle through the crowd,

Parramatta's Jarryd Hayne and South Sydney's Greg Inglis, were going nowhere.

And here is what it was all about.

Sonny Ball.

Days before Burgess announced his decision all sixteen NRL chief executive met in Auckland where the NRL updated them on their salary cap review. By then, they knew the threat to lose Burgess was real. This was some big news. With Williams, Hayne and Inglis, Burgess was in that small group of the most marketable players in the game. You bet they knew the fallout of losing Burgess.

Towards the end of the meeting Andrew Fraser, a former political advisor brought in to run the cap review, told the club bosses the League was introducing a marquee player system that would give NRL chief executive Dave Smith sole discretion to upgrade a player's contract, from the NRL's central cash reserves, to give the code the flexibility to keep them in the game. It was just the ploy needed to keep Burgess in the game if they could get it done in time. It might even help the NRL convince Williams to return once his current rugby contract was over. The money would be available only to players the NRL considered of marquee value and would require the players to undertake work for the NRL.

At this, Canberra chief executive Don Furner waited patiently for the punchline.

'You're kidding, right?' Furner finally asked.

He wanted to be clear on things. The payment meant Smith could separately contract a player in 'exceptional circumstances' and then had the power to shift the player to a club where he believed the game needed him most. The money would be above the NRL salary cap imposed on clubs. Furner was clear on that, right?

'So what you're telling me,' he then asked, just to be sure, 'is that you can sign a Sonny Bill Williams or a Blake Ferguson and then tell him he has to play in Canberra?'

A few other club bosses around him laughed.

'You know why they're laughing, right? It's a joke. There's no way you're going to make those players come to Canberra. This is just a rule that will make the rich clubs richer.'

Fraser protested, but he was cooked.

The marquee player payment was eventually introduced despite all protests and good sense. Just to show what the league was up against, though, the new deal was regarded as a great win by supporters of the game. Pay them whatever it takes to keep them in the game, Sam and Sonny Bill and anyone else that might consider leaving.

Of course, it should never be used. The trick was getting people to understand why.

All season long, as Burgess and Williams charmed and excited the NRL in equal amounts, the frustration of them leaving the game grew. In truth, few knew of Smith's new powers, the small irony being that many argued for it while it was already there.

Late in the season Darren Lockyer revealed that, like Wendell Sailor, Lote Tuqiri and Mat Rogers, he was also approached by the ARU about becoming a Wallaby for the World Cup. Lockyer chose to stay loyal to rugby league but urged the NRL to broaden its thinking in retaining players.

'When the ARU had cash, they wanted to buy rugby league players and they went out and did it,' Lockyer told Peter Badel at the *Courier-Mail*. 'We've got some financial stability right now. I'm not saying we should be reckless, but we should have a serious strategy about keeping profile players in and bringing them to our game, especially ones that have a positive impact. Rugby, from a business point of view, has learnt from the large spending of a previous era. Even though the NRL has a billion-dollar TV rights deal, we have to be diligent in our spending. But there are opportunities for our game to make an investment in players and know we will get a return.'

It was exactly the new power the NRL had given itself, even though it was yet to exercise it. Sonny and Burgess were both signed by the time the new power was ratified.

Again, the argument was overtaken by emotion. Nobody wanted to see players the calibre of Sonny or Burgess leave the game. It was natural to feel disappointed. There also remained an undercurrent among some, and particularly former, players that the NRL was sitting on a great pile of gold coins that it refused to share with the players. Again, it was a convenient argument that overlooked the meeting in 2007 when David Gallop, under threat of strike action by the players, and particularly Willie Mason, invited every NRL player to a Coogee forum and opened the game's books. Only sixteen players turned up.

Gallop knew the game was paying what it could afford.

He knew several more things.

He knew tinkering with the salary cap to keep players from leaving would not necessarily stop them leaving.

He knew such thinking was an emotional argument. It removed logic, and without logic it played into the hands of managers and players interested in raising their value.

He knew signing a player to a marquee payment over and above the salary cap disadvantaged the other fifteen teams that did not benefit from the NRL's discretion.

And he knew what that meant. It meant the goodwill initially felt by saving the likes of Sonny Bill Williams or Sam Burgess from leaving for rugby union would fast evaporate when fans of the fifteen other clubs realised there was no benefit for them.

This is how much it had changed for Williams. How much he changed the game. Five years earlier the boss of the NRL was declaring he would be barred for life for walking out on a deal that, under the salary cap, could not pay him enough and now the new boss was striving for flexibility in the cap to keep him in the game.

★

ASKED once to explain his retirement, the jockey Willie Shoe-
maker explained it was 'tough to get out of bed when you're
wearing silk pyjamas'. For years, this was Sonny's great talent.
No matter what his success, what his reputation, he worked
harder than anybody else on the little things in the game that
turn into big things. The one-percenters, he called them. It was
the first step towards winning the respect of his teammates. It
was something he might not have learned at Canterbury, but if
he did not, it was certainly honed there.

Still.

His second season at the Roosters was not as good as the first.
Life had changed a lot. He was more content now. Quietly the
previous August he slipped off and married his new girlfriend,
Alana Raffie, a wedding kept so quiet none of his Roosters
knew about it and those close to him that did, like Anthony
Mundine, did not attend. They got married during a small
break in the season and it would not be revealed until more
than six months passed.

Nobody could accuse him of not trying in his new season,
but something was missing all the same. The brilliance was
still there, just not as consistently. The Roosters played most of
the season like they were waiting for the big games, big game
players, and when the big games rolled around too many games
in too short a time dulled their edge. In round twenty-five, a
Sunday, they played Melbourne in Melbourne, winning 24–12
to stay in the race to win the minor premiership. That put them
up against South Sydney in the final round, a Friday night
game. The five-day turnaround, with a day also lost traveling,
was a concern but, once again, the Roosters went to the well
and produced. The 22–18 win over Souths gave them the minor
premiership. But it came at a cost. The emotional high of the
previous fortnight, the travel and the level of competition, flat-
tened them. They went into the qualifying final against Penrith
and more than anything they need the win to earn a week off

to recharge. It was too much. They got rolled 19–18. From that moment on they could never fill the tank. It might have already been empty.

Instead of resting for a week and preparing for what would turn out to be the Bulldogs, the Roosters had to back up the following week against North Queensland and got out of the blocks quickly, leading 30–0 after thirty minutes. But it was a ruse. Their legs were heavy. Soon enough, the workload of previous weeks began to tell and the Cowboys produced almost the greatest comeback in rugby league history, coming back to level the score at 30–all before a James Maloney field goal seven minutes from fulltime sent the Roosters through 31–30.

There wasn't enough time left in their week, though. The following weekend they went down to eventual premiers South Sydney in the preliminary final. Sam Burgess was about to take the fairytale finish to his NRL career Williams was seeking.

When grand final day rolled around Burgess proved what a tremendous asset was about to be lost. From the first tackle of the game he clashed heads with Canterbury prop James Graham, his England roommate when they tour, and suffered a depressed fracture of the cheekbone. His brother George took a look at him. 'I'm going to need your help here,' said Sam, who knew something was wrong. He didn't. He was mighty. He led South Sydney to their first premiership in 43 years.

SIX days before the grand final Jarryd Hayne returned from America. He went alone and called it a study tour and nobody knew how much he was studying.

The night Hayne returned he overcame his jetlag and headed to the Dally M Awards at Star Casino where he was named, along with North Queensland's Johnathan Thurston, joint winner of the Dally M Player of the Year Award. It was the second time he was named the NRL's best player.

Two weeks later Hayne was fronting another press conference. He just announced he was quitting the NRL to pursue his dream of playing in the NFL. Once again, questions were put to NRL boss Dave Smith about the possibility of using the marquee payment to help retain him. Smith pointed out that for Hayne it was not about money. It was about a dream.

BY then Sonny had left the NRL and was preparing to tour with the All Blacks. Again it marked his wonderful versatility. Again it revealed him being afforded privileges few others received. The New Zealand Rugby Union gave him an 'exemption' to be selected for the All Blacks despite the usual criteria requiring a player to have at least played in the national provincial championships to be considered available for selection.

He was immediately fast-tracked into the squad as they prepared their tour opener against the United States at Soldiers Field in Chicago on 1 November. It was home to the Chicago Bears and the first time a rugby game was played at an NFL venue.

The first time Sonny touched the ball he went 20 metres downfield. By the time he walked off after 58 minutes, hobbling slightly with a corked thigh, he had scored two tries and had a third disallowed in the 74–6 win.

The All Blacks had no doubts he would be fit for the All Blacks first Test against England a week later.

With the Rugby World Cup less than a year away it would be the last time the All Blacks played at venues such as Twickenham and Millennium Stadium before the tournament started and four years since he last played there. His selection was all about preparation for the Rugby World Cup. The All Blacks did not disappoint. They backed up their rout of the USA with wins in all three Tests on their northern hemisphere tour, beating England 24–12, Scotland 24–16 and Wales 34–16.

SONNY BALL

The Rugby World Cup was less than twelve months away and how much it meant to him was clear. While he was in Cardiff preparing for Wales, his first child, a little girl called Imaan, was born.

He watched the birth on Skype.

EVEN though he was now a rugby union player Williams was not completely lost to rugby league. Or cricket. Before he was gone, once more he turned up on Channel Nine, this time in their cricket coverage during a break. It was classic Sonny Ball. A former Test cricket captain interviewing a current Test rugby player about his upcoming boxing match on Nine's upcoming rugby league *Footy Show Fight Night*. Sonny was all things expected, humble and uncertain and just a man out to better himself. He was interviewed by former Test captain Mark Taylor. Taylor, quite rightfully, was in minor awe at Williams' talent and desire to continue testing himself in various sports. He had the patter down, humbling himself by talking up his opponent, New Zealand–based American Chauncy Welliver. Williams mentioned that he was fighting another heavyweight and repeated an old truth of the fight game, as he would several times: that in the heavyweight division one punch could change it all.

The fight was January 31 in the new year, 2015, and again highlighted Nine's devotion to him. The network announced it was getting back into the fight game, planning to take more fights on free-to-air and Nine boss David Gyngell told Khoder Nasser he was willing to put on the fight, meet all production costs and beam the fight into the New Zealand pay-per-view market, for one small return: he wanted a guarantee that when Williams fought fellow NRL player Paul Gallen it would be shown on Nine.

Deal, Nasser said. Gallen would fight on the undercard to build interest. Another NRL player, Willis Meehan, also fought on the night and proved to be better than both of them.

Welliver was another fat guy who was resilient and upright but without the workrate to trouble Williams at all. Welliver's great claim as a career opponent was that he worked as a sparring partner for the likes of former world champions Wladimir Klitschko and Mike Tyson. He stood an inch shorter than Williams but went into the ring thirty kilograms heavier, at a hundred and thirty-five kilograms.

His great edge was experience. Williams was having just his seventh fight. Welliver was 55–10–5 with twenty-two knockouts. It was significant.

And it was not much of a fight. All that was really revealed was that Welliver could take a punch as he took many and struggled to deliver some.

Sonny outclassed him from the first round to the last, winning all eight rounds on two judges' cards and seven of the eight on the third.

Once again, it was a triumph of athleticism over genuine skill, but once again it made you sit and wonder what might ever happen if in the right hands, with a fulltime approach.

27

EVERYBODY'S PLAYING SONNY BALL

NOBODY transitioned between codes like Sonny Bill Williams. He did it so easily he encouraged others.

At some point Sam Burgess admitted during his first cold English winter as a rugby player that Sonny's success had encouraged him to have his own crack at chasing his dreams. Make them personal, chase them hard.

Everybody was listening.

At some point he might have also questioned it. At least initially, Burgess struggled to make anything like the impact Sonny made in rugby. With each fresh struggle whispers filtered back to Australia that he was second guessing his decision. Like Sonny the year before, Burgess was the reigning Rugby League International Federation's International Player of the Year. Another blow for rugby league.

Picked in the centres like Sonny, it was hoped he would bring the same damaging power when he ran as well as the soft hands for the offload. Some of it was there. He was certainly not making the kind of statement Williams made when he first shifted, underscoring again that while many of the skills were transferable, they remained two different games.

While Burgess was chasing fresh dreams the team he left behind, Sonny moved on from his fight against Welliver to play his first game for the Chiefs just six days later in a trial against 2014 Super Rugby champions NSW Waratahs at Campbelltown. Burgess' old team, South Sydney, returned from a pre-season training camp in America. The *Sun-Herald* broke the story that Greg Inglis had employed an overseas agent to gauge interest from European rugby clubs, potentially making him the best player in the game

The following day Inglis' manager Allan Gainey confirmed he was receiving interest on a 'weekly basis' from overseas clubs. How big a disaster this was for the NRL is obvious. Inglis was the only one of the big four Sydney-based stars left. And now, about to fly to England to captain South Sydney in the World Club Challenge against Wigan, he confirmed he was 'looking around'.

Once again, Willie Mason came to the fore. By now playing at Manly, Mason threw up the idea of a centralised funding system. This time, the proposal was to structure an NRL fighting fund to pay the game's top ten players over and above their club contracts.

Like all the others it contained an inherent unfairness. Even if there was just one of the top ten players at each club, that still left six clubs without extra funding, creating an imbalance in the salary cap. Forty other inconsistencies flowed from there.

Soon talk began that Smith might finally open his purse and let a few moths flutter out before exercising his discretion to keep Inglis in the game. How would this look? Again, many thought it was not only a good idea, but necessary.

For how long?

The NRL salary cap was $6.5 million and now the League was going to tell the other fifteen clubs that the game's best team was going to be able to spend an extra $1 million above everyone else to keep their best player?

NRL boss Dave Smith refused to be brought in on whether the NRL would turn to the war chest, although his quote that the marquee allowance would be used only once every 'five to ten years' got a trot. Thankfully, Inglis ended it when he was asked whether he deserved a slice of the war chest sitting there.

'No, I don't think so,' he told Nick Walshaw at the *Daily Telegraph*. 'There are two ways to go about this, the right way and the wrong way. I want to go about things the right way. As I've said, this isn't about money. What the NRL has done for me, I'm extremely grateful for that. And I want my decisions to be based in the best interests of rugby league.'

SEVERAL months later, in late April, the Australian Rugby Union announced a marked shift in territory. With the stroke of a pen the ARU overturned almost twenty years of history, its complete professional life, and agreed to allow players from overseas leagues to play for the Wallabies.

Many believed it was all done to allow ARU coach Michael Cheika to select Matt Giteau for the coming World Cup. Giteau had not played for the Wallabies since 2011, when then coach Robbie Deans overlooked him for the Rugby World Cup in New Zealand. He moved to France and in his first three seasons helped Toulon, Sonny's old team, to a Top 14 title and two runners-up titles as well as a Heineken Cup for Europe's best club side. He was also the Top 14 Player of the Year.

The fine print meant the ARU could pick any player that had played sixty or more Tests for the Wallabies or held a Super Rugby contract for at least seven years. It basically formalised New Zealand Rugby's sabbatical rule. And it worked both ways. It allowed players to head overseas for rich guest stints and not give up their Wallaby ambitions and it meant the Wallabies could still pick the best players.

The ARU had realised the benefit of Sonny Ball. ARU chief executive Bill Pulver said the policy banning foreign-based players limited the talent pool. If ever anybody was uncertain about what mattered, which was winning, the answer was clear.

All this while Sonny was playing for the Chiefs, who fell behind the Wellington Hurricanes, at least in the early stages of the Super Rugby competition, in the New Zealand conference. Not that they worried. The Chiefs were all about qualifying. The Chiefs stayed on track for a wild card berth, even as Sonny missed early games such as the win over the Cheetahs, after a sickening concussion the week before when he clashed heads with Stormers prop Vincent Koch, and the win over the Blues when he suffered a slight knee injury. Such was the talent in their side they approached their season like the Roosters. Let's just get there in shape and go from there. They knew they were big name players.

Most focus, of course, was on the Rugby World Cup in September. A competition where three of the top four nations (New Zealand, Australia and England) would go into the tournament with the most talked about players in their team being ex-NRL players (Williams, Israel Folau and Sam Burgess).

The All Blacks have a soft draw for the World Cup, starting 18 September 2015. They share Pool C with Argentina, Namibia, Tonga and Georgia and have never lost a Test to any of them. If there is any fear in their preparation it is that the draw is too soft. Against such lightweights, it goes, the All Blacks will not get sufficiently match hardened before progressing to the next stage.

The warning there is that the previous two World Cup finals were fought out by teams who went through the tournament after advancing from the same pool. New Zealand and France played out of the same pool in 2011 before meeting in the final, as did England and South Africa in 2007. That 2007 World Cup remains particularly painful for the All Blacks. They advanced from a weak pool in the tournament and met a battle-hardened France in Cardiff, and were famously upset 20–18.

★

SONNY BALL

SONNY Bill Williams will be 30 by the time the 2015 Rugby World Cup comes around. He might become one of those few men to win two World Cups, which is usually enough to reserve a place in rugby immortality.

Whether he will, in the traditional sense though, remains up for debate. Such is the power of Sonny Ball. This conversation has been had many times in rugby union. They have had the same conversation in rugby league.

While nobody will ever doubt his impact in either code and both fought heavily to be the beneficiary of it, and it cast some shadow, the thought is that he never truly belonged to either code to be *of* it.

That's the funny thing things about the codes. Both of them.

While each is ruthless in their own way, professional and tough, they look after their own. For the truly great ones, the game tends to reward those that gave.

While there is no doubt Sonny has been well rewarded throughout his career, something nobody will ever argue, the flipside is he does not truly qualify as a great in either game because he never fully committed to either game.

Instead, he will eventually settle somewhere out on the edge, still respected enormously by both codes but never quite there, never quite *of* them.

Then again, if anybody can change that . . .

EPILOGUE

AS the Rugby World Cup neared, along with the far away hope of Olympic gold in Rio in 2016 as one of the few All Blacks who could transition to Sevens Rugby, so also did the deadline for *Sonny Ball*. It was time to call Khoder Nasser and ask him to get me in contact with Sonny and see what they both wanted to say in this very big book. I had an old number for Nasser and was no longer sure he retained it. I called but nobody answered. An automated voice asked me to leave a message. Uncertain it was his number I hung up and determined to call later. Half an hour later my phone rang. It sounded like Khoder.

He had no idea it was me and said he had a missed call on this number.

'It's Paul Kent,' I said, 'how are you?'

'Good mate.'

'Great. Thank you for ringing me back. I wanted to have a chat to you . . .'

'I didn't know who it was, mate.'

'You probably wouldn't have called if you did, eh?'

He laughed. 'Who knows . . . Anyway, what's up?'

'I'm writing a book on Sonny.'

'Yeah.'

'And I wanted to talk to you about it.'

'Oh, it's going to be difficult, mate.'

'Why is it going to be difficult?'

'Because Sonny will do his own one day. All right, my man?'

'Sorry?'

'Is that all right? Because I think he will do his own one day and I'd rather leave all that for that.'

'All right. What I'm saying is I'm writing it, I've been asked to write it and I wanted to talk to you about it and certainly wanted to give you the opportunity –'

'No, you can understand where I'm coming from.'

'I can understand exactly where you're coming from. To be honest I expected this answer but by the same token I wanted to give you guys the chance to explain your side of things. Obviously mate, on many things and the way they have been reported over the years.'

'That's no problem. You do what you've got to do, my man. But I just think it's best to leave it for Sonny.'

'Okay, that's no problem. Let me ask you this then, will Sonny talk to me?'

'Impossible. Because he is going to do it.'

'Because what?'

'He's going to do it.'

'How far away is he going to do it?'

'Well, that would be telling wouldn't it.' He laughed again. 'Paul, I don't want to be a smart-arse but that's just the way it is.'

'Mate, I understand. Look, I know that's the way the world works. I don't see you as a smart-arse, I expected Sonny will do it one day. I think whatever he does is going to be vastly different from whatever I do, as you can appreciate. I just wanted to talk to you about certain things over the years, if you could just give me your –'

'Mate, it's best not to start because if I start it never ends. So I'll just let you keep doing what you're doing and we'll do what we do, when we do. All right, my man?'

'All right, mate, not a problem.'

'Thank you, my man.'

'Thanks Khoder, see you mate.'

'See you, bye.'

Of course I expected nothing less. I understood, too. Some day he will write a book and there is never any doubt it will be vastly different from this one.

All I could do next was wait for the weekend's newspaper. You could set your watch by it. Sure enough, that Sunday there it was in the *Sun-Herald*. After a small rant from Nasser about others profiting off Sonny, with no irony at all, Weidler wrote that Nasser 'told the author to "F. . . off" when asked for a comment.'

I could not believe my luck. It was the perfect end.

I just got Sonny Balled.

ACKNOWLEDGEMENTS

IT should not surprise anyone that many people were happy to talk to me about Sonny Bill Williams and provide all the information they have, but few were willing to talk on the record. They each had their motivations, the predominant one being that Sonny might one day come back into their lives and they did not want to do anything that might jeopardise that.

Still, I want to thank all those I spoke to, on and off the record, for their information and insight.

I will thank Matt Johns and Ray Warren, who were both willing and game to put their names to blurbs on the back cover.

I do not want to thank the New Zealand Rugby Union who, at the last moment, denied permission to use any photos of Sonny in All Blacks regalia for this book, yet another example of Sonny Ball.

To the writers that cover both codes, and by association Sonny Bill Williams, only you know what you went through.

To my employers at the *Daily Telegraph* and Fox Sports, thank you for your support and for your permissions.

To Triple M and Channel Nine, who both allowed me to use interviews that form essential parts of the Sonny Ball story, thank you.

I want to thank Angus Fontaine and Libby Turner at Pan Macmillan for their support and guidance and, most of all, their perseverance. They drove it.

And I want to thank my wife Fiona and daughter Evie for their understanding. They have always been magnificent.